American Conveyancing
Patterns

Lexington Books Special Series in
Real Estate and Urban Land Economics

William N. Kinnard, Jr., Editor

William N. Kinnard, *Income Property Valuation*
Robert A. Sigafoos, *Corporate Real Estate Development*
D. Barlow Burke, Jr., *American Conveyancing Patterns*

American Conveyancing Patterns

Past Improvements and Current Debates

D. Barlow Burke, Jr.
American University Law School

Lexington Books
D.C. Heath and Company
Lexington, Massachusetts
Toronto

Library of Congress Cataloging in Publication Data

Burke, D.   Barlow, 1941-
American conveyancing patterns.

Includes bibliographical references.
1. Conveyancing—United States. 2. Settlement costs—United States.
3. Land titles—United States. 4. Vendors and purchasers—United States.
I. Title.
KF670.B8   346'.73'0438   77-4628
ISBN 0-669-01731-0

Published simultaneously in Canada.

Printed in the United States of America.

International Standard Book Number: 0-669-01731-0

Library of Congress Catalog Card Number: 77-4628

Contents

	Preface	vii
	Introduction	ix
Part I	*Our Conveyancing Patterns*	1
Chapter 1	**The Costs of Purchasing a Home**	3
	Settlement Costs at the Closing Table	3
	Classifying Settlement Costs	6
Chapter 2	**Two Case Studies of Our Conveyancing Patterns**	13
	Introduction	13
	Contracting for Purchase	15
	Traditional Patterns of American Conveyancing	17
	Conclusions	39
Part II	*Three Types of Improvements*	57
Chapter 3	**Conveyancing Legislation**	59
	Introduction	59
	Making Titles Marketable by Legislation	60
	Conclusion	69
Chapter 4	**Establishing Tract Indexes**	79
	Tract Indexes	79
Chapter 5	**Establishing Title Registries**	103
	Conveyancing Improvement in the Twentieth Century	103
	Conclusion	119
Part III	*Federal Scrutiny of Our Conveyancing*	131
Chapter 6	**Federal Investigations into Conveyancing**	133
	Introduction	133
	Past Governmental Attention to Closing Costs	134

The Inquiry Begins   136
The HUD-VA Study   140
Congressional Consideration   147
The Real Estate Settlement Procedures Act
    of 1974   153
The Backlash   170
Future Use of the Act   175

Afterword   215

Index   219

About the Author   225

Preface

This book grew out of a study that the author undertook in 1971 for the federal Department of Housing and Urban Development as that agency was preparing a report on mortgage settlement costs. The study and the report to Congress were precursors of the debate that led to the enactment of the Real Estate Settlement Procedures Act.

The writing was undertaken over several years. The case studies in Chapter 2 were written in 1974, after travel generously made possible by a grant from the Ford Foundation. The Foundation also underwrote the travel to gather information for Chapter 5 and Chapter 6's appendix on English practice. That last chapter was written during 1975 and 1977, was updated this year, and is intended as a case study in the legislative history and implementation of a statute rather than a RESPA hornbook.

D. Barlow Burke, Jr.
Washington, D.C.
October, 1977

Introduction

The purchase of a home involves many types of costs that a consumer will encounter in no other type of purchase. Purchasers are called on to deal with brokers, attorneys, surveyors, assessors, credit appraisers, and bankers and other types of lenders as well as the vendor of the property. The purchaser's relationship with each specialist is governed by a series of interrelated contracts that are hard to keep track of in their totality. In an economy in which consumers are accustomed to swifter extensions of credit than normally attend the purchase of a home, the process of settling on a house seems strange by comparison. Settlement costs are all paid at the settlement. They are not even a tax-deductible expense of purchase,[1] and they come out of the purchaser's pocket before he has the comforting thought that his purchase allows him to use the property and still receive any build-up in its market value should he decide to sell (at which time he may find that he needs all that equity to purchase his next residence).

The transfer of an interest in residential real property in the United States begins with the execution of a contract of sale. After that, the methods for transferring residential real estate in the United States move the vendor-purchaser contract through some rather specialized institutions. The product of the process is a *conveyance*—the delivery of a deed giving a provable title from the vendor to the purchaser, some of whose risks in accepting the title are often indemnified by some third party.

The subject of this book is the patterns of residential conveyancing used for realty in the United States. Its aim is first to describe the costs and tasks performed during such a conveyance and then to suggest how these tasks might be better performed and how the state and federal governments might encourage this.

The Significance of the Subject

Before summarizing the arguments made in this work, it is customary to attempt to convince the reader of the significance of the topic. In this case, the task is not accomplished in a single sentence because its significance is the result of a confluence of several factors. A primary concern is the settlement costs imposed on a conveyance.

Large sums change hands each year to pay for settlement services. By the author's calculation, about $1.9 billion was paid by vendors and purchasers for these services in 1974.[2] One or another agency of the federal government has been concerned about these costs for the past five years.[3] No precise idea of which costs are "too high" has been formulated, but legislation to regulate the settlement process in the hope of reducing costs has emerged. The history and analysis of that legislation is a major part of this work.

The concern with costs arises out of a suspicion that the services offered the parties to a conveyance are not subject to the discipline of competition. Antitrust actions against local associations of real estate brokers,[4] and recently against bar associations, are continuing evidence of this concern.[5] There is also a continuing tension in the conveyancing industry itself. Intermittent squabbles occur between bar associations and realty brokers and between attorneys and title insurers. Such conflicts periodically produce enthusiasm for making major segments of the settlement process more efficient.

The question of whether or not settlement costs are too high aside, a study of the conveyancing patterns around the country leaves the attentive onlooker with the feeling that the system is archaic and cumbersome. Technology brings this lesson home to the public; more particularly, it is the absence of technology used in the process at a time when many commercial relationships are being transformed by scientific advances applied to business.[6] Technology is available—computers and automatic data-processing equipment for title searches and recording; photogrametry, remote sensing, and aerial mapping for surveying to establish property boundaries[7]—so the obstacle to applying these techniques is lagging institutions. The absence of technology is more acute because attorneys, alone of the professions, confront the public without the visible support of technology of which the public is generally aware.

A third factor is the frequency of use of less-than-fee easements and covenants encumbering the title to realty in the process of development or urbanization. These interests facilitate the provision of water, sewer services, and utilities to improved realty;[8] developers' covenants often control the appearance of buildings and the relations between home owners in the same subdivision;[9] or perhaps they are used to implement private or public programs for environmental protection or historic preservation.[10] All such instruments must be searched out and examined upon a conveyance. The multiplication of these interests promises to increase in the future, increasing the difficulty of conveyancing as well.[11]

Moreover, and fourth, in fast-growing jurisdictions with developable or urbanizing land where less-than-fee interests proliferate on titles, there is also likely to be an increasing interest in the collection of title information about land.[12] This information can be used in a wide variety of situations: in land speculation,[13] public land planning,[14] and inventories of natural resources. In a debate over the relative advantages of disclosure of and secrecy in land ownership, the public and the business value of title information envelops any proposal to change the methods by which land title information is kept and disseminated. Debate should be particularly lively in jurisdictions where concentration of land ownership or land speculation is a matter of public concern.[15]

Fifth, and finally, there is a perceived need for comprehensive legislation in the field of real property transfers. The Commissioners on Uniform State Laws recently promulgated the Uniform Land Transactions Act. They drafted seven articles, but they adopted only three.[16] The adopted articles deal with contracts of sale and mortgages, while one of the major ones the commissioners initially rejected dealt with the subject of this work—recording and title assurance.[17] Another two years of study were necessary before the rejected articles reappeared as the Uniform Simplification of Land Transactions Act, as amended in 1977.[18] In later chapters this work will discuss some of the choices made, but not made plain, by the drafters for the commissioners. Similar choices may soon be facing state legislators.[19]

Overview

The author will argue that the dominant patterns of conveyancing are the result of a historical process in which one task was added to another. New types of information needed by purchasers, widespread financing of residential property, and specialization of the tasks involved in a conveyance all induced changes. New personnel came to dominate the evolving, accreted pattern of a locality or region. This cumulative process has resulted in fifteen to twenty charges levied on a conveyance. After providing a glossary of frequently made charges, Chapter 2 will present a historical introduction to conveyancing and discuss two case studies of the dominant patterns of conveyancing. General descriptions and case studies of American conveyancing patterns reveal a picture of long executory periods and services useful to lenders and purchasers, provided by increasingly complex institutions. Past attempts to improve these patterns through legislation have engendered problems of their own; the problems are procedural and constitutional in nature, but they also give rise to an uncertain relationship between conveyancing law and equity. Marketable title and curative acts, respectively, exemplify these problems. Both are discussed in Chapter 3.

The objectives manifest in the history of our conveyancing patterns and past attempts to improve them are guides to likely future changes. In discussing successively more comprehensive changes, increased attention will be paid to the constitutional implications of the change. One objective has been to reduce the work (discussed in Chapter 4) and the documentation (Chapter 5) required in a transfer. The ultimate in this trend is one document, registered and assured publicly. Implementing the idea of a title certificate is the subject of Chapter 5.

How can the federal government aid states in improving their conveyancing patterns? A case study of recent federal activity dealing with federally underwritten mortgage transactions will address this question in Chapter 6. Any help must be complimentary to suggestions made in the states since the turn of the century, and some alternatives for federal action will be discussed in this light. Like computers, conveyancing improvements come in "generations." Federal activity is arguably the start of a new generation of changes in conveyancing patterns.

The underlying theme of this work is that any change in our conveyancing patterns is going to be difficult to accomplish but that a full range of alternatives should be explored now. Any changes must be evaluated in terms of escalating housing costs. If we are to continue to be a nation of predominately owner-occupant households, we must of course keep housing of many types affordable. For example, there may be no alternative to our becoming a nation of leaseholders if nonfinanceable settlement costs prevent sale of the fee title. Hence attention now to the real estate settlement process will help keep our land tenure patterns flexible in the future.

The Sequence of Chapters

A final word on the sequence of the chapters is in order. The first two describe our conveyancing patterns. The next three explain and analyze three discrete recommendations for improvements that could be made in those patterns. They are presented in the order in which they should be adopted. Together they constitute some prerequisites and a program for federal action in aid of title records maintained by the states.

The first recommendation, really a precondition of federal aid, is that states enact marketable title and curative legislation. Their enactment raises some constitutional issues (see Chapter 3) which must be resolved before more accessible, comprehensive title records can be established. For this reason, this legislation is explored first. Implementing these statutes also shows the uncertainties of the relationship between codified laws and the equitable powers of the judiciary. Thus Chapter 3's constitutional issues are necessary to an understanding of Chapter 4's discussion of tract indexes while its law-equity problems are the precursors of Chapter 5. Further, the comprehensive tract indexes discussed in Chapter 4 are more easily implemented after passage of the title legislation discussed in Chapter 3, just as Chapter 4's tract indexes can be a forerunner of Chapter 5's title registries. The last chapter describes federal scrutiny of our conveyancing to date. This narrative shows the narrowing of federal options, principally settlement cost regulation, leaving inaction as the chief alternative to the federal government's aiding the improvement of our title records. Chapters 3-5 then become the guidelines for future federal action.

Notes

1. Rev. Rul. 55-442, 1955 Cum. Bull. 529; Frank V. Comm'r, 20 T.C. 511 (1953).

2. United States League of Sav. Assns, *Savings and Loan Fact Book 1976*, Tab. 20, at 28; Tab. 30, at 38; chart 41, at 76, form the basis of this calculation: $503.4 billion of residential debt in savings associations, turning over every eight years, with 3 percent of the amount turned over annually going to pay for settlement costs.

3. *See* ch. 6, *infra* at n. 6-15.

4. United States v. Natl Assns of Real Estate Bds., 339 U.S. 489 (1950).

5. Goldfarb v. Va. State Bar, 421 U.S. 773, rehearing denied 96 S.Ct. 162 (1975).

6. J. White, *Banking* 700 (1976).

7. Symposium, "Computerization of Land Title Records," 43 Cinn. L. Rev. 465 (1974).

8. Patterson v. Arthurs, 9 Watts. 152 (Pa., 1839) held a public road not an encumbrance on title, and state courts have analyzed the issue using this case as a starting point.

9. Neponsit Property Owners Ass'n v. Emigrant Indus. Sav. Bank, 278 N.Y. 248, 15 N.E.2d 793 (1938).

10. Note, "Conservation Restrictions: A Survey," 8 Conn. L. Rev. 383 (1976).

11. United States v. Albrecht, 496 F.2d 906 (CCA8, 1974) enforced federal wildlife refuge restrictions against bona fide purchaser of land without notice of the restrictions.

12. R. Fellmuth, *The Politics of Land* 3 (1973).

13. Lindeman, "Anatomy of Land Speculation," 42 Am. Inst. Planners J. 142 (1976).

14. Popper, "We've got to dig deeper into who owns our land," Planning (Oct., 1976), at 17.

15. M. Clawson, *Suburban Land Conversion in the United States* 111-140 (1971).

16. Uniform Land Transactions Act (1975).

17. *Id.*, Draft (Feb., 1975) at 7-1 through 8-11.

18. Uniform Simplification of Land Transfers Act (1976), §6-101.

19. *See also* Mass. Land Records Comm., Program Statement (Jan., 1976) at 37-39; "Feasibility of Computerized Land Title Search in Fairfax County, Virginia" (Feb., 1975) at 16-38.

Part I
Our Conveyancing Patterns

The Costs of Purchasing a Home

Settlement Costs at the Closing Table

Transfer costs pay for contracting for a purchase, financing an acquisition, proving title, or organizing the closing. Generally speaking, many of them pay for information.[1] Brokerage fees pay for information about relevant property markets;[2] financing fees pay for information about a prospective borrower's credit or the property for which he seeks a loan;[3] title proof fees pay for information on the title;[4] and closing fees pay for exchanging and disclosing the information previously gathered, as well as the rental of a place to do so.

Transfer costs are usually grouped chronologically according to the four steps of the conveyancing process. This classification reflects neatly the roles of the real estate broker, the lender, and the title attorney, all meeting in the final closing ceremony. This may involve the purchaser and vendor, or the lender and the purchaser; settlement costs and services can benefit each, depending on whether it is the sale or the mortgage that is being closed. If the mortgage and the deed are closed simultaneously, the costs of financing the purchase will often include, in part, those required to prove the title.[5] Further consideration of particular settlement services must take into account such dual uses and must reflect in each instance the uses for which the information is generated.

Real estate settlement costs are those charges paid at the closing for obtaining both the mortgage loan and the title itself.[6] Noninformational charges are included as well: processing fees, loan discount payments or mortgage points, and prepaid items; and real estate and mortgage brokerage commissions, which are semi-informational in nature.[7] This definition is not intended to cover all possible financial adjustments made at a closing. Excluded are amounts paid for "fixtures" and large appliances and sums prorated on the day of settlement such as prepaid utility bills and local taxes.[8] In addition, deductions from the purchase price may be made at closing for repairs or improvements called for in the contract of sale or to eliminate defects found in the title. These financial adjustments are made according to preexisting contractual agreements and might not be customarily imposed on a transaction.

What are settlement costs? Listed chronologically,[9] they are

1. *Attorney's fees* are charged for preparing a contract of sale; usually a flat rate between $15 and $25 is charged, except when special drafting of contract provisions is needed. If no special provisions are used, the

preparation involves filling out a preprinted, standard contract. Where no attorney is involved, forms supplied by real estate brokers are often used.

2. *Escrow fees*, paid to an escrow agent, are imposed on large residential transactions in some areas of the country, on large commercial transactions everywhere, and on most residential transactions in the southwest and Pacific states;[10] $100-$150 is paid by both vendor and purchaser to a stakeholder who collects and holds the documents and money during the executory period as a neutral third party.[11]

3. *House inspection fees* of $80-$150 are increasingly used in transactions involving existing, rather than new, houses.[12] They are for on-site inspections to discover any defects or any repairs that are necessary.

Many costs are related to procuring a mortgage loan and reflect the lender's quest for a sound investment,[13] backed by a secure title and a first-lien. Even if no mortgage is involved in the transaction, some of these fees, for work directly beneficial to the purchaser, may appear on the purchaser's and vendor's closing sheet. But if a third-party mortgage loan is involved, they will customarily be paid by the purchaser in his capacity as a borrower. Such fees[14] are

4. An *FHA or VA application fee* is charged if the loan is to be underwritten by one of those two federal agencies. This is charged for a conditional commitment to insure the mortgage loan made by the lender; it involves an estimate of the value of the property by federal appraisers. The charge is 1 percent of the loan amount.[15]

5. A *credit-report fee* is charged for the report on the purchaser's (borrower's) financial and credit status, made either by the lender or a credit-reporting agency. It is generally a flat $5-$10 charge and involves normally a few telephone calls.[16]

6. *Title-examination fees* are paid to those who examine and review the many types of public records relating to the title of real property. This fee, charged by whomever searches the title, is either a percentage (0.5-1.5 percent) of the purchase price or loan amount, depending on whether the owner or lender initiates the search, or is a flat charge of $75-$90, plus a further flat rate ($1.50-$2.50) for each entry found in the records. However computed, title-examination fees constitute a major item on any closing sheet.[17]

7. A *survey fee* is charged for preparing a document certifying that the legal description of the property, the perimeter boundaries and dimensions of the property, are as stated. If the property is improved, the location of any improvements (house, etc.) are also noted. Fees for this item vary widely and cost anywhere from $50-$250. They may or may not result from a formal survey of the property by transit and rod, and no markers are left in the ground to indicate the perimeters of the parcel.[18] The survey is often a

cursory sight-check of the property by a registered surveyor. It is initiated by the mortgage lender as part of its loan application process.

8. A *title insurance premium* is charged by a private title insurer for issuing a title insurance policy. The fee is usually based on $2.50-$3.50 per $1,000 of the mortgage loan or purchase price, respectively, depending on whether the insured is the lender or the owner.[19]

9. Lenders also charge an *origination fee*, a *mortgage application fee*, or *initial service charge* for processing the loan. On FHA-VA loans, it is limited to 1 percent of the face value of the mortgage. For conventional mortgages, percentage fees are also common practice.

10. *Preparation-of-documents fees* are charged for filling out printed, standard forms for the mortgage, note, or transfer deed. Acknowledgment forms and notarial fees may also be included. Normally such fees are levied at the flat rate of $15-$25 per form, by a realty broker, attorney, lender, title insurer, or escrow agent.

11. Any one of the parties listed above as preparing the documents may also conduct the closing, for which they charge a *closing fee* of about $50 for renting the office space and for handling the transaction.

12. *Inspections for termite or insect infestation* may be conducted by exterminators, particularly in coastal, southern, and southwestern states from Maryland to southern California. Certification that the property is free of such infestation or that past damage has been repaired is exchanged for this fee.

13. State and local *transfer taxes* are in many jurisdictions levied each time ownership is transferred or a mortgage is imposed on property. Tax rates vary but are generally so much per $1,000 of sale price, loan amount, or assessed value.[20]

Other charges may also be imposed at the closing, e.g., for photographs of the property, amortization schedules,[21] preparation of truth-in-lending statements,[22] and mortgage-brokerage commissions.

At the closing, adjustments reflecting the expenses of operating and maintaining the property will be made. They are

14. Amounts are paid by the purchaser to the lender for escrowing *real estate taxes* until due for *hazard and fire insurance*[23] on the property for the lender's benefit and premiums for *life insurance*[24] on the borrower in favor of the lender. These charges are prepaid to the lender by the borrower and are paid out by the lender when due.

15. *Interest* accruing between the closing date and the date of the first mortgage payment must be paid by the borrower to the lender.

16. *FHA-VA insurance premiums* are also usually prepaid at closing.

Also due on closing, in addition to the down payment, are

17. *Real estate brokerage commissions* from 5 to 7 percent of the purchase price of a residence are payable by the vendor at closing.[25]
18. *Loan discount payments*, or "points," are assessed by the lender to improve his yield, particularly in FHA-VA transactions. One point is 1 percent of the mortgage loan in various areas of the country. They are paid by the vendor to the conventional lender in tight-money periods, and to the FHA or VA underwritten mortgage lender as a matter of course, as a payment for extending the loan to his purchaser.[26]

At the end of closing, the transfer and mortgage documents are amended, and old mortgages and encumbrances are marked *paid* on the records. Public officials charge *recording fees* for their administrative expenses. The first page of the documents will cost $1-$5 to record; each successive page will cost $1.00-$1.50.

Classifying Settlement Costs

It is the purchaser who, in most regions of the United States, pays most of the settlement costs just listed. However, if both the purchaser and the lender benefit from the information generated by settlement services, in an ideal world both would pay some fraction of the costs. For the lender, the primary incentive to lend money is his return on the principal amount of the loan. The information provided to the lender informs his business judgment. If he were to pay a greater share of settlement costs, such charges would probably become part of his overhead expenses and become a factor in computing the interest rate on the loan. Thus the purchaser would be able to finance or amortize some of the informational settlement fees such as credit reports, surveys, and one half of the title-search charge that reduce the business risks of the lender. Arguably, mortgage preparation, a portion of the escrow and closing fees, mortgage title insurance premiums, and FHA-VA premiums might be included as well. Some other fees such as origination and loan discount payments might fall into this category because they are virtually interest payments in the opening months of the loan.

There remains one half of the title-examination fee, house and insect-infestation inspections, and deed-preparation charges to be paid by the purchaser. Some portion of the escrow and closing charges—say, one third, provided the deed and mortgage closing are held simultaneously—should be paid by the purchaser as well.

Ideally, then, the purchaser should pay directly for information valuable to him as a new owner, and the lender should pay initially and directly for information that reduces his risk, later to have them amortized by the purchaser.[27]

Categorizing settlement costs and services according to the primary beneficiaries of each one has two advantages. The first is that amortization of those costs that reduce the mortgagee's risk motivates the lending institution to bargain with its servicers for the lowest costs. As the conveyancing patterns studied in Chapter 2 show, when the mortgagee can pass on many costs intact to the purchaser, he has no incentive to hold the line or to reduce real estate settlement costs; whereas when some of those costs cannot initially be amortized, the party with the greater bargaining power has some incentive to reduce the cost of those services for which he must pay directly. Thus the lender may have a reason to help make conveyancing patterns in his region more efficient.

Another advantage of distinguishing between the types of information engendered by settlement services as either risk reducing or ownership-related is that it becomes clear that both the purchaser and the mortgagee benefit from the plethora of charges. One characteristic of the patterns of the two jurisdictions described in Chapter 2 is that the purchaser receives an itemized list of settlement charges at the closing. His review of this settlement sheet with its various charges is his only contact with those who provided the services. He may assume that he has employed those who rendered the services, but often he did not, although he pays for them: The mortgagee is the sole employer of such servicers. In law there arises a privity of contract between the servicer and the mortgagee, but not with the purchaser.[28] The legal consequence of this is that the mortgagee can, and the purchaser cannot, sue the servicer for negligence or incompetence. The case law is still solidly behind this proposition,[29] but is starting to reverse itself on the theory that the mortgagee would not have been involved had not the purchaser energized his interest with a loan application.[30] Where the payment of some fees remains the purchaser's responsibility, the possibility of a court finding privity on the basis of this payment is much stronger. For similar reasons some services beneficial to both the purchaser and the mortgagee should be split between them, for where the burden of the charge is shared, both can establish the privity needed to sue a servicer who fails to discharge his employment obligations. Furthermore, splitting costs will give both purchasers and lenders an interest in improving present conveyancing patterns.[31] It is those patterns, which are the context for the settlement costs listed in this chapter, which are the subject of the next.

Notes

1. D.D. Moyer & K.P. Fisher, *Land Parcel Identifiers for Information Systems* 1, 3 (1973) considers the multiple informational uses of land title data. In truth-in-lending laws the purchaser-borrower is to be given meaningful information about the cost of financing. *See* 12 C.F.R. §226.4, -.5 (1974). Disclosure of conveyancing information has been a source of controversy since the Statute of Enrollments in 1536. *See* T. Plunkett, *Concise History of the Common Law* 615-16 (5th ed. 1956).

2. A broker's skill lies also in the conduct of negotiations, but that might be seen as controlling the flow of information between the parties. Statutes in some states require that documents accepted for recording in land title records have the purchase price shown on their face. *See, e.g.*, Neb. Stat. Ann. §76-214 (1971); *see also* Minn. Stat. Ann., §507.09 (1969) (name of grantee and drafter required).

3. *See* text at n. 14 *infra*.

4. The extent to which it must be a title "of record" or just a marketable or partially non-record title depends generally on the sales contract.

5. The case-study jurisdictions exemplify some of this variety. South Dakota closings are arranged so that the title and the mortgage closings are held concurrently, but in the District of Columbia the closing of the title occurs before that of the trust deed.

6. HUD-VA, *Report on Mortgage Settlement Costs* (1972); Burke, "Conveyancing in the National Capital Region: Local Reform with National Implications," 22 Am. U. L. Rev. 527 (1973).

7. HUD-VA, *Report, supra* n. 6, at 7.

8. These expenses are adjusted or prorated on the closing date. Standardized closing sheets will have prepared blanks for insertion of the prorated amounts due from each party to the sale and the federal Department of Housing and Urban Development had its own form in widespread use in mid-1976.

9. These averages are taken from the HUD-VA *Report, supra* n. 6 and are on a scale encompassing South Dakota and Washington, D.C., the jurisdictions studied in detail in ch. 2.

10. B. Burke & N. Kittrie, *The Real Estate Settlement Process and Its Costs* III-E-6, -7 (1972) (hereinafter Burke and Kittrie).

11. Comment, "Independent Escrow Agents: The Law and the Licensee," 38 S. Cal. L. Rev. 289 (1965).

12. "Protection Adopted for Resale Houses," Washington Post (May 17, 1975) §E5, col. 1.

13. Marvell, *The Federal Home Loan Bank Board* 112 (1969) makes the case that savings and loan associations, which lend 44 percent of all residential mortgage credit, are extremely conservative. This percentage and other useful data on the savings and loan industry is published annually by the U.S. Savings and Loan League, *'76 Fact Book* 32 (1975); *see also* Bentley & MacBeth, "Mortgage Lenders and the Housing Supply," 57 Corn. L. Rev. 149 (1972), for a discussion of lending practices and credit standards.

14. In general, the following nine definitions are taken from HUD-VA, *Report on Mortgage Settlement Costs* 3 (1972).

15. Recent comprehensive treatment of the role of the Federal Housing Administration and the Veterans' Administration are found in R. Pease & D. Kerwood, *Mortgage Banking* (1969) and L. Graebler *et al., Capital Formation on Residential Real Estate* (1962).

9

16. Bentley & MacBeth, *supra* n. 13 at 158-159, for a discussion of credit standards in New Haven, Conn.

17. The attorney's work could include the title search, review, and certification, with separate charges for drafting and preparing the documents, billed either at a flat rate or, if special problems or research were involved, at an hourly rate. The bulk of these transactions are probably routine, yet the client pays for a review of the title against the possibility of a problem. In this context it is arguable that routine cases subsidize the difficult ones. Similarly, for brokers, a sale may take one hour, or it may take days or even weeks; their commission allows the easy sale to subsidize the difficult. The same applies to the percentage charged for a lender's administrative work. *See* para. n. 9, *infra.*

The fees earned in the higher priced transactions may subsidize the transfers of less costly housing. This subsidy is possible if the work can be held constant no matter what the sales price or mortgage amount. An hourly charge would eliminate this subsidy but might raise settlement costs on the lower end of the scale. However, with minimal housing prices as high as they currently are, the segment of the population helped or hindered by this subsidy may render it socially insignificant.

On the other hand, charges based on percentages allow a client to compute beforehand his major transaction expenses. In the case of the attorney's minimum-fee schedules and FHA-VA application fees, this was indeed one reason for their initial use.

Where a profession has been assigned quasi-public duties, another type of subsidy may operate. In the case of attorneys, their monopoly over the provision of legal services is a franchise granted by the state in return for certain duties, including assigned cases, the representation of indigents, and *pro bono* representation of various kinds. Paid services the legal profession routinely performs, *e.g.*, conveyancing, may subsidize this unpaid but socially useful work, just as a hospital with a public ward will have to recoup some of its expenses out of the fees paid by patients in its private beds. Any discussion of changes in fees should take into account the legal profession as a whole.

Regardless of the extent to which these subsidies actually determine settlement costs, the immediate point is that it is difficult to accept percentage-based fees at face value, for they may be unrelated to the actual work performed during any particular transaction. This ignores a possible further bias in favor of vendors and the status quo, for settlement costs borne by the purchaser are an obstacle to any change in ownership. Samuels, "The Coase Theorem and the Study of Law and Economics," 14 Nat. Res. J. 1, 19-25 (1974).

Another reason for consumer skepticism about charges made by attorneys and lenders is that in many cases the work duplicates that performed in other transactions involving the same title. If a lender has dealt with or an attorney has previously searched a title, his percentage charge does not reflect his previous work. An attorney may, for example, search the title of lands soon to be subdivided by a developer. To get this work, he may charge less than the full cost of the search, on the theory that his future searches of the title to the parcels in the subdivision will be easier since they will involve only an up-dating of his prior work. In this situation, the home purchaser is subsidizing the developer by reducing the latter's need to use seed money to pay for a title search. If the prior owner was a land speculator and the land has lain idle, the passage of time and the tolling of limitation and prescriptive periods may have quieted the title. Further, if subdividing increases the value of the land, a sliding scale of fees means that the attorney will later receive a larger fee for less work. These considerations suggest that, where a title is repeatedly involved in a series of transactions, subsidies between these transactions are a strong possibility.

However, one must not be bewildered by the inequity of one client paying for services performed for another. To the extent that fees subsidize difficult, low-paying, or unremunerated work, little provable inequity results. This is especially true if one considers percentage charges as an indemnity payment, relating the size of the fee to the risk assumed. Loan-processing charges, attorneys' title-search fees, FHA-VA loan-commitment fees, and title insurance premiums are often defended in this way.

18. Burke, *supra* n. 6, at 559. FHA and VA regulations require a survey.

19. Q. Johnstone & D. Hopson, *Lawyers and Their Work* 273 (1967); Q. Johnstone, *Title Insurance*, 66 Yale L. J. 492 (1957).

20. Burke, *supra* n. 6 at 553; Federal Land Bank v. Crosland, 261 U.S. 374 (1923), considers the constitutionality of transfer taxes; a separate problem so far has been their inequity, a subject left to economists.

21. Silverstein v. Shadow Law Sav. and Loan Assn, 51 N.J. 30, 237 A.2d 474 (1968), discusses how interest on mortgages is computed; *see also* Note, "Legal Aspects of the Use of 'Ordinary Simple Interest'," 40 U. Chic. L. Rev. 141 (1972).

22. P. Barron, *Federal Regulation of Real Estate* 83-107 (1975).

23. Carberry, "Mortgagors Challenge Demand that Taxes Be Paid into No-interest Escrow Accounts," Wall St. J., Oct. 26, 1971 at 40.

24. Goodman v. Perpetual Bldg. Assn, Civ. Action No. 2720-66 (D.D.C., Memo. Opin. filed Apr. 10, 1970).

25. The brokerage commission is actually due and payable in most states when the broker has secured a purchaser ready, willing, and financially able to buy, but in practice these purchaser characteristics are shown by his closing the transaction. *See* C. Berger, A. Axelrod, & Q. Johnstone, *Land Transfer and Finance* 3-50 (1969).

26. The practice in the FHA-VA market had its origins in the 1950s in a period of tight money, Hood & Kashner, "Real Estate Finance: The Discount Point System and Its Effect on Federally Insured Home Loans," 40 U.M.K.C. L. Rev. 1 (1972). In the current mortgage market, it has been used for conventional loans. The origins of these payments suggest that they are a substitute for

interest. Their purpose is either to bring the FHA-VA controlled interest rates in line with conventional rates or to anticipate future rate increases and raising of the usury ceilings in a time of monetary inflation. Comparative studies support this, for in countries using variable interest rates, the use of points declines. Anderson & Eisenmenger, "Structural Reform for Thrift Institutions: The Experience in the United States and Canada," New England Econ. Rev., Jul.-Aug., 1972, at 3, 13.

27. There are, of course, some settlement costs such as origination and loan-application fees, realty and mortgage-brokerage commissions, and point payments that do not fit into these informational categories. They pay the lender's overhead expenses and may (under many usury laws) be passed on to the borrower; they are not deemed as interest for purposes of the usury statutes. Vee Bee Serv. Co. v. Household Fin. Co., 51 N.Y.S.2d 570 (1945), aff'd 269 App. Div. 722, 55 N.Y.S.2d 570 (1945).

28. New Jersey Bar Ass'n v. Northern N.J. Mtge. Ass'n, 32 N.J. 430, 161 A.2d 257 (1960); Grievance Comm. v. Dean, 190 S.W.2d 126 (Tex. 1945); *see generally* Pollack & Maitland, *Hist. of Eng. Law* 216 (2d ed. 1952).

29. Annotation, "Attorney's Liability, to One Other than His Immediate Client, for Consequences or Negligence in Carrying Out Legal Duties," 45 A.L.R. 3d 1181 (1972).

30. Williams v. Polgar, 43 Mich. App. 95, 204 N.W.2d 57 (1972), noted at 21 Wayne St. L. Rev. 139 (1974).

31. Whitman, "Home Transfer Costs: An Economic and Legal Analysis," 62 Geo. L. J. 1311 (1974).

Two Case Studies of Our Conveyancing Patterns

Introduction

What follows is an outline of the residential conveyancing process and an examination of title delivery and conveyancing in two specific jurisdictions. The purpose is to make the process more vivid and to draw general conclusions about trends in the title-transfer industry so that subsequent chapters can assay proposals for change in light of these descriptive materials. The two jurisdictions selected are Sioux Falls, South Dakota, and the District of Columbia. The former was selected because it uses a relatively simple method of conveyancing, one that is less costly for purchasers and vendors than other methods. The latter was selected for its relative complexity and high cost. After a brief description of a residential transaction and a discussion of the pattern it presents, the two case studies will be used to describe the roles of the people involved in a transaction.

The simplest conveyances are gifts and "as is," or quitclaim, sales. In most every other conveyance, there are four steps: contracting for purchase, financing the acquisition, proving title, and organizing the closing. Purchasers and vendors of real property first agree on the property to be transferred. A prospective purchaser is shown the property by a real estate agent, broker, or his salesman. If the parties agree on the rudiments of a sale (a property, a price, and a delivery date), they sign a contract of sale or other written agreement stating these essentials. This document is executory in that it specifies standards prescribing the conduct in which the parties are to engage as preconditions to settling or "closing" the transaction. The period of time during which these actions are taken is called the *executory period* and involves obtaining financing, receiving clearance by zoning or public officials if necessary, selling the purchaser's existing residence, investigating title to the land, and negotiating and preparing the transfer documents.

In some regions the vendor must present to the purchaser any title information he has; sometimes it is the responsibility of the purchaser to assemble this information. Either way, the purchaser must have the information reviewed and found satisfactory.

Assembling title information is usually a process of searching local public records relating to property. A history of transactions involving the property in question is assembled, based on the names of the parties involved. Then a check is run on each party during his period of ownership or interest to see if that interest was sold or encumbered in any way. A list of the documents involved in this chain of transactions and a verbatim report or summary of each is then reviewed by an attorney. He informs the purchaser if the title is reasonably secure and the property safe to buy.

Normally the purchaser will finance his acquisition of the property. (In some areas mortgage lending is done only on the basis of a completed contract; in others, the mortgage commitment precedes the contract.) Since 1900 most residential purchases have been financed by third-party lenders.

Caveat emptor is a rule of law and prudence. One of the parties or the mortgagee may therefore call for assurances of merchantability from an attorney, a house inspector, a credit-reporting agency, an abstractor or title company, a surveyor, a title insurer, and an escrow agent. The list of possible servicers for any particular conveyance is a long one and varies from region to region. Each person called on receives a fee for his service. Some charges represent work a party contracted for directly. Others are "passed on" by the lender to either party. If fees are paid by the vendor, they may still be passed on to the purchaser in the price of the residence itself. If so, the purchaser may amortize them as part of his mortgage financing. He pays for the plethora of services even though he may not deal directly with the personnel providing them. Such fees are usually itemized and paid at the closing of the transaction. The closing or settlement, the final event in the executory period, is a ceremony in which the vendor and purchaser adjust the financial burden of ownership and trade the deed for the purchase price. The sale and the mortgage are usually closed simultaneously.

Because of the great volume of real property processed daily, standardized forms for contracts, mortgages, and deeds, as well as regularized business relationships, have been developed to facilitate transactions. These relationships exist most frequently between realty brokers and lenders, lenders and attorneys, attorneys and abstractors and title insurers. They may appear to the prospective purchaser as a group of people whose incomes depend on the transfer of real estate. Confronted with such a group, a purchaser may come to suspect that although he pays for their services, their primary loyalty is to the other businessmen who can offer them business in the future. Collectively, these people may be dubbed the "real estate transfer industry."

The main function of this industry is the delivery of secure titles and owner-occupied housing to purchasers. It is a delivery system comprising realty brokers, attorneys, abstract companies, title insurers, lenders, credit reporters, surveyors, property and termite inspectors, appraisers, and state and local officials who provide public records and recording services for documents. The system requires the cooperation of both the public and private sectors. The status of the title is ascertained largely from public records to which the documents of each transaction are added just after the closing. This protects the interests of both the purchaser and lender by giving public notice of their interests to others inquiring about the property.

The attorney has many ways to become involved in the transaction; yet no matter how he enters, he always enters on behalf of someone. This client orientation is entirely in keeping with the traditions of his profession, but it means that in his review of the documents he has a built-in bias. In addition, he may, as will be seen, enter the transaction in several organizational roles that might also affect his judgment.

Contracting for Purchase

In the vanguard of the real estate industry is the broker. Having previously contracted with the vendor to list the property for sale[1] (the listing contract may be written or oral[2]), the broker has some motivations that affect the early stages of a conveyance. For example, since the broker's contract is with the vendor,[3] he is the agent of the vendor alone. The broker's commission comes out of the purchase price and is payable, unusual contract clauses aside, at the closing.[4] The legal rules make it clear that the broker is due his commission when he produces a purchaser "ready, willing, and able to buy," or is the effective cause of a sale.[5] The execution of a sales contract usually satisfies the rule.[6] His expertise lies in obtaining listings, bringing the parties to the bargaining table, and conducting the contract negotiations.[7] The fact that the vendor must usually be paid before the broker receives his commission gives the broker an incentive to stay close to the proceedings during the executory period. Often a broker or board of realtors will try to protect a commission by combining the contract of sale with a written offer, or binder contract, making the purchaser's deposit subject to the payment of their commission.[8] It forges one more link in the chain of events between his efforts, the closing, and the purchaser's money. This combined binder-contract sometimes disserves the parties to the contract[9] because the length of the executory period itself, the type of financing the purchaser must make a reasonable effort to obtain, the legal description of the property, the quality of the title, and the warranties the vendor gives are all the subject of the sales contract.[10] A contract prepared by a broker, as the vendor's agent, is likely to contain only general standards at best. The purchaser may be pressured to accept a title of lesser quality, unfavorable financing, or fewer warranties than he would have liked.[11] On some matters the law has evolved minimum standards for contracts. For example, it implies that the parties intended to contract for a marketable title, one that is reasonably free from doubt and protracted litigation.[12] But whether this minimum protection is sufficient to protect either party, or indeed whether it can be contracted away, is an open question in some states.[13] Similarly, if the contract is not specific about the type of mortgage loan, its interest rate, and total settlement costs, terms will be set by conventional practices or going market rates.[14] So too with the terms of the mortgage contract, e.g., the right to prepay or accelerate the debt. That the purchaser may want to sell his present house first[15] or want special financial arrangements[16] is not likely to be explored by the broker. He has no incentive or duty to add special provisions or to counsel both parties about the particular circumstances of their transaction.[17] One of the economic functions of contracts "is to reduce the complexity and hence cost of transactions by supplying a set of normal terms which, in the absence of the law of contracts, the parties would have to negotiate expressly."[18] A second, somewhat conflicting notion is that they "furnish prospective transacting parties with information concerning the many contingencies that may defeat an exchange...."[19] The broker, however, uses a shortened contract because of his interest in having the contract executed; he leaves the terms general[20] rather than allowing the parties to think about the pitfalls that might arise. The parties' executory agreement often remains poorly documented.

For his services the broker receives a commission, usually a fixed percentage of the purchase price of the property. Currently it is 5-7 percent to be deducted from the price the vendor receives at the closing. The customary commission is, on its face, unrelated to the time, overhead costs, and effort the broker expends. In a sense, the broker is constantly betting on a quick sale.[21] If a prospective purchaser is shown one house and decides to buy it, presumably both he and the broker are happy to stop looking.[22] Should the purchaser desire to compensate the broker for his efforts and negotiate directly for a price from which no brokerage fee would be deducted, the broker's listing contract with the seller would first have to be rescinded. This difficulty prevents the prospective purchaser from negotiating on this basis.[23] A typical search conducted by a broker for a prospect involves an inspection of his unsold inventory of housing. The time spent with each prospect is hard to predict: It may be the first or the tenth house that the prospect will decide to purchase. Or he may not like any. From the vendor's perspective, no matter how many times the broker seeks to interest prospects in his house, the same commission applies. For both the broker and the owner, the percentage commission has the virtue of certainty.

A slight risk of the brokerage business is the possibility of a charge by the vendor that the broker has breached his fiduciary duty of loyalty to the vendor. Telling the purchaser that the vendor "would settle for" a certain price is likely to result in such a charge and might mean a frustrated transaction or, worse, resort to the legal process.[24]

Brokers appear to be satisfied with percentage commissions because of the unpredictability of the time needed to complete any one sale and the uncertainty that a closing will result from a signed contract. Since it is difficult to predict his costs on the basis of his last sale or even to calculate costs when the listing contract is executed with the vendor, brokers tend to average their costs. The case law concerning brokers reflects and reinforces this. In a case brought by a broker to recover a commission, it was said,

The "amount of hours spent" by the broker was not relevant to the issue. ". . . [a] real estate broker is employed not to expend time and effort but to accomplish a particular result. . . ."[25]

So actions by brokers in *quantum meruit* to obtain compensation for their time and effort, in the absence of a specific agreement, are routinely dismissed.[26]

Traditional Patterns of American Conveyancing

Beyond the activities of the broker, the title delivery and conveyancing systems around the country divide into categories in which the attorney organizes the closing and searches and reviews the title perhaps with the aid of an abstract company; or a title insurance company organizes the closing, does the title work, and issues a policy of title insurance.[27] Attorneys participate in most conveyances under either system, either as private practitioners or as salaried attorneys working for a title insurance company. The transition from the first system to the second happens when the private attorney cannot obtain the services of an abstract company because its title records have been purchased by a title insurance company.[28] Such acquisitions do not occur regularly in rural areas where attorneys may organize their files similarly to those of a small abstract company or where individual abstractors free-lance for attorneys. But a watershed is reached when the bar in fast-growing counties relies heavily on a few abstract companies for compilation of title evidence. When the source of title records changes hands,[29] the system leaves the sphere of the private attorney and enters that of a title insurance corporation. Attorneys are then denied access to title records except when they desire to purchase title insurance.[30] The title insurance corporation might continue to work with local attorneys who would organize the closings;[31] or it might establish abstracting, insuring, and escrow departments within its own corporate structure.[32] If it organizes in this way, the title insurance company will probably become the county's sole source of conveyancing services.

The Attorney's Personal Search for a Provable Title

The traditional, if not the oldest, method of conveyancing in the United States is to have the title searched, reviewed, and closed by an attorney.[33] He acts on the initiative of a client—either a vendor, purchaser, their agent (perhaps a broker), or a lender considering a purchaser's application for a mortgage loan.[34] After a title search is conducted and the abstract reviewed, the attorney tells his client his findings. Sometimes he provides his client with the compilation of title documents and records, called an *abstract of title*,[35] but more often his findings and legal conclusions about the title are summarized in a letter. If no substantial defects are found, this letter certifies the legal marketability of the title. It assures the purchaser that the title is safe to purchase,[36] able to be mortgaged,[37] and is not subject to encumbrances that cannot be satisfied out of the purchase price.[38]

The attorney's client may come to him outright or be referred to him by a broker, developer, or lender.[39] The attorney, perhaps dependent on these referrals, becomes interested as much in the flow of clients as in their representation. If the attorney's primary client is a lending institution, the attorney will review the documents from the lender's point of view and then, since repayment of the loan may be affected by an encumbrance, from the purchaser-borrower's.[40] A lender, wanting a secure investment,[41] may have different interests than an owner-occupier. For example, few lenders are concerned with easements on the property to the extent that owners are.[42] Similarly, preparation of the owner's transfer deed is incidental to the primary client's business of lending mortgage money. With the exception of the mortgage, the documents involved are likely to receive scant attention. This is not to say that the deed will be incompetently drafted but that the purchaser's interests will be represented indirectly. In this situation many purchasers must assume that "what's good enough for the bank is good enough for me too." The closing may even be held at the bank.

The presence of an attorney may not be the key to classifying conveyancing patterns. The assumption that the attorney alone prepared for the closing became commonplace in the nineteenth century and belongs to the rural past of the country.[43] In the attorney-dominated system, when conveyancing was the monopoly of private practitioners, the attorney himself searched the public records. Today this is true only in New England and some rural areas.[44] By 1900 attorneys were hiring laymen to compile title abstracts.[45] They or their firms might hire[46] an abstractor, whose principal task would be to search titles and to write reports on his findings; or a skilled legal secretary might do this. In law at the turn of the century and today, the attorney is liable to his client for a negligent[47] or incompetent title search[48] and often insures against this and any added liability to third parties.[49] Most attorneys spend what time they do give to conveyancing in reviewing the work of lay abstractors.

The Abstractor's Search and the Attorney's Review

Well before the end of the last century, many abstractors found it advantageous to organize their businesses into independent companies.[50] Their product is an *abstract of title;*[51] as the term implies, it is not the older, English compilation of all documents in one file but rather is a summary of them. At first laymen probably compiled complete title documents for perusal and review by the attorney.[52] Later as the delegation of work broadened and became an accepted practice, the compilation became an abstract that summarized[53] chronologically each title transaction discovered in the course of the title search.[54]

An abstractor's business must be efficiently organized to survive, and to achieve this title plants are often established.[55] At minimum these will be the past document compilations or summaries produced by the company. At most they will be duplications of all the public title records, rearranged and cross-indexed. The entire name index of public records might be converted to parcel-indexed records, but usually the reorganization is not that sweeping, and only those public indexes and records most frequently used are parcel indexed. In any event, these plants have as their principal asset a partially reorganized set of public records.[56] If a complete set of records is kept, abstracts are very likely kept in a separate file for reuse and updating, thus preventing duplication of a full title search with each new transaction.

When the abstract company is employed by an attorney, he is able to shift liability for any searching errors to the abstractor.[57] In some states the business of abstracting is subject to bonding and other state regulations.[58]

Whether the attorney or an abstract company performs the search, the scope of the search is a matter established by professional custom,[59] albeit greatly influenced by law. So is the length of time covered in a title search. Laws passed recently in sixteen states have established a period of time after which certain interests in land are either nullified or barred from enforcement, rather than establishing a time period to be searched.[60] The contract could define the scope of the search and so could conceivably involve more records than are found locally. In practice, this is seldom the case. Standard contracts do not specify any particular records as those to be searched. Records are searched because they are easily or locally accessible to the searcher. With time the scope of the search becomes a matter of custom.

Case Study: Sioux Falls, South Dakota

Areas where attorneys search land title records are hard to find, and where they do exist (as in New England), they are unrepresentative of national practice. South Dakota, and particularly the region around Sioux Falls, exemplifies the pattern in which abstractors compile and attorneys review title information.

The Environment for Conveyancing. South Dakota, with 666,000 people,[61] ranks forty-fourth in population among the states. It is sixteenth in area,[62] with 75,955 square miles of land.[63] Approximately 94 percent of its land is farms,[64] and 56 percent of the population lives on them.[65] In 1971 building permits authorized 2,600 housing units valued at $34 million or $13,000 per unit.[66]

(Only the District of Colombia and three other states had fewer starts.[67]) The total number of year-round housing units in 1960 was 222,000.[68] About 23,000 transfers occur annually.[69] In 1969 the median income of a South Dakota family was $7,494, substantially below the national average of $9,590.[70] The average hourly earnings of industrial and manufacturing workers was $3.13, below the national average of $3.57.[71] In 1971 South Dakota ranked thirty-sixth among the states in average personal income.[72]

South Dakota was established on land originally acquired by the Louisiana Purchase, a large part of the northern section of which became the Dakota Territory in 1861. In 1877 the Territorial Code adopted by the legislature of the Dakota Territory provided for a registrar of deeds. In 1889 South Dakota won statehood. Although some titles in the southeastern part of the state date back to the 1840s, most of the land titles can be traced to the U.S. government in the 1860s or later. It has been the practice in initial searches to trace a title back to the government patent, but this is becoming costly in urban areas.[73]

During the territorial years, conveyancing policy was a product of federal homesteading policy.[74] The United States disposed of land through direct grants as well as through the Homestead Act of 1862 and its later amendments.[75] The first claim, recorded in January, 1863, was filed in Yankton, South Dakota, by one Mahlon Gore. His entry is described as part of Sections 9 and 10, Township 92 North, Range 49 West, located about 10 miles northwest of Elk Point in Union County. (His claim was promptly jumped by one Henry Fisher, and Gore lost possession of the land.)[76] The rectangular system of land description used in the Northwest Territory and the West enabled land to be described by reference to government surveys.[77]

Settlement proceeded from the southeastern portion of the state to the east bank of the Missouri River. Engineers from neighboring states surveyed the land; by 1876 they were working in the region between the Big Sioux and James River; and by the 1880s most of the east river country (that part of South Dakota to the east of the Missouri River) had been surveyed.[78]

Federal homestead laws created one unusual problem in the area west of the Missouri River. Individual land tracts, opened to settlement under the Homestead Acts, were usually too small to be economically viable farms, and the land eventually passed to large landowners. Some ranches are the result of the consolidation of as many as fifty to one hundred small tracts. The need to search each tract back to its root in a government patent[79] makes the title search today very expensive.

Railroad and land companies worked hard to promote settlement in South Dakota.[80] Residents of eastern states could take advantage of cut-rate fares to visit the territory, best known in the 1880s and 1890s for its liberal divorce laws. When the visitors were there, efforts were made to sell them on the lush prospects of Dakota land.

Every community had one or more land locators who hauled homeseekers over the countryside in a livery rig to point out lands still open for filing. The locator charged a fee for such service. His goal was to get the new prospect to register for a claim and collect his fee. The locator also speculated in lands and relinquishments. The landsman's office was baited with pictures and samples of crop exhibits said to have been grown in the locality. Some of the locators were high pressure salesmen. A settler's later complaint or dissatisfaction brought no return of the fee.[81]

Some might argue that the land locator was a predecessor of the present-day real estate agent.

By law, homesteaded land had to be improved within three to five years. Much fraud and evasion of the requirements for improvements were overlooked by the land offices. A homesteader would sometimes swear that he had a livable residence on his land when in fact he had rented a shack on wheels for $5 a day and parked it there. After the homesteader obtained title, the shack would be hauled away. If the land proved too much for the homesteader to manage, he could sell his rights to a speculator before abandoning the place.[82]

Brokers. Real estate brokers in Sioux Falls, South Dakota, currently charge a commission of 6 percent of the sales price of a house,[83] and they, along with surveyors or engineers, often appear in rezoning cases. Lawyers seldom appear to obtain rezonings or draft contracts of sale. (Indeed, there are only two attorneys who can be identified by city planning officials as having familiarity with zoning matters.)[84] Most vendors of residential property in Sioux Falls possess commercially prepared abstracts assuring their titles.[85] Realtors often obtain this title abstract and deliver it to the purchaser's lending institution,[86] which passes it on to a title attorney. This practice has the weight of law behind it, for in the case of *Haloorson* v. *Birkland,*[87] the South Dakota Supreme Court held that a purchaser has a right to rescind a sales contract when the vendor does not furnish an abstract of title.

The unauthorized practice of law by real estate brokers, often found in regions with shifting conveyancing patterns, has not been discussed in the opinions of the appellate courts of South Dakota.[88] This may be due to the holding in a 1944 case: In a suit for injunction by the state bar association to restrain a layman from practicing law, the South Dakota Supreme Court held that the privilege to restrain the unauthorized practice of law runs solely to members of the public generally and is not a right of private attorneys. The state bar did not suffer such injury that it could maintain an action for injunction.[89] At present the South Dakota Code, which regulates admission of attorneys to practice[90] as well as their rights and duties,[91] provides that any person engaging in the unauthorized practice of law may be restrained by injunction;[92] as yet, this statute has not been invoked against real estate brokers. An attorney who holds himself "to be in the real estate business or solicit real estate business"[93] may receive a broker's license upon application, without examination. Thereafter, there is no prohibition on an attorney acting as both broker and conveyancer for the same transaction.

As of 1975 brokers are not entitled to their commission "until the transaction has been consummated or terminated."[94] No cases have clarified this statute so it is not clear whether a contract or a closing is the prerequisite for a commission. However, the broker remains involved in a transaction until the closing.[95] As in other regions where the broker remains the premier real estate specialist, many closings take place in his office.

Abstractors. Conveyancing in South Dakota today is almost totally dominated by the abstractor-attorney title-search review pattern. Personal search is used on rare occasions.[96] One commentator surmised that occasionally abstractors make their own evaluation and assurance of title in the absence of an attorney.[97] Almost all titles in South Dakota are supported by commercial abstracts, usually without accompanying title insurance,[98] although regulatory statutes do exist for title insurance rates and policies.[99]

The licensing and regulation of abstractors[100] began as early as 1899 with a statute requiring a bond to engage in abstracting. Further legislation in the 1920s required competent personnel, an "adequate" title plant, and examination by a state board.[101] It provided for a board of examiners and set forth the scope of the examination that abstractors must pass to become registered.[102] In addition, the abstractor was (and is) required to file a bond in an amount ranging from $5,000 to $15,000, proportional to the population of his county.[103] He was required to maintain an adequate abstract plant,[104] which after the 1920s meant an adequate index rather than the land records themselves. The law also authorized the board of examiners to set a fee schedule and made it unlawful for abstractors to exceed it.[105]

South Dakota law expressly does away with the requirement of privity of contract as an element of an abstractor's liability. The abstractor is liable to any person relying on the abstract to his detriment.[106] However, his liability is limited to damages proximately caused by his errors, omissions, or defects in the abstract.[107] Thus in one case where the abstractor made an entry of a recorded but nonexistent mortgage in an abstract, sureties on his bond were not held liable to a plaintiff who purchased the mortgage. The court said that the abstract makes no representation as to the genuineness of the documents it contains. Thus plaintiff's injury was not proximately caused by the abstract but by reliance on a fraudulent mortgage.[108] Additionally, there is a limitation of actions on abstractors' bonds to ten years from accrual of the cause of action, which is deemed the date of the abstract or certificate of title.[109] Finally, the abstract has, by statute, been given evidentiary value in court: The abstractor's certificate is *prima facie* evidence in judicial proceedings of the existence of its documentary contents.[110]

With commercial abstracts of such legal value, title insurance has not gained widespread acceptance and use in South Dakota. Perhaps one factor contributing to this is the statutory provision that an out-of-state title insurance company must have an abstractor countersign a title insurance policy.[111] In areas where one uncooperative abstractor has a monopoly, this requirement might effectively preclude a company from establishing a business.

South Dakota abstractors have formed a state title association that has worked out a form certifying that an abstract is a complete list of all county records affecting the title, that there are no unsatisfied liens or tax assessments due that would affect title, and no unsatisfied judgments shown by the county records.[112] The certificate is the same throughout the state except that changes are sometimes made in large cities to cover special conditions. The forms have been accepted in the industry, and their adoption saves a great deal of trouble for both attorneys and abstractors.

When the abstract company receives a vendor's abstract, it extends it for a minimum fee of $15 plus $1.00 to $1.50 for each entry required in the extension.[113] The typical abstract extension costs from $17 to $20. Of the two abstract companies in Sioux Falls, one of them does nearly 80 percent of the abstracting business in the city.[114] The other is commonly believed to exist in order to sell title insurance. In Sioux Falls abstract companies do not hire attorneys to review abstracts, although one of the companies is currently owned by a lawyer not actively engaged in the practice of law.[115]

Attorneys. The bar, by convention and formal agreement with the Board of Realtors, usually charges $50 to review an abstract.[116] There is also a charge based on the value of the property contained in a minimum fee schedule applicable in the area, but conventionally the bar does not use it except in cases where the value of the property (and a lawyer's possible liability) is extremely high.[117] An attorney actually reviews a title twice in the course of a transaction: once to issue a "preliminary certificate" on the basis of which the mortgage loan will be extended and closed, and again after a final search is made just before the closing.[118]

Under South Dakota's marketable-title act, the period of search is reduced to a relatively short period of twenty-two years plus the period of time back to the next prior title transaction.[119] Also beneficial to the attorney who issues a title opinion are the bar-promulgated title standards, found in an appendix to the marketable-title statute.[120] They are guidelines on whether the examining attorney should object to particular defects or irregularities. Their general tenor is evident in Standard 1.1, which provides that attorneys should make objections only when irregularities or defects can reasonably be expected to expose the purchaser or lender to the hazard of adverse claims or litigation. Subsequent standards (there are thirteen in all) provide, *inter alia*, the following: There should be a presumption of delivery of a deed even if the recording date is delayed; a warranty deed will convey after-acquired title; in the case of deeds from corporations, the attorney can assume that the corporation was legally in existence and that the deed was not *ultra vires*; curative acts are to be considered valid constitutional legislation; under certain specified conditions, minor name variances from one instrument to another are not fatal defects; a duly executed probate sale conveys title free of any judgment or lien outstanding against any heir; omission and inconsistency in dates does not of itself render title unmarketable unless a peculiar significance in connection with surrounding circumstances compels reasonable suspicion; and, as a prerequisite for relying on certain provisions of the marketable-title act, an attorney need only produce an affidavit of possession stating the holder is in possession of record title and that there is no conflicting claim of record. The aim of these standards is to minimize "fly-specking" a title and to establish a state-wide standard for determining what renders a title unmarketable.

It is the attorney who generally decides whether title insurance is appropriate in a particular transaction. This decision is taken solely on the basis of cost.[121] A large development or subdivision is likely to be covered by a title insurance policy; otherwise the developer would be forced to buy many abstracts when he could achieve his ends (obtaining construction and take-out loans) by the purchase of one title policy. Moreover, a title insurance company is likely to give a developer a bargain rate on his subdivision, charging only $75 for a title policy.[122] Compare this to a $40 abstract on each lot, plus a $50 charge by the attorney for his review of the abstract. However, the purchaser in the development may be the worse for this[123] because the title records stay with the title insurance corporation and no abstract is passed to the purchaser of the house. He receives only a title policy when and if he purchases title insurance. Thereafter, upon each transfer of the lot in the subdivision, every buyer must pay $100 to $150 for title insurance on the property.[124] It is very difficult to change back from a title insurance system to an abstract system for any particular lot since the purchaser would have to buy an abstract based on a search back to the government patent. Later purchasers would, however, pay only $15 plus entry fees for the extension of the abstract.[125]

South Dakota is divided east and west by the Missouri River. West of the river, title insurance is more in use than it is in the east country,[126] to protect owners against a claim that the land is still in the public domain or subject to government rights[127] or to old homestead claims. Title insurance has not gained a foothold in eastern South Dakota,[128] although it is making some headway in Sioux Falls on valuable commercial properties.[129] Even so, some recent hotel developments downtown have not used title insurance, but have relied instead on an abstract with which the conveyancing lawyer was thoroughly familiar.[130] On FHA and VA loans, many in the conveyancing bar believe that those government agencies require title insurance. (They do not.) This is not the case with Farmers Home Loan Bank and the Federal Land Bank programs.[131]

Financing: Installment Land Contracts. A long-established important method of financing realty purchases which eliminates many conveyancing expenses before the purchaser takes possession is the *installment land contract;*[132] South Dakotans call it a *contract for a deed.*[133] Its basic feature is that the vendor retains legal title during the life of the contract as security for the purchase price which the purchaser pays by installments directly to him.[134] According to one author, "[A]lthough exact figures on the percentage of land sale transactions involving a contract for deed are not obtainable, all available data for South Dakota and other midwest states indicates that a 'long term' installment land contract rather than a mortgage is used in a substantial number of both urban and rural sales."[135] Figures of the Agricultural Research Service of the U.S. Department of Agriculture show that the percentage of farm real estate transfers financed by installment land contracts increased from 18 percent in 1946 to 41 in 1960.[136] Considering that over 90 percent of South Dakota is farmland, the popularity of this method becomes evident,[137] and the tight market for mortgage money that has existed periodically since 1960 has added to its appeal. For the price of having a mortgage form prepared ($15 in 1965), and usually without paying many settlement costs, the purchaser gains possession of the land.[138]

The popularity of the installment land contract lies basically in the combination of two facts:

1. For a purchaser an installment land contract offers a low-equity financing (none to 20 percent of purchase price is a typical down payment) which is often unavailable through conventional mortgages (which may require a down payment of up to 30 percent).
2. For the vendor remedies under South Dakota's vendor-purchaser law are more desirable than those offered the mortgagee under the mortgage law, which is highly protective of the mortgagor.[139] Vendors enjoy a tax advantage as well.

Thus in a time of increasing prices for land, machinery, seed, and fertilizer, a young farmer can start farming the land years earlier by using an installment land contract, and developers who can finance sales themselves have more potential purchasers. In addition, the free assignability of the contract benefits both a purchaser who wishes to sell quickly and a vendor who wishes to rid himself of a defaulting purchaser by forcing him to assign his rights to someone else.[140]

The vendor's primary remedy upon default is strict foreclosure.[141] This enables him to realize his security interest more quickly than a mortgagee who may be limited by statute to foreclosure by judicial sale despite a power-of-sale clause in the mortgage.[142] Another significant factor is the mortgagor's one-year right of redemption after judicial sale,[143] compared to the thirty to sixty days allowed an installment contract purchaser by a court in its discretion.[144] Mortgagors are immune from a deficiency judgment[145] while the same prohibition does not apply to a contract.[146] Thus the installment land contract has a strong appeal to both vendors and purchasers despite some disadvantages to both in that the vendor cannot realize the total price of his sale immediately and the purchaser is less protected than he would be as a mortgagor.

Under South Dakota law, after signing an installment land contract, the risk of loss in the absence of fault by either party is on the one in possession of the land.[147] Unless the contract provides otherwise, the purchaser has a right of prepayment without penalty.[148] The vendor is bound to deliver a conveyance in form sufficient to pass title,[149] and unless the agreement provides otherwise, there is an implied contractual warranty by the vendor that he owns the realty and that he has a right to convey and will later convey marketable title though not necessarily a warranty deed.[150] When the contract is executed, unless it states otherwise, the vendor is under no obligation to provide an abstract of title.[151]

South Dakota courts have not addressed the question of whether a contract purchaser may put a vendor in default by discovering a defect upon tendering the purchase price. With a statutory right to prepay, a purchaser can tender the purchase price in advance of the date contemplated in the contract unless the contract provides otherwise. In this situation only the financially able purchaser would be able to put a vendor with an uncertain title in default in advance of the contract date.

This right is somewhat limited by the holdings of other cases. In *Weitzel* v. *Leyson*[152] the South Dakota Supreme Court held that one may contract to sell land he does not own, and the contract will be valid and binding if the purchaser knows of the present lack of title. The contract contemplated delivery of deed upon payment of the purchase price; the payment date was unspecified. Thus when the vendee tendered payment before the vendor had acquired title, the court held that the vendor has a reasonable time after tender of the purchase price (fifteen to thirty days) to execute and tender a deed to the purchaser and that during this time he cannot be put in default by a tender of purchase money. However, the important rule in this case is that when the purchaser knows of the vendor's lack of title at the time of contracting, the vendor cannot thereafter be put in default on that account.

In a later case, *Falde* v. *Chadwick*,[153] the purchaser under an installment contract, after making initial and installment payments, was informed that the seller did not have marketable title. He immediately deposited at the bank the balance due the vendor and offered to pay it over when vendor tendered marketable title. The vendor let the twelve-month period contemplated in the contract elapse and then brought suit to declare a forfeiture against the purchaser. The court dismissed the plaintiff's action on the ground that the vendor's obligation to convey marketable title was now concurrent with the purchaser's obligation to pay the purchase price. Since the vendor's title rested on a tax deed which would not, if delivered, give purchaser a marketable title, the vendor could not place the purchaser in default unless he were able to convey a marketable title. Thus the court again avoided passing on the vendee's original attempt to require the vendor to show marketable title before paying further installments.[154]

Financing: Mortgages. The other common method for financing real estate in South Dakota is the mortgage, with a clause giving the mortgagee a power to foreclose his lien on the land by advertisement[155] instead of by judicial proceedings and a public sale.[156] After the purchaser-mortgagor defaults in payment, a weekly notice of intent to foreclose must be given for four weeks running, and then the county sheriff conducts a sale of the property.[157] For properties of less than three acres, an especially short, 180-day redemption period after sale is permitted.[158]

Loans are often closed separately, after a preliminary review of the title by an attorney. A loan settlement statement, ". . . indicating in detail the charges and fees which the borrower has paid or obligated himself to pay,"[159] is furnished at this time by all state-chartered savings and loan associations.

After a closing, at which the title is finally reviewed and attempts at curing defects are accepted or else the defect itself is waived by the purchaser, the vendor and purchaser exchange a deed for the purchase price. They also prorate any prepaid taxes and utility charges between them.[160]

Recording. Recording the transfer documents, in South Dakota as in other jurisdictions, provides protection for purchasers of real estate[161] in two ways: by providing a series of public records to which the purchaser may turn in order to assure himself that his vendor[162] in fact owns what he is attempting to sell,[163] and to put persons interested on notice that the purchaser has bought and does own the property.[164] Recording fees and transfer taxes are quite low in South Dakota. The recording fee is usually no more than $2 per document, and the transfer tax no more than $1 more.[165] Public records, which are maintained at the county level,[166] deal with past events but are prospective in effect. South Dakota's recording law is meant to put future purchasers of the same property on notice that someone else has purchased first. It protects such a purchaser when he pays something of value for the property without notice of anyone's prior purchases, and when he is first to record his interest.[167] Some abstract companies offer escrow or closing services, but few people use them.[168] Most closings occur in the offices of a realtor or a lending institution.

County records are arranged in chronological order in three sets of books: deeds (including future nonpossessory interests in land),[169] mortgages, and miscellaneous documents.[170] An index to these books is maintained according to the description of the parcel.[171] Forty-one of the sixty-four counties in South Dakota make entries on these records by longhand or typewriter; sixteen use photocopying; one uses microfilm.[172] Legal descriptions, presented for recording, must be platted according to numbers assigned by the county auditor;[173] no metes-and-bounds descriptions are recordable here,[174] with the result that there are no surveyor's fees to raise settlement costs in this area.[175] If a metes-and-bounds description is all that is available, the county auditor will survey the property for a $25 fee.[176] However, some metes-and-bounds descriptions may be made recordable by referring to the meted boundaries in relation to the boundary lines of a neighboring numbered lot.[177]

In 1917 South Dakota authorized the Torrens system of title registration, as many other states had, but subsequently repealed it. The cost of initial registration proved too expensive, especially for owners of agricultural land, and the system was rarely used. Also in remote areas there was no person competent to register the titles.

In the early 1960s the local bar in Sioux Falls investigated creating a title insurance guaranty fund.[178] A fund run by the Florida bar was studied extensively, but in the words of the chairman of the committee undertaking the study, title insurance, whether run by the bar or a corporation, was found to be "a fraud on the public."[179] When losses were found to be less than 1 percent of the premiums collected, the local bar recommended against establishing a fund.[180] The same chairman of the local committee estimates that the total cost (excluding broker's fees) of conveying a residential property in Sioux Falls is about $100.[181]

The continuing dominance of attorneys in South Dakota conveyancing can be traced to the low number of transactions, which discourages title insurers from establishing a title plant operation, to the title standards[182] discussed previously, and to the marketable-title act with its short search period. Roots of title twenty-two years from date are rendered marketable in this state,[183] and for routine searches the abstractor need only search many titles back for a period somewhat over twenty-two years. Exceptions to this act require that some searches cover more than twenty-two years, but the act helps to limit the liabilities of the conveyancing bar and therefore is relied on.[184]

The principal reasons that conveyancing in South Dakota remains a modestly priced process are that it has no title insurance, no surveying costs, few large developers, and a liberal homestead exemption.[185] Many fees are also established by statute. Abstractors' fees were at one time detailed by statutory provision; recently such provisions have been eliminated, and fees are now set by the state board of examiners.[186] Title insurance fees remain prescribed by statute.[187]

Conversely, pressures for change come from the merchant builders, the possibility that title insurance corporations could buy the abstract companies,[188] and the disappearance of abstracts from the hands of the public.[189]

Conveyancing attorneys perceive that lending institutions might prefer to have title insurance policies in their files,[190] and to counter this, they offer speedier service in the form of preliminary title certifications upon which the lending institution and the parties can close the conveyance.[191] The attorney thereafter issues a final title statement to the lender, but he remains in privity with the bank, not with the purchaser. Unlike abstract certificates, no standard form exists for an attorney's certification.[192]

State Bar Concern with Conveyancing Practices. Like attorneys in other states, South Dakota practitioners have long been concerned with preserving their conveyancing work. In the early 1960s the state bar journal and the proceedings of its annual meetings reflect the concern that attorneys felt with the changes in conveyancing practices then taking place or perceived for the near future.[193] Throughout these periodicals and reports are comments on the minimum-fee schedule for conveyancing and the threat of title insurance moving into the state.[194]

In 1961 the minimum-fee schedule was revised. In its report the state bar association found that for deed preparations the average of the state's seventeen fee schedules was $8.25, with a range from $5 to $15.[195] For mortgages the average was $19.33. On the basis of this, the minimum-fee schedule was amended to allow charges of $12 for contracts of sale, $15 for mortgages, and $7.50 for deeds. Fifteen dollars was the standard fee set for reviewing an abstract with twenty-five entries; each additional entry cost $.30; the synopsis of a court proceeding cost $3.75 more. This $15 fee was applicable when the property transferred was valued at $7,500; $1.80 was charged for each additional $7,500 in value or major fraction thereof.[196] The compilers of this bar survey stated, .

The methods of minimum fee computation on abstract examination varied widely. Some use a flat fee plus an extra charge for each page or entry. Others combine a flat fee with a percentage of values. Still others use a flat fee only; and others an hourly rate with percentage value.[197]

The introduction of this new minimum-fee schedule for conveyances coincided with an upgrading of the importance of the schedule for the state's attorneys. In the same report the state bar said that lawyers should adhere to the minimum-fee schedule: "To do otherwise would be pure mockery and for an attorney to continuously disregard the minimum fee schedule would be strong evidence of unethical conduct."[198] This emphasis on the minimum-fee schedule reflected a trend in the 1960s to make such schedules mandatory for practicing attorneys.[199]

In 1962 or 1963 the state bar began an inquiry into the feasibility of establishing a lawyer's title guaranty fund in South Dakota.[200] A special bar committee conducted an in-depth study of the experiences of neighboring states with such funds[201] and visited these states.[202] The first report of this committee appeared in the proceedings of the 1963 annual state meeting and recommended the establishment by statute of such a fund for South Dakota.[203] In 1964 the same committee reported that it had had no success in amending the state insurance code to allow for establishment of a lawyers' fund.[204] They also reported that no attorney-legislator supported the state bar's bill. It died in committee. One gets some idea of the political difficulties of establishing such a fund. It appears that at one point the lawyers thought they had reached an agreement with the state abstractors' association but that the intercession of the title insurers' representatives made this agreement impossible in the end.[205] No legislation resulted from the bar's efforts.

In 1965 the minimum-fee schedule was again amended: Attorneys would review abstracts with up to twenty-five entries for $20; each additional ten entries or fraction thereof cost $5; a synopsis of court proceedings was $6 more, and all supplementary or preliminary (for lenders) opinions of the attorney cost $7.50 each.[206] This was the first time a charge for a supplementary opinion appeared in a minimum-fee schedule. One other new charge, for attending a closing, was added for a flat fee of $15.[207]

The preparation of forms was subject to new schedules also: Contracts for deeds cost at least $15, a deed cost $5, a mortgage cost $15, a contract of sale cost $15. In this same year the lawyers' title guaranty fund committee reported that there had been no action on the fund's establishment in the legislature.[208] The state bar journals made a valiant call for continued efforts, but no lawyers' title guaranty report appeared in subsequent minutes or proceedings, and it can only be concluded that the matter died at that point.

The 1965 effort was the last wholesale overhaul of the minimum-fee schedule; no later amendments to the schedule are reported in the state bar journal, and it was abolished in 1970.[209] One commentator on South Dakota practice has indicated that the minimum-fee schedule usually lagged behind the actual charge for conveyancing work.[210] For instance, another commentator wrote in 1961 that the typical charge in the southeastern part of the state for the opinion of the title attorney was $25,[211] at a time when the minimum-fee charge was $15 or $20.[212] It has doubled since then.

Suggestions for Reform. After all is said and done, this state still has the lowest closing and settlement costs in the nation, and therefore it might be assumed at the outset that the best features of its conveyancing system should be preserved.[213]

As a first and probably most desirable objective, the state bar might push for legislation preserving present patterns of conveyancing. Such legislation might include a requirement that any title insurance company doing business in the state of South Dakota be required by the state insurance code to provide and compile a complete abstract of title to the property it services.[214] If vendors were required to present a complete abstract to purchasers, the present system of abstracts changing hands between vendors and purchasers would probably continue. An additional provision of such a statute might require that title insurance companies be required to provide policies with standardized coverage and to present abstracts to the purchaser of the property in question.[215] Title insurance companies might also have the common-law liability of an abstractor of title assigned to them by statute.[216] This would codify what is already the legal liability of abstractors on their bond and put title insurance companies and abstractors on equal footing.[217] This legislation would mean that any title insurance written in South Dakota would be based on a company's title search rather than on that company's acceptance of another's search.

Title Insurance

If conveyancing patterns in urbanized areas of the United States are any guide, title insurance might be the next addition to South Dakota's abstractor-attorney pattern. In the conveyancing systems discussed so far, the liability of the attorney or abstractor exists only for errors in the conduct of the title search.[218] Undiscoverable defects in title, called *nonrecord* or *off-record risks*, are not a basis for their liability. However remote, these risks such as fraud, forged documents, claims of a wife or heir, and misindexed public documents[219] do exist. Title insurance provides coverage against both on-record errors and the risk of an off-record title defect.[220]

Title insurance is partially premised on a title search,[221] and most title insurance companies have searches performed as a normal part of business, to reduce their risks.[222]

The major development in American conveyancing so far during the twentieth century has been the movement toward the widespread adoption of title insurance. It had its origin as abstractor's insurance, and that gives it something of an unsavory aura. An expert title searcher sells insurance to protect the person needing his services against the expert's incompetence. Since most claims (so far as is known) arise out of a mistake or omission in the search, this still appears to be its primary function. Purchasers buy it to obtain the title-search services of the company. Eliminating off-record risks, which do infrequently occur, is a secondary aim, but this may be only a rationalization of the industry's history, particularly when the policy's exceptions and exclusions from coverage are considered. This ambiguity in its purpose, coupled with its uses by lenders to operate a secondary market in mortgages, means that title insurance is seldom treated as a reform of our delivery patterns, although arguably it is one. Moreover, it is conducted by a private business, whereas "reform" is usually thought of as government inspired, and its opposition by major segments of the bar and the abstracting industry has obscured its contribution. Nonetheless, it has revealed the deficiencies of our system of recording title records. It has coped with a deficient system about as well as is possible in our large urban centers like Washington, D.C.

Title insurance was a reform in two other senses as well; first it reduced the documentation needed for title proof since within its clauses defining specific reservations and exceptions to the fee simple (which are not insured against), the title policy functions as an abstract. In the hands of purchasers, policies thus replace abstracts which go into a company's title plant, never to re-emerge. Again this is a mixed blessing. Companies offer reduced rates when an abstract is produced, but well they might since the compilation of abstracts is the company's business. Second, title insurance is a limited reform in that it is a policy of indemnification—litigation insurance, really, should a conflict arise over an insured title. It is not, however, a guarantee of title.[223] The insurer reserves the option to defend its insured title through litigation, which may take a considerable period of time.[224] He sometimes even reserves the right to buy the property if the full face amount of the policy is claimed.[225] Failure to notify or put the matter in the insurer's hands may void the policy,[226] as could a misstatement on the application or "an act of the insured's" in derogation of this right.[227] An act of a purchaser's attorney may also be imputed to the insured for this purpose.

The policy of title insurance will contain standard exceptions: It will not guarantee a survey or insure against public liens and taxes.[228] Furthermore, title insurance provides proportionate financial compensation only up to the full amount of the policy.[229] With appreciating land values, it is adequate financially only when the purchaser's equity is insured and within the face amount of the policy.[230] With the typical mortgage with installment payments, the purchaser's equity will of course be lowest in the early years of coverage. This means that many purchasers, basing their policy on the purchase price of the property, are overinsured in the early years of their tenure.

There are two types of title insurance companies operating in this country today. The difference between them lies in whether their policy is based on a search conducted and reviewed in-house or on an attorney's title certification given in either of the two systems discussed previously.[231]

Title Insurance Based on an Attorney's Opinion. Under this system title insurance is purchased by the lender or purchaser as added protection against a negligent search or an incompetent abstract review. There are two types of title insurance policies: *lender* (or *mortgagee*) and *owner*. The rates for these vary across the country, but generally are $2.50 for lender's and $3.50 for owner's coverage. Today evidence indicates that more policies are issued to lenders than to owners.[232]

Regardless of which policy is required, most companies, especially those in rural and suburban areas, operate partly on the basis of an independent attorney's title opinion. They accept title opinions only from those attorneys whom they recognize as experts either by reputation, after undergoing a trial period, or by designation as an agent of the company. Title insurance usually guarantees the marketability of the title except for any defects the attorney's search uncovers as well as some routinely listed exceptions.

If a defect later appears, the company has discretion to pay the claim, defend the insured in litigation, or bring suit to clear the title. It has the right to hold the independent attorney or searcher liable for the amount of the policy claim based on search errors,[233] and is also subrogated to any claim possible under the insured's covenants for title. The extent to which a company asserts such rights is not known, but it is probably small; the title insurance company might lose future business if the word spread that it sued its own agents. A more likely sanction is for a company to refuse to deal with the attorney in the future.

Title Insurance Plants. Title insurance was originated to indemnify abstractors against search errors.[234] As the business evolved, the coverage was broadened to include off-record risks, as well as to insure more people.[235] In places having a large volume of transfers in the course of a year, i.e., a large city, the insurers have eliminated the middleman, the independent attorney-agent, and absorbed the three functions of title work.[236] They can search and abstract the title, review the abstract, and insure the title.[237] The insurance company can thus perform most title-delivery services incidental to the business of insuring, law permitting,[238] and the company becomes, with its attorney employees,[239] the pivot point in the conveyancing process.

In areas where the three functions are combined, the insurance companies have acquired abstract company records or attorney's files and have established their own title plants. In the larger, more advanced companies, these are computerized and indexed both by parcel number and by the parties involved in any legal proceedings. These records are becoming costly to maintain and to update since the daily input to the system can run to thousands of documents.

The charge from a title insurance company includes a title-search fee and an insurance premium. Often other services are offered and could be included such as boundary checks, on-site inspections, mortgage-guarantee insurance, and escrowing of money and documents.[240]

Escrow Agents

In the cities of the Pacific and southwestern states, a new type of real estate transfer specialist has appeared since World War II.[241] Some say that the advent of the escrow agent was due to the shortage of conveyancing attorneys during the war; others say tight mortgage money caused his appearance in times when brokers and title insurance agents were casting around for sidelights to help them maintain their previous income levels. In legal theory the establishment of an escrow allows the transfer to "relate back" to the establishment of the escrow, thus defeating claims arising after escrow but before the closing. It prevents a later sale at a higher price and aids both the purchaser and lender.

The escrow agent is the mutual agent of both vendor and purchaser. In California, for example, after the principals have signed identical contracts of sale, they must agree on a set of irrevocable instructions to the escrow agent. After the parties instruct the agent, the contract may fail for vagueness, but the transaction may nonetheless be completed on the basis of these instructions. The agent will gather and hold all the documents and money until the closing, compute any adjustments, and then distribute them appropriately to the parties. The use of escrow agents is almost universal in California and other areas where conveyancing is highly organized, although there is no legal necessity to "go into escrow," as trade jargon puts it.

Additional reasons account for the use of escrow agents. The use of identical contracts of sale executed separately by the parties and the recognition that these contracts provide only vague standards to govern the relationship and conduct of the parties during the executory period require a neutral repository. In the absence of attorneys, a disinterested third party liable to both vendor and purchaser is necessary to guide them through the conveyancing process. This makes the escrow agent a central figure in the transaction and puts him in a position to refer business to attorneys, abstractors, title insurers, and others. He in turn is likely to have business referred to him by brokers. Most escrow agents work in departments of banks and title insurance companies, although independent escrow companies are performing a larger percentage of the work every year.

When an escrow agent is used, the purchaser must take care that the escrow instructions, often drafted after a question-and-answer session with the broker, conform to the contract of sale. Where they conflict, these irrevocable instructions will control. When the instructions are drawn up, the purchaser customarily submits a check to the escrow company for his earnest money.

The use of an escrow agent obviates the need for a closing ceremony, and usually none is held. The agent will, however, prepare closing documents if asked to by the parties, using blank forms "generally printed and commonly used." The use of more complicated forms constitutes the unauthorized practice of law. Even though escrow may be used often in large commercial transactions in various parts of the country, its use in residential transactions in the West means that there the work of organizing the closing is now separately performed for a fee. This is the latest step, though perhaps not the last, in the division of labor in title delivery among the broker, lender, attorney, abstractor, title insurer, and now escrow agent.

Case Study: The District of Columbia

South Dakota and the District of Columbia have very different patterns of conveyancing. In the District of Columbia, the title-delivery and conveyancing pattern is highly specialized, with little involvement by private attorneys, and includes title insurance company abstracting, title insurance, and a nascent escrow industry. Conveyancing has not been a staple part of a private law practice in the District of Columbia for the past twenty years, even though attorneys still dominate the process in its suburbs. This study will be concerned with Washington, D.C., proper, the central city of its Standard Metropolitan Statistical Area (SMSA).[242]

The Environment of Conveyancing. The District of Columbia is a 67-square-mile city of 750,000 people in an SMSA of 2.8 million,[243] the fourth largest in the northeastern megolopolis. Its population declined by about 1 percent between 1960 and 1970, but the real estate market remained active. Large sections of the city have undergone public urban renewal, and other, equally large sections have been and still are undergoing private renewal. In a city 70 percent black, this private renewal represents a Caucasian resettlement of areas such as Georgetown in the 1940s and 1950s, Capitol Hill in the 1960s, and Adams-Morgan and Mt. Pleasant in the 1970s. This renovation is concurrent with development of black suburbs in Maryland, and may also be due to the presence of the federal government, which employs 40 percent of the District of Columbia work force, and to the in-filling of the District of Columbia's vacant land. Like other large cities, the District of Columbia has recently experienced an increase in condominium housing starts and conversions of rental apartments to condominiums. Condominiums are treated as vertical subdivision plats for conveyancing purposes. Each apartment is assigned a separate "lot" number.

In the District of Columbia the typical home buyer is the head of a household, is between twenty-five and forty-five years old, and has children under fifteen years of age. New-house prices average $37,000 to $40,000, and settlement costs (excluding brokerage fees) average 1 percent to 3 percent of that price. The total cash outlay required at the closing averages 10-12 percent of the price.

The federal enclave encompasses, for title-search purposes (but virtually no other), the federal city and Washington County.[244] Most of the land has been developed since the 1930s and 1940s, but redevelopment has uncovered some vacant land; as the District of Columbia continues to redevelop low-income areas, still more land will be available.[245] The median value of housing has been rising rapidly, particularly since 1960.[246]

Brokers. In the District of Columbia it is the broker who organizes the closings and arranges for financing.[247] He must show the property to the purchaser[248] and bring the vendor and purchaser together to earn his commission.[249] He will also recommend a title insurance company if the buyer has no preference. Most independent brokers use only one company. The only document that the broker prepares is the contract of sale; there is a case holding that this is not the unauthorized practice of law in the District of Columbia, and perhaps he could legally do more,[250] but as a practical matter, most brokers feel well advised to limit themselves to that.[251] The broker may review the documents before closing, particularly if there is no attorney involved. Few transactions today do involve attorneys except those employed by title insurance companies.[252]

The preeminence of the broker in the District of Columbia is perhaps a result of "exclusive-right-to-sell" contracts signed by vendors, which large brokerage houses often use.[253] Reportedly, many of these firms also maintain an inventory of unsold houses which they have accepted in trade from owners moving into new premises.[254]

Currently brokers are under a permanent restraining order obtained by the Antitrust Division of the Department of Justice[255] prohibiting them from divulging their fees to one another. The standard fee is 6 percent paid by the seller and is only rarely negotiated. The effect of the restraining order has been to freeze any past collusion into silence. The local Board of Realtors has expressed reluctance to collect information from their members for fear of charges of anticompetitive acts. Consequently, little is known about this practical side of the brokerage business.

Attorneys. Those attorneys who are involved in the residential purchase and sale have highly specialized law practices. They charge $20 for preparing a deed and $25 for a deed of trust, which has been the predominant security agreement in the District of Columbia since the early 1960s.[256] It has judicial sanction in the District of Columbia's housing market. Purchasers do not get a choice whether they prefer to finance through a mortgage or deed of trust.

When an attorney conducts the title search or hires an abstractor to do it for him, he is usually acting as an agent for a national title insurance company.[257] In this capacity he receives a commission, roughly 35 percent of the premium, for the insurance policy sold. The number of attorneys doing this type of work is very small compared to the total number of attorneys licensed in the District of Columbia. Most attorneys perform settlement work at an hourly rate and as a result, have priced themselves out of the conveyancing industry.

Title Insurers. In the District of Columbia, as elsewhere, purchasers have the legal responsibility to examine the public land records,[258] and title insurance is the only method of title assurance available. All institutional lenders require it. Moreover, abstracts of title have been replaced by title insurance policies as comprehensive title evidence. A decade of uncertainty created by legislative action necessitated the change from abstracting to title insurance. Its inception is traced by some to an inconclusive 1957 reform of the dower law, which raised the possibility that unrecognized or fraudulent dower claims might cloud many titles.[259]

There are five large insurance companies, with their own title plants, that service most of the realty transfers in the District of Columbia; there are four smaller firms. They perform the title search, review the abstract, underwrite the transaction, and hold the closing.[260] Four of the large firms have records dating back to 1912, while the fifth has records from around 1792.[261] These plants are not duplicates of the public records but rather contain a digest of each document filed prior to 1968, arranged and bound chronologically and indexed by lot and square. From such records a chain of title can be run. If the exact wording of a document is required, the searcher must go to the courthouse.

In 1968 a procedure serving the five large companies for "taking off" "hard copies" from the public records was started. This type of take-off makes a photocopy of the entire instrument in the recorder's office. One firm is responsible for take-offs, while another digests the judgment records in the courthouse using index cards which they file alphabetically except when a judgment includes a direct lien on a parcel, in which case it is indexed by lot and square. All five companies receive these copies and digests and share the expenses. (The title companies pay no rent for the space used by their take-off personnel in the recorder's office.) Filings of deeds, deeds of trust, and deeds of release are made at the rate of 125 daily. Upon receipt of these copies, four of the five users file them by lot number. The fifth files them by date and indexes them by lot and square. The records in the recorder of deeds office are filed by lot and block number.[262]

As of July 1, 1973, four of the five large title insurance companies that had combined their take-off process formed a jointly run title plant. Now title searches are run both in a company's title plant and in the joint plant where all participants station their own title searchers.

The period searched varies from company to company. Two of the five large title insurers claim to search back to 1792; two others say sixty years; the fifth boasts an eighty-year period. The work requires the cooperation of personnel stationed in the courthouse and the joint title plant—no one person completely searches a title. Once a request for service is logged, the title company orders from the appropriate governmental agency a report on the taxes due. Usually two folders are prepared for each case: one for its title examiners, the other for its escrow department.[263] After receipt of the title folder, a clerk will check to see if the company has previously issued insurance on the parcel. If so, the search period will commence from the date of that last issuance. If not, a "chain clerk" will compile a "chain of title" using indexes in the title plant. If digested documents will suffice, then the title plant files can be used. If a document is dated after 1968, then hard copies exist in the title plant. A third employee will search for the names of owners in an alphabetical judgment index at the plant and refer matters found to employees at the courthouse as it becomes appropriate.[264]

The jobs, basically clerical in nature, are specialized by tasks which involve chaining, running down transfer records, and running down name judgments or searches on all parties named in the chain. Companies admit that handling the operation in this way induces employee tedium but claim that the lack of trained personnel makes it necessary. Company executives maintain that few workers can understand the whole of a title search and admit that the possibility for error rises under their present mode of operation. As a result, the companies periodically reexamine their search operations.

After the search is completed, the assembled materials are given to an attorney working for the title insurer who writes a "title opinion." This is a letter or memorandum stating the extent to which the company will extend title insurance on the property and listing any special exemptions to the coverage the company may want to insert in the policy. This opinion becomes the basis of an interim title binder which is a commitment to extend indemnity to the customer. Once he has the interim title binder, the customer will know the legal description of the property usable on the loan documents, any imperfections in title that must be cured before closing, and any exceptions or clouds on the fee.

Fees for the services just described do not vary among the five large companies. They charge $75 for the search, plus $2.50 per $1,000 of sale price. Title insurance (indemnity) is extra: $2.50 per $1,000 of mortgage insurance ($3.50 for owners' policies). In addition, there is a $2.50 fee for a tax certificate and $5.00 for the interim title binder. If the owner's and the mortgagee's policies are issued simultaneously, the rate for both is based on the cost of the owner's policy plus an additional fee of $7.50-$10,[265] all of which the purchaser-borrower pays.

Title-search and insurance fees and premiums are all paid at closing, yet the title insurance policy is rarely sent to the purchaser until afterward. This is the most widespread consumer complaint about District of Columbia conveyancing.[266] The purchaser neither knows the exact extent of his coverage, nor does he have a chance to examine the state of his title.

Lenders. The majority of residential purchase loans in the District of Columbia are extended by savings and loan associations.[267] They charge the borrower-purchaser an application and processing fee (1 percent of the loan amount), and they also charge fees for preparing loan documents ($10-$20), for an appraisal ($20-$50), and a credit report ($6).[268] Commercial banks rarely extend these loans except to established customers and then at high (25 percent) down-payment rates.

Lenders customarily require the escrowing of a year's payment of tax[269] and hazard[270] insurance at closing. Some pay interest on these escrowed funds.[271]

Escrow Companies. Implicit in the description of the title company's operations is that its escrow department will hold the closing (and 70 percent of closings are held there),[272] although several independent settlement or escrow companies may hold the settlement, particularly in poor areas of the District of Columbia. The recent alleged embezzlement and indictment of officials in one escrow company may slow the growth of these independent companies, however. Fees for escrowing the sale are, in the case of one title company, $16 for the first $1,000 of the sale price, $1 for each additional $1,000 up to $25,000, and $.50 per $1,000 thereafter. The preparation of forms costs $15-$25 (if the deed and deed of trust are prepared by the title company); fees for reviewing documents prepared elsewhere ("noting fees") are $3-$4.

Special warranty deeds are proffered most purchasers at the closing. Title companies report that a last-minute presettlement run-down of title is customary, and then after the legal documents are recorded, a final search is made of the public records. Closings held in the offices of the title company will not finalize the transaction because the papers are subsequently referred to the lender for review. Only after that process is complete does the sale become final,[273] and funds, receipts, and the title insurance policies are finally released and disbursed.

After the old lender receives payment of the vendor's existing loan (if any), he executes a "deed of release" in the standard form. This form is duly recorded and is the final document memorializing a closing on the public records.

Conclusions

The title-delivery process in Sioux Falls costs about $1,000, but in Washington, D.C., the same process costs over $1,400. A proliferation of charges occurs in the District of Columbia's more expensive system. The shorter legal descriptions for property and the absence of title insurance account for much of the low cost of South Dakota conveyancing.

Both of these conveyancing systems are systems of private law; even though sales contracts are often drafted by brokers, little litigation is involved. Attorneys perform office, not courtroom work: Lenders' and title companies' attorneys second-guess what courts would do on the rare occasions when they are called on to act. The difference between the systems in South Dakota and the District of Columbia is organizational. The same work is performed in each, but the volume of transactions in the District of Columbia has spawned title companies, a joint take-off system, and then a jointly operated title plant, in that order. Attorneys are involved in the process in the District of Columbia, but as title company employees, not as private practitioners. Title insurance companies are usually run by attorneys; the genesis of such control can be seen in the Sioux Falls abstract company which is attorney owned. If attorneys are to change these patterns, the inability of the South Dakota bar to enact laws for a title-guaranty fund attests to the fact that attorneys will need to establish widespread public support for their efforts.

Compiling title evidence is subject to some economic constraints that apparently are sending overhead costs beyond the reach of individual companies in large urban centers such as Washington, D.C.; although abstracting is also dominated by one company in Sioux Falls, the unprofitability of maintaining separate title plants is inferable from the establishment of a joint plant in the District of Columbia. While four District of Columbia title companies work on a consolidated basis to provide title assurance for purchasers, this essential service remains dependent on the recorder of deeds office. This is both a strength and a weakness for the title-delivery industry. The companies organize the documents pertaining to property titles more efficiently, but they are, nonetheless, duplicating public effort and are at the mercy of local officials for access to their official records and for office space to do their take-off work. The question naturally arises, why doesn't the public sector just do its work more efficiently and eliminate the middleman?

This question suggests that the title services in the District of Columbia are at a crossroads.[274] Further privitization of the process may force the recognition that title companies require regulation as do providers of other essential quasi-public services, e.g., public utilities. On the other hand, the duplication of "public" and "private" records could be eliminated if all public records were made accessible and were organized in a block and lot or other efficient system. The crossroads has been reached, but the future course is unclear.

There is no standard for evaluating the relative efficiency of abstracting in Sioux Falls and title searching for insurance purposes in the District of Columbia. Apparently in both places private plants are more efficient than public records. Analysis based on standards of efficiency is difficult not only because of the lack of alternatives offered the parties but also because it is increasingly hard to enter the abstracting field due to the cost of maintaining adequate records. The only starting point for further analysis is to investigate past attempts to control the volume of records that must be maintained for title searches.

Whatever can be said about the efficiency of the present conveyancing patterns, it is duplicating work to reevaluate the same title data on the occasion of each successive transfer. Elimination of duplicative title searches—in whole or in part—would be an improvement in any of the patterns described in this chapter. Subsequent chapters will examine possible changes in our conveyancing patterns that will eliminate successively greater amounts of this duplicative work. Absent such improvements, our conveyancing patterns seem designed to maximize the work and profits of the conveyancer rather than to serve his clients.

41

Notes

1. G. Lefcoe, *Land Development Law* 351 (2d ed. 1974). W. Kusilier, *Legal Aspects of Real Estate Brokerage* 164 (1964); R. Kratovil, *Real Estate Law* 66 (1969).

2. Comment, "Recovery on Oral Real Estate Broker's Contracts," 31 S. Cal. L. Rev. 425 (1969).

3. Lefcoe, *supra* n. 1 at 352.

4. Ellsworth Dobbs Inc. v. Johnson, 50 N.J. 528, 236 A.2d 843 (1967).

5. Lefcoe, *supra* n. 1 at 359.

6. Humphrey v. Knoebel, 78 Nev. 137, 369 P.2d 872 (1962); McCue v. Deppert, 21 N.J. Super. 591, 91 A.2d 503 (1952).

7. *Cf.* Fishbein v. Zexter, 270 A.2d 510 (R.I. 1970) where the broker was found to have acted as a "finder," or property locator but did not bring the parties to an agreement "on the principal's terms." *Cf.* MacWilliams v. Bright, 273 Md. 632, 331 A.2d 303 (1975).

8. Binder agreements are a first step; they are offers to purchase "subject to contract." This establishes a privity of contract with the purchaser.

9. Burke, "Conveyancing in the National Capital Region: Local Reform with National Implications," 22 Am. U. L. Rev. 527 (1973).

10. C. Berger, A. Axelrod, & Q. Johnstone, *Land Transfer and Finance* 240 (1969); A. Casner & B. Leach, *Property* 685 (1969).

11. Some state statutes provide that every deed shall contain minimal warranties. *See, e.g.*, Mass. Gen. L., ch. 183, §§8-28A (1969); J. Warren, *Conveyances* 553 (1938); 3 Am. L. Prop. §§12.124-12.131 (1952).

12. 3 Am. L. Prop. §11.48 (Casner ed. 1952). Some standards such as a "marketable title" and completion within a "reasonable time" are implied at law only where the contract is silent.

13. O. Browder, R. Cunninghan, & J. Julin, *Property* 1044 (2d ed. 1973). In the Washington, D.C., area, standard contracts require "title of record or in fact." "Record title" generally means a title completely established by the public records, but whether the title "in fact" is conjunctive or disjunctive is a question not yet litigated.

14. Kovarik v. Vesely, 3 Wisc. 2d 573, 89 N.W.2d 279 (1958), discussed in Raushenbush, "Problems and Practices with Financing Conditions in Real Estate Purchase Contracts," 1963 Wisc. L. Rev. 566 (1963).

15. *See* Raushenbush, *supra* n. 14.

16. 3 Am. L. Prop. §11.78 (Casner ed. 1952).

17. *See, e.g.,* Lien v. Pitts, 174 N.W.2d 462 (Wisc. 1970).

18. R. Posner, *Econ. Analysis of Law* 44 (1973).

19. *Id.*

20. G. Lefcoe, *Land Development Law* 378 (2d ed. 1974).

21. On modest, middle-income sales," it is volume that counts." G. Lefcoe, *Land Development Law* 377-78 (2d ed. 1974).

22. Ellsworth-Dobbs Inc. v. Johnson, 50 N.J. 528, 236 A.2d 843 (1967); *cf.* Gaynor v. Laverdare, 291 N.E.2d 617 (Mass. 1973).

23. McCue v. Deppert, 21 N.J. Super. 591, 91 A.2d 503 (1952).

24. Haynes v. Rogers, 70 Ariz. 257, 219 P.2d 339 (1950).

25. Steward Village Shop. Ctr., Ltd. Part v. Melbourne, 274 Md. 44, 332 A.2d 625, 629 (1974).

26. *Id.*

27. *Cf.* Payne, "Ancillary Costs in the Purchase of Homes," 35 Mo. L. Rev. 455 (1970).

28. Commander Leasing Corp. v. Transamerica, Inc. (10th Cir., filed Apr. 16, 1973) reported in Trade Reg. Reptr., para. 74,443, held that an abstract company once purchased by a title insurance corporation is thereafter regulated exclusively under the applicable state's insurance laws and regulations. *See also* Chicago Title Ins. Corp. v. United States, 242 F.Supp. 56, app. dis. 385 U.S. 1022 (1967).

29. Johnson, "Examination of Title Abstracts," 46 N.D.L. Rev. 175 (1970).

30. *Cf.* Chicago Title Ins. Corp. v. Great W. Financial Corp., 70 Cal. Reptr. 849, 444 P.2d 481 (1968); *see also* Annot., "Rights in Abstract of Title Held by Mortgagee," 44 A.L.R. 1332 (1927).

31. Such a title insurance company is called a "national title insurer" by some commentators; that is, it operates without a set of local land title records or a title plant. *See infra* text at n. 58.

32. *See* Q. Johnston & D. Hopson, *Lawyers and Their Work* 276 (1967).

33. National Sav. Bank of District of Columbia v. Ward, 100 U.S. 195, 25 L.Ed. 621 (1879); Page v. Trutch, Fed. Cas. No. 10,668 (1876); 1 Century Dig., "Abstracts of Title," §§3, 4 (1896). The oldest type of system, if the early published appellate opinions are conclusive evidence, is a title search by public officials, followed by an attorney's review of the abstract. The earliest cases show the abstractor liable on his bond for a "false" certificate or abstract of title. Lusk v. Carlen, 5 Ill. (4 Scan.) 395 (1843); McCaraher v. Commonwealth, 5 Watts. and S. 21 (Pa. 1842); Ziegler v. Commonwealth, 12 Pa. St. (2 Jones) 227 (1849). Later cases imposed a standard of negligence or falsity; Wacek v. Frink, 51 Minn. 282, 53 N.W. 633, 38 Am. St. Rep. 502 (1892); Morano v. Shaw, 23 La. Ann. 379 (1871) (recorder not liable to third party); Peabody Bldg, and Loan Ass'n v. Houseman, 89 Pa. St. 261, 33 Am. Rep. 757 (1879). Thus Illinois and Pennsylvania cases imposed early liability on recorders' bonds. Post-Civil War cases in Louisiana, Minnesota, New York, and Pennsylvania spoke in terms of negligence. The advent of such cases coincides with the formulation of the rules of searching titles. Heinan v. Lamb, 117 Ill. 549, 1 N.E. 75 (1886); Dodd v. Williams, 3 Mo. App. 278 (1877).

34. Page v. Trutch, Fed. Cas. No. 10,668 (1876).

35. Union Safe-Deposit Co. v. Chisolm, 33 Ill. App. 647 (1889). Such an abstract may either be a compilation of each document in the chain of title in full, a precis of documents, or a precis of the important sections of each. "An Abstract of Title," 14 Am. L. Reg. 529 (1875) provides a full description of a common-law abstract. *See also* 1 Am. Jur., "Abstracts of Title," §1 at 155 (1936); Annot., 52 A.L.R. 1460, 1472 (1928).

36. Simis v. McElroy, 160 N.Y. 156, 54 N.E. 674 (1899), *and see* materials in A. Axelrod, C. Berger, & Q. Johnstone, *Land Transfer and Finance* 467 (1969); Mertens v. Rerendsen, 213 Cal. 111, 113, 1 P.2d 440, 441 (1931); 25 Cal. Jur. 626; *cf.* Hocking v. Title Ins. and Trust Co., 37 Cal.2d 644, 234 P.2d 625 (1951).

37. Hebb v. Severson, 32 Wash.2d 159, 201 P.2d 156 (1948).

38. Douglass v. Ransom, 205 Wisc. 439, 237 N.W. 260 (1931).

39. *In re* Kamp, 40 N.J. 588, 194 A.2d 236 (1963).

40. National Sav. Bank v. Ward, 100 U.S. 195 (1879); Annot., "Attorney's Liability, to One Other Than His Immediate Client for Consequences of Negligence in Carrying Out Legal Duties," 45 A.L.R.3d 1181 (1972); *contra*, Williams v. Polgar, Mich., 1974, 215 N.W.2d 149, noted at 21 Wayne St. L. Rev. 137 (1974).

41. Such a review is conducted once the application, or offer, has been received but before the loan commitment is issued so no contract to loan money as yet exists. Annot., "Measure of Damages for Breach of Contract to Lend Money," 44 A.L.R. 1486 (1925); Annot., "Measure of Damages for Breach of Contract to Lend Money," 36 A.L.R. 1408 (1925); specific performance is not generally available upon this contract. Rogers v. Challis, 54 Eng. Rep. 68 (Ch. 1859).

42. Their interest is in the "conveyance" of a nonpossessory security lien. *See* Lambert v. Home Fed. Sav. and Loan Ass'n., 481 S.W.2d 770 (Tenn. 1972).

43. For a short survey of this nineteenth-century legal lore, *see* A. Casner & B. Leach, *Property* 352, 363 (1969). B. Partridge, *Country Lawyer* 7, 8, 9, 10, 113, 290 (1939), provides a view of conveyancing in the 1880s and 1890s in upper New York State.

44. B. Burke & N. Kittrie, *The Real Estate Settlement Process and Its Costs* (1972).

45. Watson v. Muirhead, 57 Pa. St. (7 P.F. Smith) 161, 98 Am. Dec. 213 (1868); Dickel v. Nashville Abstract Col, 89 Tenn. 431, 14 S.W. 896, 24 Am. St. Rep. 616 (1890).

46. Tyler, "Pitfalls in Title Examination," 35 Mass. L. Q. 20 (1950), describes one jurisdiction's organization for this work.

47. Savings Bank v. Ward, 100 U.S. 195 (1879); Lattin v. Gillette, 95 Cal. 317, 30 P. 545 (1892); J.H. Trisdale Inc. v. Shasta Title Co., 146 Cal. A.D. 863, 304 P.2d 832 (1956); Roady, "Professional Liability of Abstractors," 12 Vand. L. Rev. 783 (1959).

48. Annot., "Liability of Attorney Passing Defective Title," 5 A.L.R. 1389 (1920).

49. *See supra* n. 40.

50. Access to public records was at first a problem, particularly where public recorders performed searches for fees. West Jersey Title and Guaranty Co. v. Barber, 49 N.J. Eq. (4 Dick.) 474, 24 A. 381 (1892). *See also* Belt v. Prince George's County Abstract Co., 73 Md. 289, 20 A. 982, 10 L.R.A. 212 (1890). Some states solved the problem with legislation. Minn. Gen. L. 1878, ch. 8, §179. Wisc. Stat. Ann. 59.55 (1864, as amended) shows attempts by recorders to set up abstract businesses by removal of public records.

51. *See supra* n. 35.

52. Taylor v. Williams, 2 Colo. App. 559, 31 P. 504 (1892); Kane v. Rippey, 22 Ore. 296, 23 P. 180 (1892).

53. Union Safe-Deposit Co. v. Chisolm, 33 Ill. App. 647 (1889).

54. Banker v. Caldwell, 3 Minn. 94 (1859).

55. Day v. Batton, 96 Mich. 600, 56 N.W. 3 (1893); Scribner v. Chase, 27 Ill. App. 36 (1888). State v. Rachar, 37 Minn. 372, 35 N.W. 7 (1887). The independent abstract business is often treated as a separate system of title delivery. In large cities abstract businesses were established by the 1870s. *See, e.g.,* Roberts, "Urban Conveyancing in the United States," 27 Conv. (N.S.) 240 (1963).

56. Eckhardt, "Abstractor's Licensing Laws," 28 Mo. L. Rev. 1 (1963).

57. Watson v. Muirhead, 57 Pa. St. 161 (1868).

58. Eckhardt, *supra* n. 56.

59. Indeed, judicial opinions predicate some decisions on such custom. First Fed. Sav. and Loan v. Fisher, 60 S.2d 496 (Fla. 1952); Tramontozzi v. D'Amicis, 344 Mass. 514, 183 N.E.2d 295 (1962). *See also* Johnson, "Title Examination in Massachusetts," in A. Casner & B. Leach, *Property* 886 (1969).

60. P. Basye, *Clearing Land Titles* 386 (1970).

61. *Statistical Abstract of the United States*, p. 12 (93d ed. 1972), published by the U.S. Bureau of the Census, Washington, D.C. These figures are from the 1970 census.

62. *Id.*, 169.

63. *Id.*

64. *Id.*, 589.

65. *Id.*, 18.

66. *Id.*, 680.

67. *Id.*

68. *Id.*, 688.

69. U.S. Department of Agriculture, *Land Title Recording in the United States*, Table 8 (1973).

70. *Statistical Abstract of the United States, supra* n. 61, at 326.

71. *Id.*, 235.

72. *Id.*, 319.

73. Bickell, "Title Practices and the Use of Standards for Title Examination," 14 S.D. Bar J. 13 (1945).

74. W. Webb, *The Great Plains* 415 (1931).

75. Johnson, "Examining the Abstract of Title," 46 N.D. L. Rev. 174 (1970); Ruemmel, "Title Evidence in North Dakota," 43 N.D. L. Rev. 467, 468 (1967).

76. J. Jennewein & J. Boorman, *Dakota Panorama* 222 (1961).

77. This federal surveying system was also known as the Jeffersonian survey. It assumed a land area to be on a flat plane and, from a meridian base-line (or y-axis) divided it in townships of six miles square, and further divided each township into 36 sections, of 640 acres each.

78. J. Jennewein & J. Boorman, *Dakota Panorama* 223 (1961).

79. Bickell, "Title Practices and the Use of Standards for Title Examination," 14 S.D. Bar J. 13, 17 (1945).

80. J. Jennewein & J. Boorman, *Dakota Panorama* 224 (1961).

81. *Id.* at 225.

82. *Id.*

83. Interview with J.E. Moore, Sioux Falls, South Dakota, 2 p.m., April 30, 1974.

84. Interview with city planner, Sioux Falls, South Dakota, 10 a.m., April 29, 1974.

85. Interview with G. Danforth, Sioux Falls, South Dakota, 11:30 a.m., April 30, 1974.

86. *Id.; see also* Payne, "Ancillary Costs in the Purchase of Homes," 35 Mo. L. Rev. 455, 508-09 (1970).

87. 84. S.D. 328, 171 N.W.2d 77 (1969), noted in 15 S. Dak. L. Rev. 435 (1970), involving the transfer of a trailer court under a contract for deed calling for delivery of an abstract on a certain date. *See* "Contract for Deed," #43-26C, South Dakota Legal Blanks, 1974, p. 2.

88. *See* Comment, "Survey of Unauthorized Practice of Law," 2 S.D.L.Rev. 104 (1957).

89. State v. Conzad, 70 S.D. 193, 16 N.W.2d 484 (1944).

90. S.D. Comp. Laws § 16-16 (1967).

91. *Id.*, § 16-18.

92. *Id.*, § 16-18-1.

93. S.D. Comp. L., § 36-21-19 (1974).

94. S.D. Comp. L., § 36-21-35.3 (1974), whose source was Neb. Rev. Code, § 81.885.21(6).

95. S.D. Comp. L., § 36-21-42.1(15) (1974).

96. Payne, "Ancillary Costs in the Purchase of Homes," 35 Mo. L. Rev. 455, 508-09 (1970).

97. *Id.*, 509.

98. *Id.*

99. S.D. Comp. L. §58-25 (1967).

100. *See* S.D. Comp. L. §36-13 *et seq.* (1967).

101. *See* Eckhardt, "Abstractors Licensing Laws," 28 Mo. L. Rev. 1 (1963). The Model Abstractors Licensing Act was approved by the American Title Association in June 1928 and was promptly adopted for introduction in South Dakota where a variant of the original model act was finally adopted in 1929. *Id.*, 28.

102. S.D. Comp. L. §36-13-1 to 13-7 (1967).

103. *Id.*, §36-13-15.

104. *Id.*, §36-13-10.

105. *Id.*, §36-13-25.

106. *Id.*, §36-13-15 and §36-13-19. *See also* Goldberg v. Sisseton Loan and Title Co., 24 S.D. 49, 123 N.W. 266 (1909) (any person damaged by relying on an abstract may bring an action in his own name without regard to who ordered or paid for abstract).

107. *See* DuPratt v. Black Hills Land and Abstract Co., 81 S.D. 637, 140 N.W.2d 386 (1966) (Abstractors liable for any and all damages sustained by any person by reason of error deficiency or mistake in abstract and injured person could recover all damages that were the proximate result of error including reasonable attorney's fees and costs of litigation).

108. Gronseth v. Mohn, 57 S.D. 604, 234 N.W. 603 (1931).

109. S.D. Comp. L. §15-2-8 (1967).

110. *Id.*, §36-13-26.

111. *Id.*, §58-25-16.

112. P. Basye, *Clearing Land Titles* §180 (2d ed. 1970).

113. These fees are, as said, regulated by statute. Siefes v. Clark Title Co., S.D., 1974, 215 N.W.2d 648, held in a class action that plaintiff customers could recover excess of fees charged above the statutory rate. S.D. Comp. L. §36-13-25 (1971) allows this rate to be set by a board of abstractors. For the current abstracting fees, *see* Siefes opinion, *supra* at 650.

114. Interview with G. Danforth, *op. cit.*, n. 85.

115. *Id.*

116. *Cf.* "The methods of minimum fee computation on abstract examination varies widely. Some ask a flat fee plus an extra charge for each page or entry. Others combine a flat fee with a percentage of values. Still others use a flat fee only; and others an hourly rate with a percentage of value." State Bar Proceedings, 30 S.D. Bar J. 45 (1961). By the time during which Goldfarb v. Virginia State Bar, 421 U.S. 773 (1975) was pending, the schedule was not binding on attorneys and was for information purposes only.

117. *Id.*

118. Interview with J.E. Moore, *op. cit.*, n. 83.

119. S.D. Comp. L. §43-30-1, -2 (1967); *see also* S.D. Comp. L. §15-3-1

(1967) (adverse possession period of twenty years); S.D. Comp. L. §15-2-7, -27 (1967) (statute of limitations for mortgages established at fifteen years); S.D. Comp. L. §15-2-13 (six-year statute of limitation on contracts or trespass to realty). Other curative laws appear at S.D. Comp. L. §43-4-3 (rights of reentry), -12, -13 (easements and covenants), -29.

120. 13 S.D. Comp. L. 165-178 (1967), with citations from out-of-state courts. The most recent amendment of these standards shows the difficulty of gaining acceptance for these standards. Calling past versions of a standard on mortgage statute of limitations "ambiguous and confusing," the S.D. Bar's Standards of Title Committee proposed that a "mortgage past due more than 15 years from its due date or recorded extension thereof, or if no due date is stated therein or is unascertainable therefrom, 30 years from the date of the mortgage, is ineffective and void and the record thereof may be disregarded." The Committee commented: "The Federal Land Bank of Omaha has refused to accept the predecessor of this Standard and will probably refuse to take this one either." "Committee Reports, Standards of Title Committee" 42 S.D. Bar J. 49 (June 1973).

121. Interview with G. Danforth, *op. cit.*, n. 85.

122. *Id.*

123. "Compensating balances," accounts maintained by a developer with his construction lender, are another form of lender assurance. These are common in South Dakota. Danforth, "Usury: Applicability to Collateral Fees and Charges," 16 S.D. L. Rev. 52, 69 (1971). Compensating accounts for all types of loans are validated by S.D. Comp. L. §52-8-12 (1967).

124. Interview with J.E. Moore, *op. cit.*, n. 83.

125. This implies that it is the loss of the abstract, which vendors and purchasers realize is of value and importance, which also prevents title insurance from gaining a foothold. Herring & Cummings, "The Case of the Disappearing Abstract and Lawyer's Title Guaranty," 30 S.D. Bar J. 15 (1961).

126. Interview with G. Danforth, *op. cit.*, n. 85.

127. *See* text *supra* at n. 79.

128. *See* text *supra* at n. 50.

129. Interview with G. Danforth, *op. cit.*, n. 85.

130. *Id.*

131. Interview with G. Danforth, *op. cit.*, n. 85. *See also* Fiflis, "Land Transfer Improvement: The Basic Facts and Two Hypotheses for Reform," 38 U. Colo. L. Rev. 431 (1966).

132. *See generally* Clark, "Installment Land Contracts in South Dakota," 6 S.D. L. Rev. 248 (1961) (hereafter cited Clark, Part I) and Part II, 7 S.D. L. Rev. 44 (1962) (hereafter cited Clark, Part II); Herr, "Evaluating Debt-to-purchase-price Ratio in Financing Farm Real Estate Transfers," 36 Agric. Fin. Rev. 73 (1976) indicates increased use of the installment contract in the 1971-73 period.

133. This name distinguishes it from a "preliminary" contract, the local word for a realty sales contract.

134. S.D. Comp. L. §44-6-1, -4 (1967). This lien is treated as a mortgage for recording act purposes. Opin. A.G., Report 1919-20, at 610. It may not be transferred, except in trust, by the vendor. *Id.,* §44-6-4. *See* Cal. Civ. Code §3047 for similar provision. The vendee acquires a lien (for so much as he pays on account under the contract on the land). *Id.,* §44-6-2.

135. Clark, Part I, at 249-50.

136. *Id.,* at 252.

137. It is also used in the urban ghetto of Washington, D.C.

138. S.D. State Bar Ass'n, "Ann. Mtg. Proceedings," 34 S.D. Bar J. 48-50 (1965) (the last minimum-fee schedule printed in these proceedings).

139. Clark, Part I.

140. *Cf.* S.D. Comp. L. §44-6-2, *supra* n. 72.

141. S.D. Comp. L. §21-50 (1967).

142. *Id.,* §21-48-9 and §21-49-1 (Supp. 1974).

143. *Id.,* §21-52-11 *et seq.*

144. *Id.,* §21-50-1.

145. *Id.,* §21-47-13. The low conveyancing costs of South Dakota have been noted by several authors. One related this to low statutory costs and the absence of title insurance. Under South Dakota law, the bar does not have the power to fix the fees charged by its members, but as has already been pointed out, the board of examiners regulates abstractor's fees, and statutes regulate title insurance rates. The statutory costs of conveyancing (transfer fees, recording fees, etc.) are low in South Dakota. One writer reporting on the cost of establishing title across the United States found that statutory costs in South Dakota did not exceed $25 as of 1970. He reported that the maximum cost of establishing title when the purchase was financed by a mortgage or insurance company, a commercial bank, or a savings and loan association was $302, $174, and $174, respectively. The median costs for these same institutions were $105, $120, and $120, respectively. *See* Payne, *supra* n. 96, at 477.

Another writer reported a similar result for fees establishing title in a transaction financed by a mortgage lender in the early 1960s:

Bank service charge	$135.00
Title opinion of attorney	25.00
Cost of adding deed and	
mortgage to abstract	6.25
Recording fee	8.40
	$174.65

See Clark, Part I, at 259-60.

146. *Id.,* §44-8-23.

147. *Id.,* §43-26-6.

148. *Id.,* §43-26-9 (Supp. 1974).

149. S.D. Comp. L. §43-26-1 (1967).

150. Boekelheide v. Snyder, 71 S.D. 470, 26 N.W.2d 74 (1947).

151. *Id*. Contracts generally provide for delivery of the abstract upon final payments. "Contract for Deed," State Legal Forms, Pierre, S.D., No. 43-26C.

152. 23 S.D. 367, 121 N.W. 868 (1909).

153. 72 S.D. 563, 37 N.W.2d 622 (1949).

154. The Iowa courts, whose influence is apparent in South Dakota case law, follow the majority or California rule of Luette v. Bank of Italy Nat'l Trust and Sav. Ass'n, 42 F.2d 9 (9th Cir. 1930). *See* Fitcher v. Walling, 225 Iowa 8, 279 N.W. 417 (1938). However, since the South Dakota courts have not considered the same question directly, one may only guess at the result. Absent a contract provision to the contrary, South Dakota law allows prepayment of purchase price without penalty; the courts might reach a result contrary to the Luette case in some circumstances where the purchaser was unaware of vendor's lack of title or unmerchantable title at the time of contracting. One might argue that in this situation, the purchaser might exercise his right to prepay at which time the obligation of the vendor would become concurrent with that of the purchaser. Boekelheide v. Snyder, *supra* n. 150, a case considering an installment land contract, held that the obligations of the purchaser to pay the balance of the purchase price and the obligation of the vendee to convey are dependent covenants and must be concurrent acts so that neither party could place the other in default without making a tender of performance. Under the Weitzel case, the court might allow the vendor a "reasonable time" after purchaser's tender to perfect his title and tender it to the purchaser. Failure of the vendor to offer merchantable title after a reasonable time might then put them in default.

155. S.D. Comp. L. §21-48-1 through -25 (1967); Hanson v. Fed. Land Bank of Omaha, 63 S.D. 622, 262 N.W. 228 (1935).

156. S.D. Comp. L. §21-47-1 through -24 (1967).

157. S.D. Comp. L. §21-48-6, -10 (1967).

158. S.D. Comp. L. §21-49-1 through -10 (1967).

159. S.D. Comp. L. §52-8-11 (1967).

160. The "closing statement" will reflect this fully. Both lenders and brokers must provide this. *Id*.

161. 4 Am. L. Prop. 527 (Casner ed., 1952).

162. Bucholz v. Hinzman, 44 S.D. 336, 183 N.W. 993 (1921) (contract purchaser not given priority over unrecorded conveyance).

163. S.D. Comp. L. §43-25-3 (1967).

164. Fullerton Lumber Co. v. Tinker, 22 S.D. 427, 118 N.W. 700, 18 Ann. Cas. 11 (1908) (held, a purchaser has a duty to search both indices to these records available, one alphabetized by names of grantors and grantees, as well as one arranged by numerical indices).

165. S.D. Comp. L. §7-9-15 (1967).

166. S.D. Comp. L. §7-9-1 (1967).

167. S.D. Comp. L. §43-28-17 (a so-called race-notice recording act). Historically, recording acts gave priority to the transferee first recording his interest, but the inequity of allowing an unscrupulous but quick purchaser to record with notice led equity courts to impose the additional requirement that the recording party be without notice of conflicting claims or that the first to record also be without notice. Hence, "race acts" became notice or race-notice statutes. 4 Am. L. Prop. 539 (Casner ed., 1952).

168. Interview with J. Moore, *op. cit.*, n. 83.

169. S.D. Comp. L. §43-28-2 (1967).

170. S.D. Comp. L. §7-9-11 (1967); the effect of maintaining two books (by name and tract) is minimal; in interviews, those interviewed described the name index as the one used most for title searches.

171. S.D. Comp. L. §7-9-8 (1967) (which sets out the form for rural, rectangularly surveyed and urban or platted land).

172. U.S. Department of Agriculture, *op. cit.*, n. 69, table 4.

173. S.D. Comp. L. §7-9-5, -6 (1967). The names and addresses of the parties must also be given. *Id.*, -7.

174. No conveyances will be accepted for recording on platted land until the plat is accepted for record and reference. S.D. Comp. L. §7-9-5 (1967).

175. Interview with J. Moore, *op. cit.*, n. 83.

176. The office of county surveyor was recently abolished. S.D. Comp. L. §7-15-1 through -8 (1967), repealed by S.L. 1974, ch. 282, §1.

177. Interview with G. Danforth, *op. cit.*, n. 85.

178. Annual Mtg. Proceedings, State Bar of S.D., "Report of Committee on Lawyers' Title Guaranty Fund," 33 S.D. Bar J. 70 (1963), recommended the establishment of a bar-related title insurer.

179. Interview with J. Moore, *op. cit.*, n. 83.

180. *Id., cf.* n. 178, *supra.*

181. *Id.*

182. *See* text at n. 120, *supra.*

183. *See* text at n. 119, *supra.*

184. *See* text at n. 22, ch. 3, *infra.*

185. Homesteads are exempt from judicial sales and liens, without dollar limits. S.D. Comp. L. §43-31-1 (1967); Note, "Creditors and the South Dakota Homestead Exemption," 17 S.D. L. Rev. 483 (1972).

186. S.D. Comp. L. §36-13-25 (1967).

187. S.D. Comp. L §58-25-2 through -11 (1967) which provides, like many other states, for a filing of rates for approval or disapproval without a hearing on their reasonableness, a term prescribed by statute. *Id.*, §58-25-3 (1967).

188. *Cf.* S.D. Comp. L. §58-25-16 (requires abstractor's signature on title insurance policy of a foreign insurer) (1967).

189. Herring & Cummings, "The Case of the Disappearing Abstract," 30 S.D. Bar J. 15 (1961).

190. Interview with G. Danforth, *op. cit.*, n. 85.

191. Interview with J. Moore, *op. cit.*, n. 83.

192. The bar has sought to extend abstractors' liability on their bonds from ten to twenty years. Annual Mtg. Proceedings, State Bar of S.D., "Real Property and Probate Law," 31 S.D. Bar J. 33 (1962).

193. *See* Herring & Cummings, *op. cit.*, n. 122.

194. Annual Mtg. Proceedings, State Bar of S.D., "Minimum Fee Schedule Committee Report," 30 S.D. Bar J. 45, 46, 50 (1961); *Id.*, 31 S.D. Bar J. 25 (1962).

195. Annual Mtg. Proceedings, S.D. State Bar, "Minimum Fee Schedule Committee Report," 30 S.D. Bar J. 45, 46 (1961).

196. *Id.* at 50.

197. *Id.*, 31 S.D. Bar J. at 45.

198. *Id.*, at 25.

199. Archer, "Advertising of Professional Fees: Does the Consumer Have a Right to Know?" 21 S.D. L. Rev. 310, 330 (1976) comments on Goldfarb v. Va. State Bar, 421 U.S. 773 (1975), discussed in chapter 6's text at n. 324; *see generally* Whitman, "Transferring North Carolina Real Estate: Part II," 49 N.C. L. Rev. 593, 595-96 (1971).

200. Annual Mtg. Proceedings, S.D. State Bar, "Report of Committee on Lawyer's Title Guaranty Funds," 33 S.D. Bar J. 70 (1963).

201. *Id.*

202. *Id.*

203. *Id.*

204. *Id.*, "Minimum Fee Schedule Committee Report," 34 S.D. Bar J. 45 (1964).

205. *Id.*, at 47-48.

206. *Id.*, 34 S.D. Bar J. 48-50.

207. *Id.*

208. *Id.*, at 30.

209. Letter from R. Oviatt, Pres., S.D. State Bar, to Sen. J. Tunney, Wash., D.C., reprinted at 42 S.D. Bar J. 32-33 (Dec., 1973). *Cf.* Oviatt, "Remarks to Senior Class Upon Graduation," 43 S.D. Bar J. 22 (Sept., 1974), which indicates that the schedule was then a "recommended" one.

210. Clark, Part I, at 259.

211. *Id.*

212. *Id.*

213. HUD-VA, *Report on Mortgage Settlement Costs* (1972).

214. *Cf.* S.D. Comp. L. §36-13-10 which requires only that indexes of the public records be maintained by licensed abstractors. This statute requires amendment. *See* Eckhardt, "Abstractors Licensing Laws," 28 Mo. L. Rev. 1 (1963).

215. This would give developers of platted lands an abstract to present to their purchaser. S.D. Comp. L. §43-21-1 (1967).

216. Du Pratt v. Black Hills Land and Abstract Co., 81 S.D. 637, 140 N.W.2d 386 (1966).

217. S.D. Comp. L. §36-13-5 (1967).

218. *See* Watson v. Muirhead, 57 Pa. 161 (1968), holding an abstractor liable for negligent errors in title searches. *See* E. Roberts *et al.*, *Public Regulation of Title Insurance Companies and Abstractors* 13 (1960).

219. Straw, "Off-record Risks for Bona-fide Purchasers of Interests in Real Property," 72 Dick. L. Rev. 35 (1967).

220. Roberts *et al., supra* n. 218 at 4.

221. Comment, "Title Insurance: The Duty to Search," 71 Yale L. J. 1161 (1962).

222. Roberts, *et al., supra* n. 218 at 6.

223. Sattler v. Philadelphia Title Ins. Co., 192 Pa. Super. 337, 162 A.2d 22 (1960).

224. Southern Title Guar. Co. v. Prendergast, 478 S.W.2d 806 (Tex. Civ. App., 1972).

225. American Land Title Ass'n, Owner's Policy Form B-1970, §5; *id.*, Loan Policy—1970, §5.

226. *Id.*, Owner's Policy, §4; Loan Policy, §4.

227. First Nat'l Bank and Trust Co. of Port Chester v. N.Y. Title Ins. Co., 171 Misc. 854, 12 N.Y.S.2d (1939).

228. American Land Title Ass'n, Owner's Policy Form B-1970, Schedule B.

229. Lawyer's Title Ins. Corp. v. McKee, 354 S.W.2d 401 (Tex. Civ. App., 1962).

230. Overholtzer v. N. Counties Title Ins. Co., 116 Cal. App.2d 113, 253 P.2d 116 (1953).

231. Johnstone, "Systems of Land Title Protection in the United States and Possibilities for Their Improvement," in G. Wunderlich & W. Gibson, *Perspectives on Property* 187, 189-91 (1973) (the description following in the text is indebted to Johnstone's); *see also* Payne, "Title Insurance and the Unauthorized Practice of Law," 52 Minn. L. Rev. 423 (1969).

232. Roberts, *et al., supra* n. 218 at 8; *see also* Burke, "Conveyancing in the National Capital Region: Local Reform with National Implications," 22 Am. U. L. Rev. 527, 540 (1973).

233. Lawyer's Title Ins. Corp. v. Edmar Const. Corp., Civ. Action No. G.A. 22904-67 (Super. Ct. D.C., filed July 20, 1971), D.C. Ct. App., 1972, 294 A.2d 865.

234. Roberts, "Urban Conveyancing in the United States," 27 Conv. (N.S.) 240 (1963).

235. Roberts, *et al., supra* n. 18, at 13-20.

236. *See, e.g.,* G. Wunderlich, "Title Examination in Virginia," Va. Poly. Inst. & St. Univ., Agric. Econ. Reprint No. 10 (1972).

237. B. Burke & N. Kittrie, "The Real Estate Settlement Process and Its Costs," (1972) at III-A-7.

238. *Id.*, at III-E-1.

239. Q. Johnstone & D. Hopson, *Lawyers and Their Work* 296, 308 (1967).

240. *Id.*

241. *See generally* C. Donahue, T. Kauper, & P. Martin, *Property* 523, 1474 (1974), and materials cited therein.

242. The following section was adapted, though greatly rewritten, from Burke, "Conveyancing in the National Capital Region: Local Reform with National Implications," 22 Am. U. L. Rev. 527 (1973).

243. 19 Ency. Brit. 621 (1974).

244. D.C. Code tit. 1, §§101, 106, 107, 625 (1967); *id.*, tit. 49, §302. Historically the District of Columbia has encompassed as many as five local governments at one time since 1790.

245. M. Clawson, *Suburban Land Use Conversion* 229-33 (1971).

246. The SMSA median new-house price was $35,500 in January 1972. Bridemeir, *Housing Costs in Area Jump by Over $1000*, Washington *Post*, April 3, 1972, §C, at 1, col. 6. Since 1950 the District's share of new housing starts in the D.C. SMSA has declined drastically, from about 2,000 per year to less than 100. Overall, however, the metropolitan area is still one of the strongest single-family markets in the country, and in the decade 1960-70 produced an average of 14,000 units per year. Sumichrast, *New Housing May Set Mark*, Washington *Post*, July 31, 1971, §D, at 1, col. 1.

247. B. Burke & N. Kittrie, *The Real Estate Settlement Process and its Costs*, at III-B-34. As to brokers, *see* Stambler & Stein, *The Real Estate Broker—Schizophrenia or Conflict of Interests*, 28 D.C. Bar Assn. J. 16, 19 (1961).

248. Representations by the broker on the condition of the house are, however, not imputed to the vendors when the broker offers his opinion, *e.g.*, as to termite infestation. Pywell v. Haldane, 186 A.2d 623 (D.C. Munic. App., 1963). This case gave rise to house inspections and fees for same thereafter.

249. Dunn v. Shane, 195 A.2d 409 (D.C. App., 1963); however, each party may sign at different times. Braun v. Yaffee, 193 A.2d 895 (D.C. App., 1963).

250. The typical contract will protect the brokerage commission at the same time that it binds the parties. *See, e.g.*, Sales Contract—District of Columbia (Lerner Law Book Co., Washington, D.C., Form 3063). This form calls on the purchaser to produce a title "good of record and in fact." The vendor undertakes to cure promptly all defects in title, pay for the title examination if title should prove defective, and render a special warranty deed to the buyer at closing. The closing may take place at either the title company or the broker's office, as designated in the contract. *Id.* A broker may negotiate for financing by statute. D.C. Code tit. 45, §1402 (1967).

No District of Columbia cases hold that the broker is practicing law when doing this, although many attorneys interviewed seemed to assume such matters had been judicially determined. The courts of the District of Columbia seem to have adopted a rule that where preparation of papers is "primary" (as opposed to "incidental") to its business, preparation will not constitute the unauthorized practice of law. Merrick v. Am. Sec. & Trust Co., 107 F.2d 271 (D.C. Cir. 1939), *cert. denied*, 308 U.S. 625 (1940) (involving a trust company).

251. This is done as a matter of custom and specialization of labor, however; for if the broker does not attend to the specifics of the closing, it is put in the hands of another layman, either in the title company or broker's office. D.C. Code tit. 45, § 1401 (1967).

252. Some District of Columbia lawyers still maintain themselves on an approved list of attorneys found capable by title companies of performing title searches. *See* Lawyers' Title Ins. Corp. v. Edmar Constr. Co., Civil Action No. G.S. 22904-67 (Super. Ct. D.C., filed July 20, 1971), aff'd 294 A.2d 865 (D.C. Ct. App., 1972), wherein a title insurance company was held liable for funds required to procure a deed of release, where an attorney on its approved list failed to do so.

253. There is also a Multiple Listing Service, run by brokers in the District of Columbia, which has spurred the use of exclusive-right-to-sell contracts, signed by a member broker on behalf of all other participating brokers.

254. A broker-vendor who is asked by the purchaser for advice at closing but refuses to give it has breached a fiduciary obligation to the purchaser. Hammett v. Ruby Lee Minar, Inc., 60 App. D.C. 286, 53 F.2d 144, *cert. denied* Marar v. Hammett, 284 U.S. 682 (1931).

255. B. Burke & N. Kittrie, *supra* n. 237 at II-B-24.

256. D.C. Code tit. 45, § 601 (1967). Litigation settled the matter under the D.C. Code. Young v. Ridley, 309 F.Supp. 1308 (D.D.C. 1970). Corporate officers of the lender may, in addition, act as trustee. Admiral Co. v. Thomas, 164 F.Supp. 569 (D.D.C. 1958), *rev'd on other grounds*, 271 F.2d 849 (D.C. Cir. 1959). The borrower may, however, have lost important rights in this transaction. *See* Deed of Trust (Lerner Law Book Co., Washington, D.C., Forms 2022, 5002).

257. This term is used to distinguish national title insurance companies from insurers with local title plants. A national company maintains no local plant but relies on local attorneys to search a title and writes a policy from its national office based on his findings. .

258. Anderson v. Reid, 14 App. D.C. 54 (1899).

259. *See* D.C. Code tit. 19, § 102 (1967) (Revision notes). *See also* Osin v. Johnson, 243 F.2d 653 (D.D.C. 1957), on the possibility of equitable interests clouding a record title.

260. Although many of these companies have names inherited from local companies, most are subsidiaries of nation-wide insurers.

261. The District of Columbia has no marketable-title act, and indeed, nothing in the way of curative legislation. *But see* D.C. Code tit. 45, §§ 802, 817

(1967) (abolition in 1901 of estates tail and coparcenary estates). Statutes of limitations must, therefore, suffice to help limit durations of interests.

262. D.C. Real Estate Comm., "Real Estate and Business Chance Manual" 18 (1967).

263. Before the closing, the escrow department will obtain certificates of payment from, or balances due to, public taxation and water officials; and instructions from existing and prospective lenders; in addition, the department will prepare the documents on instructions from lenders and the principals. Am. Land Title Ass'n., "Closing Cost Project," Supp. Info. (Washington, D.C., 1971).

264. The five large title insurers had discussed the possibility of combining their title plants, but until 1973 no definitive action had been taken. Most managers argue that the plant costs cause their District of Columbia business to operate in the red when taken alone, but that profit margins from their suburban business make up for this loss and put the companies in the black.

265. The majority of home buyers (estimates range between 80-95 percent) in the District of Columbia do not procure owners' insurance, but many companies will issue "record policies," certifying that their search has been competent and workmanlike. They assume basic common-law liability as abstractors, D.C. Real Estate Comm., "Real Estate and Business Chance Manual" 58 (1967).

Rate schedules are complicated documents for the average home buyer, and the rates given may always be increased for more than normally difficult searches and certifications. On new construction, for instance, mechanic's liens constitute a source of many claims on title policies. Companies in the District of Columbia handle this problem differently. For some, mechanic's liens constitute a "Schedule B" exemption to the policy coverage; however, one company will not exempt the lien if found, but will not disburse funds in escrow to the seller in the amount of the lien until a release is filed. The Insurance Code (D.C. Code tit. 35, §1302 (1967)) exempts title insurance from rate-setting procedures applicable to other types of insurance.

266. Interview memorandum, Nov. 1974, on file with author.

267. Private mortgage bankers extend a substantial portion of the credit for housing and also act as brokers for savings and loan associations in the national secondary mortgage market. *In re* Parkwood, Inc., 461 F.2d 158 (D.C. Cir. 1971), involving the District of Columbia Loan Shark Act (D.C. Code tit. 26, §601 (1967)), revealed the extent of this involvement. The case held up millions of dollars of mortgage sales from the District of Columbia area into the secondary market.

268. In 1967 these costs usually were $10, $10, and 0, respectively. D.C. Real Est. Comm., "Real Estate and Business Chance Manual" 60 (1967).

269. *See* B. Burke & N. Kittrie, *supra* n. 237 at III-B-33.

270. *See* Goodman v. Perpetual Bldg. Ass'n, Memo. Opin., Civ. Action No. 2720-66 (1970). Stern, "Debt Insurance Charges Hit," Washington *Post* (Nov.

12, 1974) at A9, col. 1, in which Senator Proxmire (D.-Wisc.) said the placement of this insurance in an uncompetitive way resulted in overcharges and the payment of kickbacks to lenders. D.C. Real Estate Comm., "Real Estate and Business Chance Manual" 40 (1967).

271. Annotation, "Rights in Funds Representing 'Escrow' Payments Made by Mortgagor in Advance to Cover Taxes or Insurance," 50 A.L.R.3d 697 (1973).

272. American Land Title Ass'n, "Closing Cost Project," Supp. Info. (Washington, D.C.) (1971).

273. The title or settlement company will, at the closing, also collect the recordation fees. The recordation tax in the District of Columbia is one half of 1 percent of the consideration for the deed. There is no tax on the deed of trust. When no consideration or only nominal consideration is recited, the tax is then levied on the fair market value of the property. Grantor and grantee are jointly and severally liable for the tax. D.C. Code tit. 45, § §723, 724 (Supp. I 1968).

274. Merryman, "Toward a Comparative Study of the Sale of Land," II Jus. Privatum Gentium 737 (1969) (compilation of essays in honor of Max Rheinstein).

**Part II
Three Types of
Improvements**

Conveyancing Legislation

Introduction

The descriptions of local conveyancing in the foregoing chapter provide a basis for assessing the development of American conveyancing. Deficiencies in early patterns gave rise to new patterns. There is no reason to think that this pattern of incremental additions to past conveyancing institutions is complete today. The evolution of these patterns, one turning into another, occurred because of the need to improve, not the quality of, but the access to existing land title records; accessibility was a continuing concern of attorneys, abstractors, and title insurance companies, in that order, and is arguably the key to improved conveyancing in the future.[1]

Assuming that these patterns will continue to evolve, perhaps the prescription for improving the accessibility of information needed for title proof and delivery is to do nothing. As an option of the policy maker, this course of action rests on an argument that the abstract and title insurance policy based on a title search are costly to compile and that the present system will continue to change in the direction of simplified title proof and documentation. Whether systems of title documents are maintained publicly or privately in the future, new forms of record keeping are a necessity.

With the prospect that the greatest improvements can be attained without public interference comes the corollary that interference may retard the pace of this change. The conveyancing industry may seek public regulation of many types to escape the changes needed in an unregulated market,[2] and effective conveyancing can be attained by professional care on the part of private practitioners.[3]

Improved access to title records was mentioned in the case study on South Dakota: It maintains tract indexes, has enacted a marketable-title act, and has suggested title standards for state-wide use.[4] The tract index is one improvement in public title records found in many states and makes the information in these records more accessible to the public.[5]

Because the development of American conveyancing has been based on remedying deficiencies in past practices, it has been backward looking and often without a guiding rationale for future change. Many jurisdictions in the United States experimented with rudimentary registration or Torrens laws in the early decades of the twentieth century,[6] but after that died out, less comprehensive proposals for marketable-title and ad hoc curative legislation[7] were taken up.

This legislation is usually premised on the "general-welfare" clause of the federal and state constitutions or on the general-welfare aspect of the police power.[8] As a rationale, however, the general welfare provides few if any reliable guides for predicting the future of American conveyancing and absolutely no guide for measuring the social effects of that change. Legislation rendering titles more easily marketable may sacrifice some personal rights. In policy terms the question (empirically unanswered) is whether more titles are made marketable in the hands of the true owner than are placed beyond the reach of the holder of an otherwise actionable or legitimate claim on them. In constitutional terms the question becomes one of harmonizing the general welfare with the due-process clauses of federal and state constitutions.[9] With this issue in mind, a review of the problems with past legislative attempts at improvement in conveyancing patterns seems in order.

Making Titles Marketable by Legislation

After the debate over the Torrens system died down as a result of a declination in use,[10] legislation to improve conveyancing attempted to reduce the documentation necessary for title proof; most of these improvements affected only the attorney- and abstractor-dominated patterns of conveyancing.

This legislation is of two types: marketable title and curative acts. A *marketable-title act* limits the title-search period to a certain period of time or date and covers all interests in documents of record and unrecorded instruments,[11] while a *curative act* only cleanses named and particularized defects on the records.[12] A marketable-title tolls a limitation period and eliminates ancient restrictions on title and documents from the record; a curative statute validates an interest once the document in which it appears has reached a statutory age.[13] In other words, marketable-title acts eliminate old records; curative statutes toll a limitation period on challenges to old defective ones. Operating in tandem, marketable-title acts shorten the necessary chain of title while curative acts forge its links.

Justifications for This Legislation

Statutes limiting the period of time a property interest can exist on the records operate like the most traditional[14] of title-quieting devices, statutes of limitations. Ordinarily, the latter would suffice for this purpose were it not for the future, equitable, and reversionary interests that our common-law system of estates permits.[15] These interests, whose holders do not have a present right to possession of the property affected, will not become subject to the statute of limitations until that right becomes possessory. Even if the period of limitations has tolled, its expiration will extinguish the right to bring judicial actions to enforce the right, but not the right itself. Moreover, subsequent dealings with the land, or the incapacity of the interest holder, might delay the tolling of the statutory period.

Extinguishment of old interests may promote a secure title and the economic welfare of its holder.[16] Any extinguishment or even reordering of proprietary interests requires a substantial justification if it is to survive constitutional attack as a measure supportive of the general welfare. Such support has existed in the West when groundwater in a valley was exploited under a rule of capture to the point that the land was drying up and individual conservation became self-defeating. Mortgage lenders in one such valley refused to loan money unless their potential borrowers had access to a stable water supply. Faced with this situation, state legislators abolished existing water rights and framed new rules for appropriating water.[17] Restrictive lending policies have similarly justified South Dakota's establishing a state program for farm loans.[18] Since lending policies result in many closing services and costs, legislation to reduce the burden of title proof renders titles both marketable and mortgageable.[19] In *East New York Savings Bank* v. *Haln,*[20] Justice Frankfurter said

when a widely diffused public interest has become enmeshed in a network of multitudinous private arrangements, the authority of the State ... is not to be gainsaid by abstracting one such arrangement from its public context and treating it as though it were an isolated private contract constitutionally immune from impairment.[21]

Marketable Title Acts

The marketable title acts resulted from the desire to shorten title searches. Adopted today in sixteen states, the first was enacted in Iowa in 1929.[22] These laws extinguished interests in land that were based on a document or set of facts preexisting either a period of time[23] (averaging thirty or forty years under existing laws, and fifteen years in England)[24] or a particular date. These two types of laws are known respectively as "automatic" or "nonautomatic" marketable-title statutes.[25]

The by-product of extinguishing presumably stale interests is to set limits on the number of years that a title search must cover.[26] Since every act contains exceptions, these parameters cannot be firm, and old interests may be preserved by filing a notice of them in the recent title records.[27] The minimal effect of these statutes is to permit evaluation of a title on the basis of the recently recorded documents in its chain of title.[28] Elimination of claims arising from mistakes or mistaken intentions of the parties will seldom survive the statutory period because in all likelihood such interests will not be rerecorded.

Marketable-title acts do not try to define the marketability of a title in terms of any particular documents or interest or to erase defects on recorded documents as do curative acts, nor do they have a legal effect on the contents of documents filed for record within the statutory search period. They do generally preserve the common law's respect for possessory rights by excepting them and assuming that a person owns what he possesses.[29] Attempts to distinguish marketable-title acts from curative laws are largely a matter of scope and subject matter rather than legal substance.[30] These laws have survived a multifaceted attack on their constitutionality.[31]

Marketable-title legislation does, however, have counterproductive side effects. Their statutory exceptions[32] could result in several types of title searches for any one piece of property, depending on the interests involved.[33] More specialized legal problems remain: First the statutory period varies with each search, for a documentary "root of title" predating the statutory period of marketability must be located.[34] Second two nonpossessory chains of title, equally valid under such statutes, may be found for any particular property.[35] Third the acts may be (mis)interpreted to protect less-than-fee interests as well as fee-simple absolutes.[36] Fourth whether they apply to party walls or boundary agreements established by acquiescence is in doubt.[37] These laws are valuable conveyancing aids, but they are complex in their own right and present unique, often fascinating legal problems. In solving one problem, they create others.

One final problem is that marketable-title acts do not in practice affect conveyancing patterns. Abstractors and other title searchers can save time and effort only when no abstract exists or when the time covered by an up-date exceeds the marketable-title period. This is so because a common practice is to search back only until a past transaction is found in which another examiner, title insurer, or mortgage lender known to require marketable title is discovered on the record. Periods of adverse possession and statutes of limitations for real-property actions may also define the period of search. Since most properties change hands more frequently and most searches do involve an up-date of less than twenty years, their real effect is to shorten long careful searches required for commercial, very valuable, or urbanizing properties.

Close attention to marketable-title legislation can yield some conclusions about what improvements are possible in the system. In the United States the average statutory period that must be searched before examining a root of title is thirty to forty years. In the transition and evolution of title-delivery patterns— from an attorney, to an attorney-abstractor, to a title insurance plant—one objective has been to eliminate unnecessary information found in the public records. In large plants data irrelevant to a title search must be quickly eliminated. Whether the records incorporated into such plants were originally organized by name or by parcel description, their reorganization, and not merely a shifting of documents to recently filed records, is a precondition to ready access. In title insurance plants much data is routinely assembled in the hope that collecting more than is needed will save time in compiling abstracts or issuing title insurance. Marketable-title acts reduce the period during which this information will be useful. They do not reduce the volume of documents that must be located during a title search or the work involved in locating them. What they do is encourage that those documents be refiled or preserved by a notice in more recent title records. If anything, the burden of take-offs necessary to maintain large title plants in marketable-title act states is likely to be greater because of this encouragement.

Normally title plant data will be used in an abstract only as frequently as the property changes hands.[38] Abstracting all the customarily-used title data on a continuing basis allows the abstractor to stabilize his business costs and assume that, in the long run, all his information (or a large percentage of it) will be useful. He looks to the future to recoup his take-off costs. Since real estate activity is particularly sensitive to other sectors of our economy, the time span of his recoupment is longer than the usual business cycle.

In the evolution of the attorney-search system to the attorney-abstract system, search practices were based on custom and were little questioned.[39] An abstract was a business expense and the work product of a search, but it becomes a capital asset when future work on the same parcel is done;[40] the abstractor or attorney who had searched or certified a title was the man who could do the work most easily a second time.[41] Conveyancing work generated abstracts and then title opinions, and, after a time, a rudimentary title plant.[42] Evidently in this country there was not that certainty of future work; and if no firm had a clear monopoly, title records were pooled first by abstractors and then by title insurers; only then and without a monopoly or near-monopoly developing in some other enterprise could the uncertainties of future work on existing title records be overcome and economies of scale be realized.[43] Only after decades of collecting title information will a title plant or an attorney be able to provide a root of title from his own records. The root-of-title requirements of marketable-title acts indicates a preference for land title records over other types—probate, bankruptcy, tax records—with which the conveyancer is not likely to have as great a familiarity and which incorporate more facts extrinsic to the documents.[44] Marketable-title acts do not attempt to reduce the number of records that must be searched. Marketable record titles are expressly "subject to . . . any interest arising out of a title transaction which has been recorded subsequent to the effective date of the root of title . . ."[45] and can in time give rise to a marketable record title. Thus a probate or bankruptcy decree can become a transaction destroying the marketability of a title under the acts. To fill in the information gaps in an attorney's or abstractor's files of conveyancing documents or plant, his office must hire extra personnel to devote large amounts of time to a transfer. Gradually, in an urban setting pooled records and a high volume of conveyancing work become the preconditions of doing this work, and the sole practitioner or small law firm falls by the wayside, unable to meet the demands of many clients, unless they all want advice on titles previously abstracted.[46] In large urban centers the trend toward making many types of information accessible has resulted in large overhead expenses for the title insurers who do business there. As abstract files evolved into title plants and were purchased by title insurers, the sheer volume of information engendered the need to pool overhead and take-off expenses among several companies. The experience of the District of Columbia's title insurers is not atypical in this respect: coop title plants have also been established in Los Angeles, Denver, St. Louis, and Seattle.[47] The expenses of searching title have put urban title insurers in a dilemma: Searching a title reduces their risk of loss but increases their overhead expenses. In balancing the reduced risk against the increased expense, companies have not been receptive recently to suggestions that they increase the coverage of their policies, especially when that would necessitate assembling new information. They have even gone so far as to resist the imposition of any statutory duty to search the titles they insure.[48]

So marketable-title acts are unlikely to affect the organizational preconditions of conveyancing work. For the attorney, many reorders of previously compiled abstracts are still needed. For the abstractor with a title plant, that plus larger amounts of title information are necessary. More highly organized title-search organizations add one more characteristic to those already mentioned—specialization of labor. The largest title firms, whether abstracting or insuring, are likely to have two characteristics, none of which is affected by marketable title acts.

1. The first three patterns described in Chapter 2 culminate in a title plant that requires *high capital investment costs.*[49] If built gradually, capital investments in records will not be noticeable because each client or customer will pay his own way. But once the accumulated title records are pooled, customers will expect the firm to have the pertinent records,[50] and at that point they must pay for the accumulation of more records. Title records must be taken off public records and reproduced, which in large urban title plants often requires photoduplicating equipment in the public records office itself.[51] Only a portion of these take-offs can reasonably be expected to become the subject of a title search within the calculable time period of a fiscal year or business cycle. As new records are deposited, older, less useful ones must be retired or microfilmed and stored. Take-off costs remain high and are relatively constant, regardless of the volume of title transfers and better equipment—faster cameras, computers, etc. Marketable-title acts do little to reduce these costs. Further, the resale market for used title plants is limited. Some very old records may have historical value, but beyond that only another title plant owner would be interested and then perhaps only selectively to supplement his records.[52] The illiquidity of the industry's investments, whether made gradually or all at once, is likely to induce a cautious attitude toward change.

2. A title plant also produces maintenance and labor costs that are constant

over time. Since the volume of real estate transactions rises and falls with the cycles of the real estate market generally, title records must have a long time-horizon in which to recoup the expense of compiling them. Marketable-title acts foreshorten the horizon, and title companies might object to them on that ground. Another objection is that since labor costs are relatively constant, the costs of using the records is unrelated to the volume of records in the plant. *Labor specialization* in title plants has already been detailed. In the more highly organized operations, a clerk writes a work order for incoming jobs; another establishes the list of names of owners who must be searched; a third does the search or hunts for the documents; and a fourth reviews the documents. Labor costs are a high proportion of all overhead costs,[53] for the work is labor-intensive. A recent survey showed that 42 percent of the gross profits of the abstract and title insurance industry went into personnel salaries;[54] another 20 percent went for commissions to field agents, mostly attorneys.

A fixed capital investment with a long time-horizon using a specialized labor force in labor-intensive surroundings—all these characteristics seem to induce the most guarded dealings with the public and to encourage dealings with a group of brokers, attorneys, and escrow agents who can be relied on to refer business and supply complementary services. This is one reason why an industry like abstracting or title insurance does not serve consumers directly; then it does not need to advertise and can solicit the consumer through intermediaries (lenders and attorneys). The latter become its public,[55] and the costs of solicitation its only advertising expenses.

With this narrow constituency for title company services and the economic costs of title plants relatively stable and unaffected by the legislation, marketable-title acts can be expected to encounter industry opposition. For example, in 1975 the Commissioners on Uniform State Laws rejected, in favor of further study, Lewis Simes' version of a marketable-title act.[56] Moreover, the acts have so far provided no evidence that they encourage the automation or computerization of title data, although this is widely assumed, and the acts may indeed be one precondition for further public-sector improvements. In very large urban centers, the initial capital needed to automate and the documents required for even a 30- or 40-year title search may still prevent the automation of all presently used title records. It is likely that both public and private efforts to modernize land title data will result in a system in which usable title data remains in both public and private hands, depending on the region and the capacities of local government. For this reason alone, the United States will continue to have a mixed system of title data collection well into the twenty-first century.

Curative Acts

To paraphrase the definition of curative acts found in Paul Basye's *Clearing Land Titles* (1970), they are a form of retrospective state legislation that reaches into the past, operates on past events,[57] and renders valid attempted land transfers that would otherwise be legally ineffective for technical reasons.[58] These laws are meant to complete transactions that the parties intended to accomplish but carried out imperfectly.[59]

It might generally be said that a curative act does by statute what an equity court would do if called upon to act.[60] One of the aims of a curative act is to provide fair dealings between the parties to a transfer in order to prevent one party from taking advantage of technical defects to defeat their prior intent.[61] Based on constitutional requirements, this defines the scope of these acts so that they can be validated under the contract clause of federal and state constitutions.[62] The general-welfare clauses of our constitutions provide another utilitarian premise for legislative action; by curing past irregularities in the land records, conveyancers are able to achieve a record chain of title not otherwise possible. Thus the acts are both fair to the parties and useful to the public.

At the beginning of this section, curative acts were referred to as "retrospective legislation." This terminology raises constitutional problems because of the possibility that if a statute validates a defective document *ab initio*, the rights of intervening third parties are subordinated to a prior event invalid at the moment of their intervention.[63] In that event curative statutes might be construed to refer to a past act but establish only present rights or duties, thus saving the right of intervening third parties. Even the most competent drafters of these statutes are ambiguous on this question.[64] The following sections are drawn from the 1971 Nebraska Code.

§76-258:

When any instrument of writing, in any manner affecting or purporting to affect the title to real estate, has been, or may hereafter be recorded for a period of ten years in the office of the register of deeds of the county wherein such real estate is situated, and such instrument, or the record thereof, because of defect, irregularity or omission, fails to comply in any respect with any statutory requirement or requirements relating to the execution, attestation, acknowledgment, certificate of acknowledgment, recording or certificate of recording, such instrument and the record thereof shall, notwithstanding any or all of such defects, irregularities and omissions, be fully legal, valid, binding and effectual for all purposes to the same extent as though such instrument had, in the first instance, been in all respects duly executed, attested, acknowledged and recorded.

§76-259:

The defects, irregularities and omissions mentioned in section 76-258 shall include all defects and irregularities in respect to formalities of execution and recording, and all defects and irregularities in, as well as the entire lack of omission of attestation, ackowledgment, certificate of acknowledgment, or certificate of recording, and shall apply with like force to instruments whether or not the real estate involved is homestead.

§76-260:

From and after its validation by the operation of section 76-258, such instrument shall impart notice to subsequent purchasers, encumbrancers, and all other persons whomsoever so far as and to the same extent that the same is recorded, notwithstanding such defects, irregularities or omissions; and such instrument, the record thereof, or a duly authenticated copy shall be competent evidence to the same extent as such instrument would have been competent if valid in the first instance.[65]

Imparting notice after validation might imply that the statute establishes only present rights and duties. If, for example, a defective conveyance is recorded and in the period before its statutory validation, the vendor in the defective transaction dies and his widow takes the property through the intestate laws, the last section of this statute is unclear as to whether the vendee or the widow takes the property. If only "... after validation ... such instrument shall impart notice," the vendee would appear to hold the better claim; however, the validated notice is given "to the same extent that the same is recorded." In the end whether a curative statute establishes only present rights and duties or relates back to the prior transfer and cuts short the rights of subsequent third parties depends on the case law of a jurisdiction, particularly on the discretion remaining in a chancellor in equity after passage of the curative act. But if third-party rights have intervened, the narrower, present validation of a previously ineffective document is often ascribed to the statute.[66]

Three rules are generally cited by the courts in upholding curative acts:[67] that the curative act operates only on nonvested rights; that the act alters the remedy but not the right to sell; and that if the legislature has power to dispense with any formality of conveyancing in advance of a transaction, it also has the power to cure transactions not satisfying its own requirements. In large measure, the first two rules are non sequiturs and constitute a word game. However, the third rule has two advantages to it: It allows the courts to examine the intentions of the parties operating through the recording laws of the state and implies that retroactive effects on the recording are not objectionable per se.[68] This is particularly true when these acts are perceived as statutes of limitations on challenges to formal defects in a transaction. Indeed, when statutory defects of the last-mentioned type are involved, legislatures can give the broadest effect to curative acts and will even cut off intervening third-party rights.

Legislation and Equity

If curative acts attempt legislatively to do equity and marketable-title acts attempt to save titles from stale claims that it would be inequitable to enforce, then the more general problem inherent in all this legislation is the imprecisely defined relationship between the statutes and the equity powers of the courts.

Should, for example, a legislature decide to draft a curative statute on the theory that intervening third-party rights are extinguished, and the statute expressly said this, would the chancellor be bound to follow it? This type of curative act attempts to codify equitable rules and binds courts to them.

Historically conveyancing developed a great part of its law in the most supple branch of the judiciary, the courts of equity. The rise of the deed of bargain and sale,[69] of an action for specific performance of a contract,[70] of the combined modern action of ejectment by an out-of-possession title holder,[71] and of the combined quiet-title action, are all examples.[72] It is also equitable jurisdiction that has subjected the recording system to many interests not of record but actionable in equity.[73]

With so much conveyancing law being made in courts of equity, the possibility of equitable interests undermining the record title is a real one.[74] Title attorneys were increasingly asked to predict how a chancellor would react to the facts revealed in an abstract of title. This second-guessing by attorneys certifying the marketability of the title[75] was difficult because of the flexibility of the equitable rules.[76] Since the chancellor might react differently depending on the position of each litigant, it was necessary to review each abstract every time the title passed into the hands of a new purchaser. For example, a prior owner may have used the property in a way that left him unconcerned about the legal sufficiency of an attempt to create an easement over the property. A new owner may wish to develop the property in a way inconsistent with the easement, but may find himself estopped from denying the user if he purchases with notice of it. Later purchasers may find themselves with a valid claim to extinguish the easement but barred by the equitable doctrine of laches from doing so. More commonly a title may have been found marketable when reviewed by an attorney for a mortgagee and later rejected by an attorney for an owner. Finally, the status of past owners who might take by operation of law, tax sale, or mortgage foreclosure, as well as by contract and conveyance, may affect the chancellor's view of the title. These uncertainties, taken together, finally gave rise to the need for abstractors and then for title insurance, the last step in the evolutionary change in conveyancing patterns.

Yet equitable interests may be of several varieties:[77] As a class, they might include the rights of undisclosed heirs; marital rights of dower and curtesy; actions to invalidate documents never delivered, signed under duress, based on forgery, or acquired through fraud;[78] constructive trusts, which are established by a finding of an equity court;[79] and a purchaser's interest in a contract of sale enforceable by an equitable action for specific performance of the contract. They may be based on documents or a set of facts, but where it is the latter, the recording system will, as far as the property affected is concerned, neither disclose the true owner of the property nor the extent of his ownership. That is, full disclosure of the ownership will not be possible until any equitable claim on the property is adjudicated or otherwise settled.[80]

Thus with the recording acts constrained by the chancellor's discretion, these statutes cannot publicize the true owner of property even if the indexing and land title record keeping made recorded information accessible to the public (which it does not). It is in this sense that the recording acts are not legislation aimed at "public disclosure" of property owners. At best, the record title tells the prospective purchaser that if he deals with anyone but a record owner, or someone tracing title from him, he may not be purchasing what he thinks he is. So the record is evidence of title, but does not prove title. It indicates who does not own the property—i.e., anyone not tracing his interest from a record owner—but does not provide full information on true ownership. This is why the recording acts are only a starting point for a title search and why many other types of public records are searched for traces of actionable claims on a property. It is also one reason why most recording acts do not make the act of recording necessary for a valid conveyance between vendor and purchaser. The reason for this uncertainty and lack of disclosure lies not in recording acts per se but in the interaction of the record title with the equitable powers of the judiciary.

Often the difficulty of making a title marketable lies not in unrecorded interests but in the fact that the resulting abstract may have conflicting claims, all of which the recorder has accepted without ever sorting them out. This is particularly apparent with tract indexes in which all claims will be cataloged in one place, but less likely with grantor-grantee indexing under which recorded documents must be filed within a chain of title to be recoverable by the abstractor's routine search. Sorting out these conflicting claims in a review of the resulting abstract is the job of the title attorney; he must decide what claims appearing in the abstract might still be actionable at law or equity.

Because of the difficulty of his task of avoiding litigation and an adverse judgment, inconsistent claims in the abstract will render a title unmarketable in the attorney's eyes, and so it is through the incompleteness of the record that unadjudicated and perhaps insubstantial claims come to have a very practical harsh effect: A recorded instrument without substance can nonetheless deny an owner the financing of improvements or even the right to sell his property.

Conclusion

The enactment of marketable-title acts and curative laws are intended to handle the problems of cumbersome title searches and the inadequacies of the recording acts. Their objective is to remedy the deficiencies of a faltering title-delivery system. It could be argued that these later changes in the recording system have not been made in jurisdictions that need them most: Few populous states have enacted marketable-title statutes; relatively few such states have adopted curative acts or uniform, bar-promulgated title standards. Title insurance aside, there has been a mismatch between the need and the solution. States like South Dakota which make the recording system more workable have preserved the best features and low costs of older systems, while other, more populous areas, including large urban centers in jurisdictions otherwise using older, unmodified patterns, have used title insurance to "paper over" their deficiencies.

Constitutional issues litigated after the enactment of marketable-title and curative acts raise, but do not resolve, questions of conflict between the general-welfare and due-process clauses of federal and state constitutions. On the one hand, the legislature in enacting these laws declares that all fee titles in the jurisdiction will be rendered more secure and marketable; at the same time individual claimants who have had rights extinguished will claim violation of their right to due process. Past legislative improvements have, in other words, an inherent flaw in that they set up this conflict. With marketable-title acts, no resolution is even attempted. In the case of curative statutes, a resolution is seemingly left up to courts of equity. Future improvements in conveyancing patterns should therefore encompass procedures either to preserve or extinguish old interests in realty; instead of leaving the matter up to courts of equity, administrative procedures might be established to bring uniformity to the process. In the context of the establishment of tract indexes for land records, the next chapter will attempt to describe both the need for such procedures and the procedures themselves.

Notes

1. L. Simes, *Handbook for More Efficient Conveyancing* 18 (1961).

2. Echardt, "Abstractor's Licensing Laws," 28 Mo. L. Rev. 1 (1963); *see also* Am. Land Title Ass'n, Revised Model Title Insurance Code (1973).

3. Indeed, many past proposals for legislation in this area are really taken from practices developed by prudent conveyancers.

Conveyancers can make title searches simpler by reciting situations putting a purchaser on notice of facts *dehors* the record. *Cf.* Wisc. Stat. Ann. § 706.09 (1975) (recitals of facts presumed valid). In an effort to define the chain, conveyancers sometimes refer in deeds or mortgages to the documents from which each derives title. They recite the reference number, the book number, and page of such documents included in the chain of title. This saves a subsequent conveyancer having to chain the title. This practice might be formalized by statute. A recent Alabama bill, "An Act to Protect Innocent Purchasers," requires that every recorded document state the book, number, and page of the previous instrument in its chain of title, and this, used with a marketable-title act, soon eliminates the need to search the grantor-grantee index in the normal case. Payne, "The Alabama Law Institutes Land Title Acts Project: Part I," 24 Ala. L. Rev. 175, 180-202 (1971). Other states have considered legislation that would require the social security numbers of the parties, the sales price, and the real parties in interest to be stated on the deed when recorded. Md. H.B. 1039 (1973); Iowa Hse. File No. 215 (1975) (disclosure of corporate and alien owners required), now Iowa Code Ann. § 172 c.5, -.7 (1975).

Services can be eliminated by such devices as well. Retaining the documents from past conveyances may allow affidavits of "no change" when obtained from neighbors to stand in the place of a new survey. J. Grimes, *Clark on Surveying and Boundaries* 498 (3d ed., 1959). Similarly, appraisals can be updated with a calculator instead of a site visit by the expert.

Recertification of past services can avoid duplicative work. When choosing an abstractor or title insurer, the company that conducted the last title search can most easily do the work and may even give a lower rate for reissuing its title policy. This practical advantage might be formalized by statute as well: A marketable title might be defined as one searched back to a time at which a state-regulated abstractor or insurer certified or indemnified the title. The earlier abstractor, attorney, or insurer might be permitted to recertify the title for a flat fee (a so-called back-title letter). Identification of the preparer on a form deed is often possible, but such identification could be required by statute.

The value of some services can be enhanced by proper supervision of them. Surveyors can be directed to leave markers or monuments in the ground. Ill. P.A. 79-649 (1975). Abstractors can be asked to extend their privity of employment to purchasers and third parties; this will extend their liability to such parties for negligent or incompetent title searches. Attorneys can similarly be asked to review and certify a title for third parties. The title insurer can likewise be asked to broaden the coverage of the insurance contract. Waivers of some standard exceptions to coverage, or else endorsement to add coverage (*e.g.*, for mechanic's liens in the District of Columbia) for an extra premium, are possibilities.

Some common off-record title risks might be minimized by further statutory reform. For example, dower and curtesy could be minimized by legislation abolishing these marital estates or vesting them only as to a decedent's property of which he or she is "seized at death." Opinion of the Justices, 337 Mass. 786, 151 N.E.2d 475 (1958); R. Powell, 2 *Real Property* para. 213.1 (1973). Several states have already enacted such changes in their landed estates. Second, mechanic's liens for the building trades might be reduced as a threat to marketable titles if the doctrine, under which the priority of the lien relates back to the commencement of work on the property, were eliminated. The lien would then take its priority as of its recordation date. Statutory reform might alternatively limit the relation back as far as the last conveyance of the property or allow the new owner to take free of claims against his merchant-builder-vendor. Simple changes in the recording laws might also reduce off-record risks from fraudulent and forged documents. The recorder could be required to notify a grantor named in a recently recorded contract, mortgage, or deed of the filing of a later document against his interest. A postcard detachable from the acknowledgment form (reducing it from legal to letter size) filled out by the latter document's presentor, should suffice for this purpose.

4. *See supra* ch. 2, text at n. 118-20.

5. For an analysis of the problems where no tract indexing is available, *see* Cross, "The Record 'Chain of Title' Hypocrisy," 57 Colum. L. Rev. 787 (1957) *and* Payne, "Continuity and Identity in Land Title Searches—A Perpetual Self-Indexing System" 16 Ala. L. Rev. 9, 12-17 (1963). *See also* Spies, "A Critique of Conveyancing," 38 Va. L. Rev. 245, 262-63 (1952) (where the author recommended that a system of tract indexes be substituted for Virginia's cumbersome grantor-grantee indexes); Cribbet, "Conveyancing Reform," 35 N.Y.U. L. Rev. 1291, 1306-16 (1960) (suggesting any effective reform of present recording systems must include effective marketable-title acts and tract indexing); *and* Basye, "A Uniform Land Parcel Identifier—Its Potential for All Our Land Records," 22 Am. U. L. Rev. 251, 263 (1973) (proposing a new system of recording based on a tract index).

6. M. Yeakle, *The Torrens System* (1894).

7. L. Simes, *Handbook for More Efficient Conveyancing* 42, 64, 74 (1961).

8. P. Basye, *Clearing Land Titles* 384-85, 463-65 (2d ed., 1970).

9. *Id.,* at 463.

10. R. Powell, *Registration of Title to Land in the State of New York* 55 (1938).

11. Basye, *supra* n. 8, at 368-73.

12. *Id.,* at 463-74.

13. In this respect a curative act operates much like the "ancient-document" exception to the hearsay rule of evidence. In practical terms, it is a substitute for an affidavit in transactions where the paper title is insufficient to give the purchaser marketable title.

14. 4 Hen. VII, c. 24 (1487) (provided a five-year limitation on challenges to a "fine").

15. P. Basye, *Clearing Land Titles* 336 (2d ed., 1970).

16. Harris v. Presbytery of Southeast Iowa, Iowa Sup. Ct., 1975, 226 N.W.2d 232, cert. den. 44 U.S. L. Wk. 3201 (1975); Payne, "The Crisis in Conveyancing," 19 Mo. L. Rev. 214 (1954); *and see* Lane v. Travelers Ins. Co., 230 Iowa 973, 299 N.W. 553 (1941).

17. State v. Dority, 55 N.M. 12, 225 P.2d 1007 (1950).

18. Green v. Frazier, 253 U.S. 233 (1920).

19. *See generally* Williamson v. Lee Optical, 348 U.S. 483, 488 (1955): "The day is gone when this Court uses the Due Process Clause of the Fourteenth Amendment to strike down state laws, regulatory of business and industrial conditions, because they may be unwise, improvident, or out of harmony with a particular school of thought."

20. 326 U.S. 230 (1945).

21. *Id.*, at 232.

22. Iowa Acts 1919, c. 270, § 1 (1919), now entitled the Iowa Code Ann., sec. 614-617 (1958). Basye, "Trends and Progress: The Marketable Title Acts," 47 Iowa L. Rev. 261 (1962). There is a mismatch of needs and solutions here. With the aim of eliminating title searches over long periods of time, marketable-title acts would seem most needed in our eastern states, while, in fact, with recent exceptions, they have been enacted primarily in the Midwest and north central states. P. Basye, *Clearing Land Titles* 171 (2d ed., 1970).

23. *Id.*, at 404.

24. P. Basye, *Clearing Land Titles* 375 (2d ed., 1970).

25. *Id.; e.g.,* S.D. Comp. L. § 43-28-16 (nonautomatic curative act).

26. P. Basye, *Clearing Land Titles* 426 (2d ed., 1970); *see also* Mich. Stat. Ann. § 26.1271 through 1279 (1974).

27. P. Basye, *Clearing Land Titles* 376 (2d ed., 1970).

28. This attempt to bring all relevant documents within recent records was first made with water-rights records in western states. Archuleta v. Boulder and Weld County Ditch Co., 118 Colo. 43, 192 P.2d 891 (1948); Quigley v. McIntosh, 88 Mont. 103, 290 P. 266 (1930). Another special problem exists on Maine's off-shore coastal islands. *See infra*, n. 59.

29. Tesdell v. Hanes, 248 Iowa 74, 82 N.W.2d 119 (1957).

30. A. Axelrod, C. Berger, & Q. Johnstone, *Land Transfer and Finance* 720 (1971); *see, e.g.,* Note, "The Massachusetts Marketable Title Act," 44 B.U. L. Rev. 201 (1964); *see also* Pa. H.B. 751 (1973).

31. Hachman, "The Supreme Court and the Constitutionality of Retro-active Legislation," 73 Harv. L. Rev. 45 (1967); Note, "Constitutionality of Marketable Title Legislation," 47 Ia. L. Rev. 413 (1962); Surlock, *Retroactive Legislation Affecting Interests in Land* (1953). Naturally the state could not legislate to cut off federal land rights, but they might do so for their own agencies and departments in an effort to promote more efficient and realistic conveyancing methods. Many states have moved in this general direction by allowing adverse possession to run against the state.

32. P. Basye, *Clearing Land Titles* 376 (2d ed., 1970).

33. In Indiana, for example, recorders maintain separate record books for recordation of preservation notices. Ind. Stat. Ann., § 56-1103 (1914).

34. L. Simes & C. Taylor, *The Improvement of Conveyancing by Legislation* 10-16 (1961).

35. Marshall v. Hollywood, Inc., Fla., 1970, 224 So.2d 743.

36. Ind. Stat. Ann. §§ 56-1101, 1108(a) (1974); *contra*, Wichelman v. Messner, 250 Minn. 88, 83 N.W.2d 800 (1957).

37. G. Lefcoe, *Land Development Law* 974 (1st ed., 1966).

38. Indeed, statistics tell us that the average family moves once every five years, and the average loan portfolio contains mortgage obligations zero to five years old. Kendall, *Anatomy of the Residential Mortgage* 14 (1964).

39. 32 Hen. VIII, c. 35 (statute barring the writ of entry after five years), misinterpreted in Morris' Leasee v. Vanderen, 1 Pa. Repts. 67 (1782) to require a sixty-year title search to preclude adverse judgments in ejectment.

40. If the same searcher does not perform the search, the whole piece of work will have to be performed anew, at increased levels of time, effort, and expense. If the abstract were already compiled, however, the task would be simpler: It would then be a matter of updating the previous compilation.

41. *In re* Kamp, 40 N.J. 588, 194 A.2d 236 (1963). The title insurance-rate structure commonly reflects this fact by providing that upon reissue of a policy to a new purchaser or beneficiary, lower insurance premiums are to be charged. *See also* Bertrand v. Jones, 58 N.J. 273, 156 A.2d 161 (1959), where plaintiff obtained a "starter certificate" from a title insurer.

42. Large title insurance corporations expand their market area by buying up abstracts, either from abstract companies or conveyancing attorneys and law firms. *See* United States v. Chicago Title and Trust Co., 242 F.Supp. 56 (N.D. Ill. 1965).

43. That is, if records are geographically comprehensive, there is a reasonable chance that orders for searches can be filled using abstracts already compiled.

44. A. Axelrod, C. Berger, & Q. Johnstone, *Land Transfer and Finance* 556-93 (1969).

45. Model Marketable Title Act § 2(d).

46. "A lawyer in private practice is economically an entrepreneur who operates a service enterprise. . . . More than one-third of all lawyers and just over half of the lawyers in private practice are individual practitioners. . . . This type of practice appears to be gradually declining in favor of partnerships, however. Most law partnerships consist of two or three members. . . ." Am. Bar. Fdn., "The Legal Profession in the United States" 11-12 (2d ed., 1970).

47. B. Burke & N. Kittrie, *The Real Estate Settlement Process and Its Costs* III-E-13, 26 (1972) (hereafter Burke and Kittrie).

48. American Land Title Ass'n, Revised Model Title Insurance Code 32 (§ 160) (1973).

49. In Seattle, Washington, $1.5-2.0 million was the cost of establishing a working title plant for King County, Washington. Burke & Kittrie, *supra* n. 47 at III-E-44. A similar effort for Cook County, Illinois, took $3.5-4.0 million in 1966-67. *Id.,* at III-C-12, n. 18.

50. A recent proposal to computerize the title records of Fairfax County, Virginia, for the Bar Association, set the cost of $.75 million in 1973.

51. Sometimes the public recording office locates a branch in the major title insurer; this occurred in Cook County, Illinois. Burke & Kittrie, *supra* n. 47, III-C-8.

52. The purchase of a title plant may be depreciated, even if not used after purchase. 4 Mertens Fed. Inc. Tax. § 23.115.

53. 117 Cong. Rec. S38182 (daily ed. Oct. 29, 1971) (Survey by the Office of Senator William Proxmire).

54. *Id.*

55. Business "tie-ins" form the links between many of these personnel. *See* E. Herman, *Conflict of Interest in the Savings and Loan Industry* 777 (1969), resulting in 12 C.F.R. § 544.5 (1974) amendments in 1970; *see also* Burke, "Conveyancing in the National Capital Region: Local Reforms with National Implications," 22 Am. U. L. Rev. 527, 528; L. Downie, *Mortgage on America* 3 (1974).

56. Commissioners on Uniform State Laws, Uniform Land Transaction Code, Working Draft, Feb., 1975, at 7-1, 8-1.

57. Curative laws should also encourage the efficient use of existing search practices. They should operate automatically (Wisconsin has an automatic type of statute that requires a thirty-year search to determine vendors' interests and a sixty-year search for covenants and easements; Wisc. Stat. Ann. § 330.15 (1958)), not on designated dates, and the date chosen for curing invalid documents should be far enough removed from the transfer so as not to encourage carelessness in drafting or recording. However, they should not be limited to particular interests in property but rather should concentrate on defects found frequently in the documents that create many interests. *See* Basye, "The Crisis in Conveyancing," 19 Mo. L. Rev. 214, 224-32 (1954). Some states—particularly Alabama, Massachusetts, Nebraska, and Wisconsin—have been active in this area. Alabama's proposed bill is contained in Payne, "The Alabama Law Institutes Land Title Acts Project: Part I," 24 Ala. L. Rev. 175, 180-202 (1971). Neb. Rev. Stat. 1943, §§ 76-288 to 76-290 (Reissue 1971). Ann. L. Mass. ch. 184 § 26-30 (1969). Wisc. Stat. Ann. § 330.15 (1958).

58. The origins of many curative acts are found in so-called special legislation enacted by state legislatures. For a description of the statutes of the approximately sixteen states (including Illinois, Vermont, Indiana, Ohio, and Connecticut) which now have marketable-title acts, *see* Basye, *supra* n. 32, §§ 172-90 (including the 1975 Pocket Part). Many state constitutions now proscribe such legislative endeavors. *See, e.g.,* Colo. Const. art. 2, § 11; Ga. Const. § 2-302; Idaho Const. art. 11, § 12; Mo. Const. art. 1, § 13; Mont. Const. art. 15, § 13; N.H. Const. Pt. 1, art. 23, Tenn. Const. art. 1, § 20; Tex. Const. art. 1, § 16. *Compare* with Ohio Const. art. II, § 28 (curative laws are specifically allowed). One early law tested in the United States Supreme Court considered the retrospective problem for a civil statute. Calder v. Bull, 3 U.S. 386 (1798) (Connecticut statute granting a rehearing after a will had been denied probate held valid since decree rendered on new trial, not the legislative act, took away the parties' rights). Conveyancers should determine what defects regularly appear on the land title records and constitute a local title problem. South Dakota attorneys made some determinations along this line when promulgating their uniform title standards as an appendix to the state's

marketable-title act. Normally state legislatures adopt this type of legislation to remedy frequently recurring irregularities. Sometimes such statutes validate transfers in which the parties' misunderstandings or misconceptions have left the formalities of conveyancing unfulfilled.

For a convenient classification of existing types of curative legislation, *see* Basye, *supra* n. 32, § § 231-364. *See also* L. Simes & C. Taylor, *Improvement of Conveyancing by Legislation* xvii (1960). They do not validate void deeds. R. Patton, *Titles* § 83 (2d ed., 1957).

59. Basye, *supra* n. 32 at 467. For a case so holding *see* Pardo v. Creamer, 228 Ark. 746, 310 S.W.2d 218 (1958) (a curative statute applying to defective acknowledgment will not supply an acknowledgment that is entirely missing). Legislation, to be curative in the best sense, should affirm the intention of parties to past land transfers and should specify the interests affected without imposing a blanket cut-off date on all interests searched. *Cf.* Pa. H.B. No. 751, § 3(a) (1973). Blanket legislation has rarely been used; Iowa, which was the first state to adopt a marketable-title act in 1919, uses this blanket cut-off date. However, the legislature has continually amended this date and the current cut-off date (as amended in 1970) is January 1, 1960. Iowa Code Ann. § 614.17 (1950) (Cum. Supp. 1977). There is precedent for blanket legislation: Maine has recently used it to handle the problem of cloudy titles to some of its off-shore islands by allowing a full decade for preserving old interests. Me. Rev. Stat. Ann. tit. 33, § § 1201-17 (1964) (Supp. Pamphlet 1975).

60. Basye, *supra* n. 32, at 468. For an early case espousing this principle, *see* Chestnut v. Shanes Lessee, 16 Ohio 599, 609-10 (1847).

61. *See, e.g.,* Ewell v. Diggs, 108 U.S. 143 (1883). "The right which the curative or repealing act takes away in such a case is the right in the party to avoid his contract, a naked legal right which it is usually unjust to insist upon and which no constitutional provision was ever designed to protect." *Id.,* at 151.

62. The constitutional aspects of curative legislation are discussed in Basye, *supra* n. 32, at 476-508. *See also* L. Simes & C. Taylor, *supra* n. 10, 253-94; and Hachman, "The Supreme Court and the Constitutionality of Retroactive Legislation," 73 Harv. L. Rev. 45 (1967).

63. Basye, *supra* n. 32 at 493.

64. L. Simes & C. Taylor, *The Improvement of Conveyancing by Legislation* (1961).

65. Neb. Code Ann., § 76-258 through 260 (1971).

66. *See, e.g.,* Eden Street Permanent Bldg. Ass'n No. 1 v. Lusby, 116 Md. 173, 81 A. 284 (1911).

67. Basye, *supra* n. 32, 502-05.

68. Watson v. Mercer, 33 U.S. 88 (1834) (Pennsylvania act curing defective acknowledgments not a violation of contracts clause because effect of act was to confirm original contracts, not impair them).

69. T. Plucknett, *Concise History of the Common Law* 578-587 (5th ed., 1956).

70. Stapylton v. Scott, 16 Vesey 272 (ch. 18-9).

71. Hutchins, "Equitable Ejectment," 26 Col. L. Rev. 436 (1926).

72. Comment, "Enhancing the Marketability of Land: The Suit to Quiet Title," 68 Yale L. J. 1245, 1265-67 (1959).

73. More specifically, modern conveyancing developed from a fusion of legal and equitable principles. A.J. Casner & B. Leach, *Property* 350-52 (2d ed., 1969). The right to enforce a conveyance in a court of equity where (1) no symbolic delivery of the land was made on the land itself, but (2) consideration was given for the transfer, developed only gradually from the sixteenth century onward. The symbolic transfer, a livery of seisin, was required at law, R. Patton, 1 *Land Titles* 3 (2d ed., 1957), but not in equity if the purchase price passed between purchaser and vendor. Thus the parties could transfer land without going on it by the so-called deed of bargain and sale, creating an equitable right in it in the purchaser. This equitable right came gradually to be the basis of the two-document system of contract and deed between which comes the executory period and during which the purchaser in our conveyancing system finances the purchase and assures himself of a good title. He does this while he has the equitable but not the legal title to the property. This means that he has the right to enforce his equity by an action for specific performance of the contract. Bell v. Andrews, 4 Pa. (4 Dall.) 152 (1796).

Both the bargain and sale and the action of specific performance were thus devices of a court of equity. The keystone of equity is discretion in the chancellor in equity to do substantial justice between the parties. What gave rise to this idea was a common-law maxim that a failure of substantial justice in a particular case is preferable to a breach of legal principle. Katz, "The Politics of Law in Colonial America: Controversies over Chancery Courts and Equity Law in the Eighteenth Century," in D. Fleming & B. Bailyn, *Law in American History* 257, 259 (1971). The requirement of consideration for a bargain and sale was, for example, dropped where intrafamily transfers were involved. R. Patton, 1 *Land Titles* 4-8 (2d ed., 1957). Where one member of a family conveyed property to another member and "covenanted to stand seized" of the grantee, equity would enforce the conveyance even though no consideration, other than "love and affection," changed hands.

Another example of equitable influences on conveyancing is the action of ejectment. Morris's Lessee v. Vanderen, 1 Pa. (1 Dall.) 67 (1782); C. Donohue, P. Kauper, & P. Martin, *Property* 293 (1974). When sought by an out-of-possession title holder, he first had to bring an equitable action for specific performance, and then once in possession by virtue of his success there, a legal action for ejectment of the wrongful possessor on the property. *Id.* A gradual fusion of these legal and equitable actions allowed an out-of-possession owner to bring the modern cause of action in ejectment.

A further example of this trend is the quiet-title action, the modern version of which is the combination of three equitable writs: the bill of peace, the writ *quia timet*, and the quiet-title action. Comment, "Enhancing the Marketability of Land: The Suit to Quiet Title," 68 Yale L. J. 1245, 1266 (1959).

74. Horton v. Kyburz, 53 Cal.2d 59, 346 P.2d 399 (1959); equities of redemption in mortgage law provide another example. Katz, *supra* n. 73 at 259.

75. Eggers v. Busch, 154 Ill, 604, 606, 39 N.E. 619, 620 (1895); Dwight v. Cutler, 3 Mich. 566, 64 Am. Dec. 105 (1855).

76. Annotation, "Marketable Title," 57 A.L.R. 1253-1554 (1928).

77. *Id.*

78. A. Axelrod, C. Berger, & Q. Johnstone, *Land Transfer and Finance* 594-95 (1970).

79. School Dist. No. 10 v. Peterson, 74 Minn. 122, 76 N.W. 1126 (1898).

80. 4 Am. L. Prop. 551-53 (Casner ed., 1952).

Establishing Tract Indexes

This chapter and the next will explore three issues: First, how title records might better be maintained to make them more accessible to users; second, if and when more types of records are included in the recorder's office, how the recording system might be adapted to handle this new comprehensiveness; and third, how the records themselves might protect the holders of realty titles. Title records are the keystone of our conveyancing patterns, and any changes proposed in how these records are kept should be carefully weighed for both practical and legal consequences. Since any change in record keeping is basic to the patterns in which it is set, the most fundamental issues—which in this country mean constitutional issues—must also be considered. For this reason increasing attention will be paid to these issues in the next two chapters.

Tract Indexes

The last step in the transactional process described in the foregoing chapters is the recording of the documents—generally a deed and a mortgage—with the recorder of deeds. This step is one of limited significance to the completion of the transaction between the parties, but it is of great significance for future transactions involving the same property, for it is from each recorded document that abstracts of title are compiled and used to show marketable title in subsequent transactions.

In none of the conveyancing patterns found in the United States does the recorder review the legal sufficiency of the conveyances presented for record. His function everywhere is a limited one: He accepts a document for record if it meets the formal requirements of the recording act. It must be in proper form, be attested and acknowledged, and be accompanied by payment of recording fees and taxes.[1]

This limited function leaves the legal review of the documents to private conveyancers of many types.[2] It also means that the recorder will not check to see if the recording is effective to give notice of the documents to later purchasers of the same property. In a jurisdiction with a grantor-grantee index, this means a recording within the chain of title; in a tract-index jurisdiction, indexing under the correct name or number. Checking for effective indexing is the duty of the purchaser.[3]

Effective indexing of documents is particularly crucial in states where indexing is by names of grantors and grantees. The index there serves as a source of information on the names of past owners. Examining the index for the name of either a past grantor or grantee will yield (because of cross-indexing) the names of the persons with whom he dealt. Thus looking under the name of the present record owner in the grantee index will yield the name of his grantor. Checking that name will give you his grantor, and so on back in time until every owner in the so-called chain of title is ascertained.

With a chain of title each owner's name can be checked in the grantor index for conveyances made by an owner between the dates he took the conveyance and the day the next owner recorded his interest.

If tracts, rather than names, were the basis of the index, the task of chaining the title would be simplified and perhaps eliminated. A name index is perhaps still well suited to a system of common-law estates in which different interests have different durational, temporal, and possessory dimensions, but tracts become more important than names where many parcels tend to be held in one way, as with single-family housing held by one individual alone or by husbands and wives jointly. Further, there is an element of fairness in confining the reach of an interest to a particular tract that balances the need to define interests in property by the names of their holders. About one third of all the recording jurisdictions in the United States use tract identifiers rather than names as the basis for indexing title records.[4]

Organizing Tract Indexes

Initial organizational problems involve the size of the recording district, the choice of an identifying parcel number, and the legal effect of the parcel identifier. The costs of conversion is an aspect of every one of these.

1. A problem inherent in conveyancing in large urban centers is the size of the recording district: In the District of Columbia, one district includes three quarters of a million people. Without reorganization, public title records are unusable by either the private or the public sector.[5] South Dakota has recording jurisdictions of just under 2,000 to 96,000 people. It has reorganized its public records, previously alphabetized by names of owners, into tract indexes.[6]

Name indexes per se are not the problem, but a multitude of names are when they must all be searched. One alternative to reorganizing public records by tract is to reduce the size of the recording district. An index established for the District of Columbia might define a tract as a city block or a neighborhood.[7] In any state law on the subject, geographic definition of the district should initially be left to local option. The object of the initial reorganization would not be to create a parcel index but merely to make the name index more efficient by reducing the search time necessary to gather names for a particular chain of title. A next step would be to eliminate chaining the title. If it were to be eliminated, all the documents recorded under the names of the parties could then be indexed on a parcel basis. This is a tract index and is widely used in those areas of the country that have noted the experience of the eastern states with alphabetical name indexes,[8] although it is not widely used in the East itself.[9] South Dakota recorders have maintained both name and tract records since the 1920s. As in South Dakota, assembling the documentary references by plat results in a tract index to recorded documents[10] and provides effective notice under existing recording laws while working within their framework.[11] If as a later step the records all were reorganized on a parcel basis, the public records would be a series of abstracts, and abstracting could be eliminated.

2. As a conveyancing tool, tract indexes are most effective when the individual land parcel is their basic unit. They are easier to automate than name indexes,[12] and when interests are to be registered, a registry is more easily established with parcel references.[13] The basic unit must be the land parcel as defined by ownership at the time the index is established, but the number assigned to it must be flexible enough to reflect later subdivision. Conversion of name to tract indexes is too costly to be anything but gradual. Tract indexes could be established with minimal capital investment by providing that the existing land records be converted as future conveyances were processed, until the tract system applied to all transfers. Prospective revamping of title records would not then duplicate work already performed by abstractors.[14] For a time grantor-grantee searches and tract-abstract searches would exist side by side. This transition, however, has certain dangers.[15]

The jurisdictions which have tract indexes, and therefore allow recorder abstracting, also maintain grantor-grantee indexes. The existence of this dual system has caused considerable difficulty in the past. Searchers have often been required to search both indexes in order to be fully protected. Thus, in the case of *Boyer v. Pahvant Mercantile & Investment Co.*, the Utah Supreme Court ruled that the buyer had constructive notice of a prior trust deed where due to the recorders' negligence, there was no notation in the said transaction of the official tract index. The court reasoned that since the transaction was properly recorded in the grantor-grantee index, it provided sufficient notice to the grantee. In so doing the Utah court completely negated the usefulness of the tract index as an abstracting tool.

A better view has been expressed in other cases which have given the tract index broader effect. In a recent case the North Dakota Court reasoned: "in our state today the tract index is the only practical index through which instruments on record can be located. It would be a prohibitive burden to locate instruments on record without a tract index. It would certainly be a travesty of justice to hold that perspective purchasers are bound by the record, if for all practical purposes the record cannot be located. The practice today . . . is to use the tract index rather than the old means of grantor-grantee indexes. Although the register of deeds still has to keep all the indexes, the grantor-grantee indexes are actually a carry over from the old system and only an additional tool available to title searchers for other purposes. (Footnotes omitted.)[16]

3. Another transitional problem involves the choice and legal effect of a parcel identifier. One commentator has written about this problem:

Where it is not done, as in the older seaboard states, parcel maps exist, usually in the tax assessors' office. While these maps may not be accurate enough in scale to settle boundary disputes, they are accurate enough to serve as a parcel or tract index. By working with the tax assessor and the recorders it should not be too difficult to obtain a reference to the recorder document containing the most recently used description. A reference to that document may then be re-entered into the tract index next to the parcel identifier.[17]

The assessor's numbers will often be the most useful and accessible parcel identifier.[18]

To be effective for conveyancing purposes, however, the parcel identifier would have to refer to a publicly filed document[19] or deed containing a discrete description of the parcel.[20] This description would include a survey which "closes," that is, encompasses, the parcel it attempts to describe.[21] A valid survey, important to the completeness of the contract of sale and deed for legal purposes, does not prove title to a parcel.[22] While surveys and title are traditionally separate, they should remain so with the establishment of a tract index. Except in special cases (which might include urbanizing lands subdivided by a developer), no such index should purport to establish definitive boundaries or incorporate a legal description by reference except as an optional supplement to the index. If legal descriptions are made a part of the index, a platted or subdivided-lands act will become a precondition to the establishment of a tract index, and conversion costs will rise. The description must also be "coordinated" with a recognizable point of reference,[23] perhaps a public monument; since there exist several systems for establishing coordinates,[24] the choice should be left to state law. Both the problems of closing and coordinating the description suggest that in establishing the tract index, the legal effectiveness of the tract description remain severable from the question of its establishment. Establishing a system of surveys each of which close and are coordinated one to another is really a problem of surveyor competence. Proof of boundaries will involve study of field notes and should not be governed by recording rules in any event.[25]

Finally, the cost feasibility of tract indexes established by gradual conversion of existing records has been debated; one commentator has written:

Where it is used, the tract index does not replace name indices, it is a supplement. Expenses, therefore, may be expected to be higher in those [recorders' offices] supplying this extra service. In fact, jurisdictions without tract indexes, on the average nationally, had expenses $3,379 lower than other offices. Much, if perhaps not all, of the saving of tract indexing goes to the user in the form of speed and accuracy in assessing information. Although complete and exclusive tract indexing might reduce public costs, under its present status it cannot. Thus, a tract index may be more properly regarded as an increase in public service and not as a factor in reducing public costs.[26]

Legislation implementing tract indexes could reduce public costs to the minimum by not converting existing records into tract or parcel abstracts. This way, no past records or indexes need be changed. For the future, recorded documents would simply be indexed by tract. Little extra capital equipment aside from new books would be necessary, and the recorder should have discretionary power to arrange the tract abstracts by either assessment number or plat reference or city block, although the first would make coordination between the assessors' and recorders' offices easier.[27] Maintaining such new records in secure loose-leaf volumes would permit subdivision and consolidation of tracts to be reflected without breaking the sequence of numbers originally adopted since new pages could be inserted for new lots as numbers were assigned. However, would there be an increased liability on the part of the recorder of deeds for misindexing?[28] It might be better, at the outset, to leave existing law for misindexing and misfilings intact; that would decrease opposition to the tract index and allow for its gradual acceptance. Initially only the method of indexing, not the record keeping itself, should be changed.[29]

The transition to the new tract index might be made easier by providing a self-indexing device in the records themselves.[30] This device would require that documents first presented for tract recordation contain a precis of the grantor-grantee chain of title on which they depend. The accuracy of the tract index could be easily checked in the future if this device were instituted prior to the tract index as a link between the old alphabetical (should it be continued) and the new tract index. Overall, the notice-giving aspects of recording are unaffected by this addition,[31] yet a tract index with a self-indexing device would increase the notice-giving aspects of recording when the chain of title involves records other than deeds (e.g., probate, tax, or bankruptcy records).[32]

Future legislation may eliminate reliance on grantor-grantee searches if the institution of tract indexes makes them a duplicative and expensive device. In 1975, 50 out of 67 South Dakota counties spent from $750 to $900 to maintain a tract system for recording an average of 30 or 35 land-related documents over two weeks (the median numbers are 23 and 22). As a recent North Dakota case[33] indicates, there is no need for the continued maintenance of grantor-grantee indexes once the tract index is workable and accepted by the conveyancing bar.

When accepted and fully utilized by the bar, a tract index can be used to record many other forms of property-related records now filed in special indexes: Mechanics' liens and *lis pendens* notices are examples. Legislation can achieve this greater comprehensiveness for land records by more broadly defining what is a "recordable" document or interest in property. However, even without increasing the number of recordable interests, a tract index will extend the notice that any recorded instrument will provide if it frees the records of chain-of-title rules. Real property freed of these rules may not thereafter be as freely marketable. A title searcher using it would be referred to many documents, in the order in which they were presented for record, regardless of whether or not together they constituted a chain of title. He would have to look at each to see its relationship to all the others and in the process might be presented with documents that were recorded without the normal chain of title that he would be attempting to establish in a name-index jurisdiction. If the legal effect of examining such a document is unclear, the question for the courts becomes whether or not examining that document provides legal notice of it, and perhaps of any document referenced therein. If the answer is that notice is provided, then conversion of a name index to a tract index may decrease the marketability of some titles while making all titles easier to search by eliminating the need to chain the title.

Some constitutional questions attend the establishment of a tract index. To a lesser degree, the same problems are also present with any review by the recorder of the documents presented for record. We have said that the recorder's authority to review instruments presented for recordation is everywhere limited. Where A presents a deed for record and the recorder refuses to record it because of (say) its lack of proper acknowledgment, and before A is able to cure the defect, B records a deed to the same property, the recorder's review has defeated the priority of A's claim to the property.[34] With a tract index the recorder would review each document for the sufficiency of the legal description vis-à-vis his ability to use it to index the document. If in the latter situation, A's legal description was insufficient and B again obtained the superior claim, A might sue the recorder for violating his due-process rights. If A had sued the recorder for turning away a deed for lack of an acknowledgment, the recorder would defend the suit by claiming that his duty was ministerial and so involved no discretion. If the recorder's refusal to record was based on an insufficient legal description, then the recorder may, de facto, also be judging the legal validity of the conveyance, which would be harder to defend as a purely ministerial act.

A solution to this problem would permit the recording of defective documents but give them a limited life on the record, allowing them to lapse if not cured within that time. This solution contains two distinct elements, each one of which might serve as the basis for more general changes in the recording laws to make the establishment of tract indexes easier.

First, states might enact statutes expunging from the index some less-than-fee or nonpossessory interests in land after they reach a certain age without having been rerecorded and refiled through a preservation notice;[35] such interests would have to be rerecorded at regular intervals. This would put a positive time limit on title searches, which would not depend on the abstractor's finding a root of title, but on an instrument's remaining on the record, unencumbered or unchallenged, for the statutory period. Because of the need to recognize and challenge unsubstantiated claims, name indexes should be replaced with tract indexes before this change is made, for easy checking of records for expungeable claims will then be possible.[36] Once found, they should be expunged or validated in shortened judicial proceedings to clear title.[37] If expunged as a result of such proceedings, slander of title action may be available to the fee holder as well.[38] Extinguishing ancient, unnoted, or unrefiled interests recognizes the principle inherent in marketable-title and curative laws: that laws retroactively invalidating once-recorded interests are not objectionable constitutionally or as a matter of policy. A short statute of limitations then confirms this removal.

The legislative need today is to recognize that title records are vital to the title itself. Records are, after all, the precondition to proof of title. Making them part of the title, not just evidence of a title,[39] is a major step toward fully effective tract indexing. Legislatures can do this in two ways, summarized as follows, by

1. making indexing a part of the record;[40]
2. making indexing and recording necessary for a legally sufficient conveyance between the parties and as to third parties.[41]

A second proposal worth consideration is to freely allow recordation of any encumbrance or less-than-fee interest but also to require that judicial action, to prove its validity, be taken to confirm it within a short time of its recordation or perhaps at the time of a challenge to it. If no such action is taken, then the recordation lapses, and any interest based on the same set of facts may not be rerecorded. This is not intended to supplant existing statutes of limitation (which would continue to clear titles in their fashion) but would provide a record title while encouraging use of the public records. This proposal should have one exception. Providing for a limited life on the record for a less-than-fee interest should not apply when that interest is noted on the recorded deed to the fee-simple title. Excepting less-than-fee interests noted or specifically referenced on a deed's face permits a market in valuable rights to preserve them and moves common-law conveyancing toward requiring less-than-fee interests to be noted on the fee-simple deed.

Both these proposals raise constitutional questions. Whether recorded titles are encumbered, recorded interests lapse or are expunged, or interests are recorded by ex parte procedures, the persons deprived of any property as a result should not also be deprived of the due process of law. Questions of due process in the indexing system must now be addressed in their turn.

The Need for Due Process in Comprehensive Tract Indexes

In the context of the proposals for tract indexes outlined in the previous section, the right of due process[42] arises in two ways: First, if the notice giving effect of an index is reduced by lapsing or expunging some recorded interests from the index, the holders of these encumbrances will allege a retroactive violation of their due-process rights. Second, the broader notice achieved by the new index may render titles less marketable, and so the fee owner will have been deprived of the right to sell, mortgage, lease, or leverage the property by its consequent unmarketability.[43] The right of due process in these two contexts is discussed in this section, although the first will be touched on only briefly since it has been developed in the discussion of the constitutional validity of marketable-title and curative legislation in the opening sections of Chapter 3. It is presented again, however, because its presence makes the important point that arguments over due process accorded by property-related records arise and must be addressed in more than one context.

Conveyancers have not undertaken these analytical tasks as yet because the emphasis in the recent past has been on clearing land titles through legislation.[44] While this legislative effort has illuminated the intractability of improving conveyancing, it has not aimed at changing our present patterns of conveyancing but rather at making them work more smoothly. Further, it has been predicated on a general-welfare-clause approach that is circumstantial in its analysis and produces no more than ad hoc rules. What is needed is principled analysis and a guiding rationale for future redesign of property records.

Due Process: Removing Interests from the Record Title. When recordable interests have existed on record for a time and are to be expunged from the index or the public abstract, the administrator determines whether or not a preservation notice has been filed. If not, his expunging of the old interest rests on a legislative presumption of either the satisfaction and release of the claim or its staleness due to unenforceability because the statute of limitations has tolled or because its holder failed to pursue it because of some defense to it. The constitutionality of retroactive expunging of a record has largely been established by judicial validation of marketable-title acts and curative acts that cut off recorded intervening third-party rights.[45]

Due Process: Encumbering a Record Title. Property-related records that might be kept in tract indexes can be classified into two types, ex parte and recordable documents. Recordable documents are those now fileable with the recorder and purporting to transfer an interest in real property between the executing parties. Keeping them in public hands for conveyancing purposes does not give them any official status (and so may not constitute state action). Ex parte documents represent an unproven and unacknowledged claim on real property and are now filed for record in some archive other than that of recordable documents, without an opportunity for the owner of the property to contest its filing. However, notice is often sent to the party against whose property the claim is made.

If future tract indexes are to include ex parte records, there must be a procedure established to adjudicate the validity of a claim soon after it is filed for record. This might be done by requiring the filer to bring a lawsuit or to substantiate his claim in a hearing before the administrator of the records. The determination made by the administrator would decide whether the claim would remain of record until released. It probably should be appealable to the courts.

The establishment of these procedures would make an ex parte filing the equivalent of a *lis pendens*. To such a filing, a presumption of constitutional validity might attach if notice to the owner is followed within a reasonable time by a hearing to decide the validity of the claim. If validated, the claim would thereafter be treated as if it were a recordable interest.

In past attempts at conveyancing reform (e.g., marketable-title and curative acts), courts can only hesitantly confirm the legislatures' reforms in the name of the general welfare because they are never certain which litigant's welfare represents the general welfare. However, courts and attorneys are more likely to feel comfortable with a due-process analysis. This analysis proceeds by asking three questions: First, is the state involved in the deprivation of due process to any significant degree (is "state action" present); second, is a due-process right involved; and third, what procedures are necessary to satisfy the right where it is applicable?

State Action: Examining Several Types of Records. The Fourteenth Amendment states: "Nor shall any state deprive any person of . . . property, without due process of law." It establishes a limitation on the states and is, in other words, used only to strike down or require "state action." It does not control private action, however discriminatory or wrongful, but reaches significant exertions of state power. Hence whether the amendment applies in a particular situation depends on whether sufficient state action is involved.

In the usual situation, the involvement of the state in the challenged activity is direct. State action is present when statutes are used as a basis for procedures transferring property between parties. Examples are bankruptcy transfers or a mortgagee foreclosing on a property by judicial means and thereby securing possession.

In the leading case of Shelly v. Kraemer,[46] "state action" was present when the state had

made available to . . . individuals the full coercive power of government to deny to petitioners . . . the enjoyment of property rights.[47]

Involved in *Shelley* was judicial enforcement of a racially restrictive covenant where

the difference between judicial enforcement and non-enforcement of the restrictive covenants is the difference to petitioners between being denied rights of property . . . and being accorded full enjoyment of those rights. . . .[48]

Matters of title are often equally crucial to the use and occupation of property, and so this holding might encompass decisions on marketability made by attorneys and rejected or confirmed by state courts in the name of "state action." However, a more recent opinion of the United States Supreme Court rejected this analogy as controlling.[49] The Court said that attorneys, although perhaps "providing arguably essential goods and services, 'affected with the public interest,' " do not have a sufficiently public function to convert "their every action, absent more, into that of the State."[50] These latter comments come from an opinion involving a suit against a publicly regulated utility company that terminated service to a petitioner without a hearing on the matter.

Where a private party acts without the direct authorization of the state, there still may be an indirect delegation of state power to him. This is a second theory of state action in which the state delegation of authority encourages private action without sanctioning it. For state action to be present under this second theory, a more complex test is used. In the words of the Supreme Court opinion on the telephone utility's termination of service, there must be a "public function," "one traditionally associated with sovereignty" and "delegated to a private party"; there must also be an inquiry into "whether there is a sufficiently close nexus between the State and the challenged action of the regulated entity so that the action of the latter may be fairly treated as that of the State itself."[51] This is an inclusive test, integrating several past cases into one broad requirement.[52] With this multifaceted test, the Court invited close analysis of the acts alleged to be "state action." It invites a balancing of the public and private aspects of conveyancing documents, memorializing private acts but made into public records to safeguard future transactions.

With the keeping of public title records, the primary consideration in determining whether state record keeping relating to titles constitutes state action involves examining the types of records and their uses. Records kept under authority of the recording acts are the lynch-pin of our conveyancing system. The question is whether their contractually private aspects or the state's encouragement of private parties to file such records will be emphasized. These records have two principal uses, one in litigation over conflicting claims to property and a second made by title abstractors in establishing marketable title. In resolving conflicting claims over the same property sold by one grantor to two separate purchasers, the recording acts perform a unique governmental function of controlling land titles, which American jurisdictions have traditionally "associated with sovereignty" at the state level. The acts were early used to restrict in-migration and to protect settlers from dispossession.[53] Indeed, the problem of the same land being sold twice through inadvertence or fraud was a pervasive problem in American history.[54] For various reasons the subsequent purchaser was preferred unless he in some sense knew or should have known of the prior sale; perhaps the subsequent purchaser was preferred because he seemed more innocent than prior purchasers; or because he was more likely to be in possession (as in western South Dakota, prior parties had the habit of moving on without formally relinquishing their claim).[55]

Their second principal use arises when an attorney or conveyancer tries to anticipate decisions under the recording acts; he is arguably anticipating a decision based on the legislature's attempt to codify an equitable rule. Most state legislatures, modifying the race-type recording acts to establish notice or race-notice acts, conceived of their actions as equitable in nature.[56]

The equitable basis for the recording statutes of most states is important, for it has been suggested that enforcement of the common law by courts is not state action,[57] and this rule is a tenable obstacle to a finding of state action when a court enforces a race-type recording act; it, after all, only modifies a common-law race to close a transaction first into a race to file first at the recorder of deeds' office.[58] But judicial enforcement of the other major types of recording acts—notice or race-notice acts—alters the common-law conveyancing rules of first-in-time/first-in-right still further.[59] A notice recording statute restricts the class of protected subsequent purchasers to those who purchase subsequently but are also without notice of prior purchasers. A race-notice statute defines the protected class more narrowly still to those subsequent purchasers who are without notice but who also record first. Under each of the three types of recording acts, however, the state has encouraged recording: In the notice state, the subsequent purchaser is protected without recording, but only so long as there is no purchaser taking subsequent in time to himself; in a race-notice state, the subsequent purchaser must be first to record; and in a race state, any purchaser to be protected must record first. The incentive to record is successively greater in each of these jurisdictions. In each the state encourages all purchasers to put at least their conveyancing documents on the public records and encourages all purchasers to accept what information can be gathered from the public records as evidence of the marketability of a title. Suits for specific performance brought by a vendor presenting a marketable abstract provide evidence of the state's encouraging use of the public records; the use of abstracts in conveyancing for governmentally underwritten purchases is further evidence. A persuasive argument can be made that state legislatures have through the recording acts encouraged parties to a conveyance to rely on statutes altering common-law conveyancing rules. The legal effects of the recording acts are thus crucial to every title search, and the acts themselves are, when made use of by conveyancers, sufficient state action to satisfy the Fourteenth Amendment where recordable (contractual or conveyancing) documents are concerned.

This does not mean that every provider of conveyancing services can assert this claim of state action. For an abstractor's purposes, the contractual nature of conveyancing documents makes them a product of private, not state, action so far as his use of them is concerned.[60] To be affected by state action, there must be a reliance on the notice-giving effect of recording, and only the purchaser is encouraged to rely on the recording. The abstractor must limit his liability for nonrecorded or fraudulently recorded documents by appropriate wording in his certification of the title.

The recorder's acceptance of ex parte records is even more easily categorized as state action. For example, mechanics' lien statutes alter the common-law rule of priority-in-time by allowing certain materials suppliers and other craftsmen who add value to property through improvements to it to file a lien on it which "relates back" or attaches as of the time they first commenced work on the property.[61] In this country these liens depend entirely on state statute.[62]

Yet another type of title-related record involves the power of the judiciary to preserve property that may be needed to satisfy the judgment of a court in pending litigation over particular property. These are *lis pendens* statutes, the filing of which informs subsequent purchasers of the property that litigation is pending, the outcome of which may affect the title.[63] Whether or not the litigation involves a common-law or statutorily created cause of action, a *lis pendens* preserves the power of the court over the property.[64] However, this is arguably the purpose of any type of land title record: The purpose of an abstract is to compile all such interests for resolution under state law and possible adjudication of all claims revealed in the abstract in a court of competent jurisdiction. Any abstract is thus connected to the judicial power of the state, surely a function "associated with sovereignty"; and where it contains summaries of ex parte documents, it becomes even more clearly the product of state action.

Due-process Rights. Once the involvement of the state is found sufficient to justify a finding of state action for various records, the analysis shifts to an examination of the interests protected and the quality of treatment offered the individual owner in the statute under scrutiny.[65] The task here is defining the individual's right to the "due process of law." That term is, of course, not amenable to precise definition.[66] "There is no table of weights and measures for ascertaining what constitutes due process."[67]

Even where a statute is based on the common law, "parties whose rights are affected are entitled to be heard; and in order that they may enjoy that right they must be notified." Further, notice and a hearing must be "granted at a meaningful time and in a meaningful manner."[68]

When the recorder accepts an ex parte interest such as a mechanic's lien for filing, he or the recording party must give notice to all interested parties who "in due course of business come to the knowledge of" either.[69] Whether this means that the recorder or the filer must notify competing claimants, the owner of the property encumbered will be ascertained in the course of filing the encumbrance in a tract index. As to the method of notice, "within the limits of practicability notice must be such as is reasonably calculated to reach interested parties";[70] the mails today are recognized as an efficient and inexpensive means of communication[71] to reach those beyond the jurisdiction of the recorder's personal service. For interested parties within the jurisdiction, personal service may be necessary but is not mandatory.[72] The need of the state in adjudicating the interest can be weighed against the practicality of giving personal service.

A mechanic's lien is an example of an ex parte document. Those claiming a mechanic's lien can file one on their own motion without the permission of the owner of the property on which the lien is asserted.[73] Here a state office lends its facilities to the publication of the lien[74] (hence a finding of "state action"). The effect of recording such a claim in rendering a title unmarketable is very likely in the case of a mechanic's lien, as greater provision for effective notice is made; normally today the lien can be filed only in a special index,[75] with information sufficient to identify the owner and property filed against it,[76] but without filing a bond to indemnify the owner or proving the claim under an employment or service contract at the same time. The lien lasts for a six-month to one-year period unless extended by enforcement action or lifted by court order in proceedings brought by the owner to contest the lien.[77] The chance to mortgage or sell the property will likely be lost until and unless the lien is removed from the records.[78]

A violation of a due-process right will most probably occur in situations where the value of the property is very high. Commercial and industrial properties will likely present the best situation for an argument that due process has been violated. The failure of such an owner to realize a sale, a profitable leveraging, or development of his property because of the presence of a recorded claim asserted on his title means that the intervention of the state's publicized records has prevented the owner's expected gain from reaching fruition.[79]

Thus a denial of a due-process right appears clearest in a jurisdiction using tract indexes for ex parte documents and allowing the encumbrance to remain of record for a period of time during which its removal has commercial value to the property owner.

It will be argued, however, that this "value" is an expectancy, not a present property right. Temporary deprivations of expectations are real nonetheless. Admittedly, the combination of statutory provisions required for this argument suggests that the finding of a due-process violation is a circumstantial matter, involving the weighing and sifting of particular facts.[80] However, in *Fuentes* v. *Shevin*,[81] the U.S. Supreme Court "attempted to erect what amounted to a presumption that notice and some form of hearing would be required prior to any state action which impinged"[82] on an individual's contractual property rights. In this case, two state statutes in Florida and Pennsylvania permitted

a private party, without a hearing or prior notice to the other party to obtain a pre-judgment writ of replevin through a summary process of *ex parte* application to a court clerk, upon the posting of a bond for double the value of the property to be seized. . . . [T] he sheriff is then required to execute the writ by seizing the property.[83]

Involved under both state statutes were a home appliance and household furniture purchased under installment sales contracts allegedly in default when the replevin process was commenced. The fact that the installment contracts did not vest "undisputed ownership" in the petitioning purchasers was not controlling.[84] (Similarly, the fact that an abstract, by analogy, presents only evidence of title, not an undisputed title itself, would not control.) "The due process clause has been read broadly to extend protection to 'any significant property interest,' " one less than a fee-simple title,[85] perhaps equitable in nature.

Moreover, it is the deprivation of the use of property, rather than the deprivation of an interest (no matter how classified) which gives the *Fuentes* holding its real impact. The removal of record encumbrances on the fee by the passage of a statutory period (as with mechanics' liens) or a limitations period, through adverse possession or marketable-title legislation, is thus no proper remedy if, even though eventual removal is certain, the potential for use of the property is unconstitutionally diminished in the interim. The rationale of *Fuentes* is based in turn on the case of *Sniadach* v. *Household Finance Corporation*[86] which held that a Wisconsin prejudgment wage-garnishment statute was unconstitutional. There the statute provided for notice given after the *in rem* seizure of a debtor's wages, which seizure was commenced by a creditor's attorney filing a request for garnishment with a court clerk. Filing the request froze the wages of the garnishee until a hearing was held, but the deprivation of the debtor, his being unable to use the money in the interim, was found to be an unconstitutional deprivation of property. Wages are as essential to the wage earner as property is to the realty developer. Wages are earned and property is purchased, with an eye toward their use. *Sniadach*'s holding only emphasizes the rationale of use-deprivation in *Fuentes*.

The effect of the *Sniadach* garnishment procedure bears a strong resemblance to the effect of filing ex parte interests on the public records. In each case the use of an asset is denied for a period pending a review of the merits of the creditor's case. Where recorded property interests are filed against a title, no review is even contemplated at the time of filing: That often occurs only when the property next changes hands. So the public recorder's acts present an even more grievous case of due-process violation than does the garnishment process found unconstitutional in *Sniadach*. The theory of use-deprivation, rather than title deprivation, insures judicial inquiry into the effect of the record and makes that inquiry more important than any study of the purpose of the laws. The purpose of the recording acts, to give notice to interested parties rather than to effect a change in title, is irrelevant to the discussion of due process at this stage.

Later cases have shown that in the field of commercial transactions, the presumptive minimum requirements of due process are hard to find. In *Mitchell* v. *W.T. Grant Co.,*[87] a prejudgment sequestration permitted the installment debtor's goods to be seized on judicial order without prior notice or hearing after the posting of a bond. The Court pointed out that a judge here issued the order on the basis of a complaint specific in its factual allegations, and a full hearing was provided promptly after seizure.

Most recently prejudgment garnishment freezing a commercial bank account with neither notice nor hearing was declared unconstitutional by the Court, 6-3, in *North Georgia Finishing, Inc., v. Di-Chem, Inc.*[88] There were two prerequisites for obtaining garnishment of the account: (1) an affidavit executed before the court clerk stating the amount owed and some reason to apprehend its loss if the writ was not issued; and (2) filing a bond for twice the amount owed to protect the debtor who could dissolve the garnishment by filing his own bond in turn.[89] No judge was involved in the process, the writ was issued on the allegation of a creditor's apprehensiveness, and no opportunity for a prompt hearing was made. Prejudgment due process was lacking as a result.

North Georgia is the latest evidence of the durability of this line of cases. It protects the temporary deprivation of a valuable property right and applies to title records that maintain ex parte filings. Mechanics' liens are only one example of interests that should be included in a redesigned tract index, but that will require validation procedures before the document presented for record can be found recordable.

Due-process Procedures. A worthwhile tract index would make many types of public records, both recordable and ex parte records, accessible at one location. The more comprehensive the index is, however, the greater the need for the recorder's or other administrative control over its use by filers. When ex parte interests are made recordable, procedures to confirm the validity of the interest must be undertaken by the controller of the records. If, on the other hand, ex parte interests are not included in the index, its usefulness to conveyancers and its comprehensiveness will be diminished accordingly, perhaps to the point where a change from existing practices would not be worth the cost.[90] As a matter of policy, increasing administrative control over the records and providing some public evaluation of interests presented for recording may be desirable, but recording ex parte documents makes it constitutionally necessary. To prevent ancient, stale interests from clogging a title, each such recording should be followed quickly by the validation of its interest and should operate initially like a *lis pendens* notice of that validation proceeding.

Lis pendens filings under the *Fuentes* case would be presumptively constitutional because they are by definition related to the granting of a final judgment in pending litigation. Most statutes today provide that the notice of *lis pendens* shall set forth the style, number, and objective of the litigation, the title of the court in which it is pending, the names of the persons whose interests are sought to be determined, and a description of the property involved. The failure to file the notice as prescribed by statute will preclude the statute from affecting the interests of *pendent lite* purchasers who in good faith and without actual or constructive notice of the action purchased the property during the litigation but before judgment was rendered.[91] When the doctrine of *lis pendens* is properly invoked, it gives constructive notice of all facts apparent from the face of the pleadings and exhibits, as well as any information that would be uncovered by a person of reasonable and ordinary prudence as he is put on inquiry notice as well. Conversely, the filing of a *lis pendens* does not give notice as to property not embraced in the pleadings and will not extend beyond the prayer for relief. Once the doctrine of *lis pendens* is operative, it remains in effect until a final judgment is rendered.[92] Generally, statutes place a time limit on the operational period of the statute and provide for extensions of it.

The public evaluation of interests presented for record might be accomplished in one of two ways: First, a system of private conveyancers might be used as masters, or alternatively, the validity of the interests might be determined by public officials.[93] Depending on the competence of their decisions, future claimants would either continue to file their documents and have them reviewed in prevalidation procedures, or else attempt to record without the procedures by using recordable conveyancing instruments.

The procedure for placing a document within a comprehensive set of property-related records would in either event provide a publicly supervised evaluation, perhaps administrative in the initial stages but with a judicial appeal possible for aggrieved parties. If recordation is freely permitted, this evaluation of conveyancing or ex parte interests should take place within a short time of the filing date. If a judicial action is necessary, the claimant should be required to bring his action within the same period. Thus the same proposals that allow the establishment of tract indexes responsive to their problems of increased record notice also satisfy the due-process requirements of *Fuentes* and allow initial access to the record for many types of claimants.

The procedures for evaluating interests before validating them on the record or removing them from it need not be uniform in each state. A claimant might be required in some jurisdictions to post a bond if the evaluation of his claim is presumptively invalid or protracted because of his own delays. Similarly, the owner might be required to post a bond or establish an escrow account when the claim is presumptively valid and the evaluation is incomplete while a transaction involving the property is pending.

This increased supervision over property-related records brings the American system of conveyancing a long way toward a registry system. The mechanism for doing so is the need for more comprehensive records, coupled with the constitutional requirements of the due-process clause. But with the mechanism for inducing change clear, there is much more to be said about the policies that should underlie any conversion to a title registry. These policies are the subject of the next chapter.

Notes

1. O. Browder, R. Cunningham, & J. Julin, *Property* 868-74 (2d ed., 1973).

2. G. Lefcoe, *Land Development Law* 872-77 (1966).

3. Cross, "The Record 'Chain of Title' Hypocrisy," 57 Col. L. Rev. 787, 789 (1957).

4. United States Departments of Agriculture and Commerce, State & Local Govt. Spec. Studies, No. 67, "Land Title Recording in the United States" 10 (1974). The jurisdictions using tract indexes are not in the most populous areas of the country. *Id.*

5. *See generally* Payne, "The Crisis in Conveyancing," 19 Mo. L. Rev. 214 (1954).

6. S.D. Comp. L. § 7-9-8 (numerical indexes); *Id.*, § 7-9-9 (alphabetical indexes) (1967). Fullerton Lumber Co. v. Tinker, 22 S.D. 427, 118 N.W. 700 (1908) (purchaser charged with notice from both sets of records).

7. In some areas the District has a "lot-and-block" system. D.C. Code, § 45-701b (1973).

8. *See, e.g.,* Hawaii Rev. Stat. tit. 28, § 502-17 (1968); Iowa Code Ann. § 558.49 (1950); S.D. Comp. L. §§ 43-22-12, 28-1 (1969); Utah Code Ann. § 17-12-6(b) (1972).

9. For a list of state statutes providing for tract-indexing systems, *see* Lore, "A Facelifting for the Recorder of Deeds: Tendering a Calumet to Real Estate Reformers," 22 Am. U. L. Rev. 639, 655 (1973). The states listed are Colorado, Idaho, Illinois, Maine, Minnesota, Montana, New Mexico, North Dakota, Utah, Washington, Wisconsin, and Wyoming. However, these jurisdictions also maintain grantor-grantee indexes. *Id.*, n. 76 at 655. *See also* S.D. Comp. L. § 7-9-8 (1967).

10. The following chart is a survey of South Dakota county recorders (fifty responding out of a possible sixty-seven).

	Averages	Medians
Filings Jan. 6-10, 1975	29.76	23
Filings June 9-13, 1975	34.90	22
Recorder estimate of average	34.28	23
Number of books per year	3.5	3
Cost per book	$ 235.53	$ 250.00
Current salaries (FY 76)	$ 16,191.83	$ 13,430.00
Current supplies	$ 3,412.45	$ 2,080.00
Total (does not add)	$ 20,347.45	$ 15,700.00
Past salaries (FY 75)	$ 13,153.39	$ 11,969.00
Past supplies	$ 2,858.97	$ 1,650.06
Total (does not add)	$ 16,327.73	$ 13,230.

	Averages	Medians
Upcoming salaries (FY 77)	$ 18,065.56	$ 14,775.00
Upcoming supplies	$ 3,964.58	$ 2,750.00
Total (does not add)	$ 22,141.34	$ 18,000.00
Number of personnel	2.12	2.0

11. "If we continue to regard the recording of a deed merely as sending it to the recorder for him to keep or transcribe on his records, we miss the whole point as to our public registry system," Basye, "Need: A Modern System of Land Title Records," in R. Cook & J.L. Kennedy, Jr., eds., *Proceedings of the Tri-State Conference on a Comprehensive, Unified Land Data System* 12 (1968).

12. *Id.;* Dunham, "A Modern System for Land Title Records with a Parcel Index as a Foundation for Land-use Data," in *Proceed. of the N. Am. Conf. on Modernization of Land Data Systems,* Wash., D.C., Apr. 14-17, 1975, at 401-10.

13. In the United States, the question is often asked whether the recording system and our system of present, future, and concurrent interests in property are not obstacles to the implementation of the registration system. R. Powell, *The Registration of Title to Land in the State of New York* 34 (1938). The answer is yes if the recording system is (or remains) an ineffective notice-giving device.

14. There is a proprietary aspect to an abstract as an attorney's "work product." Hickman v. Taylor, 329 U.S. 495 (1947).

15. A brief discussion of legal and procedural problems related to a tract-indexing system is found in P. Basye, *Clearing Land Titles* 263 (2d ed., 1970).

16. Lore, "A Facelifting for the Recorder of Deeds: Tendering a Calumet to Real Estate Reformers," 22 Am. U. L. Rev. 639 (1973).

17. Leary & Blake, "Twentieth Century Real Estate Business and Eighteenth Century Recording," 22 Am. U. L. Rev. 275, 298 (1973).

18. For a discussion of various types of parcel identifiers, *see* Basye, "A Uniform Land Parcel Identifier—Its Potential for All Our Land Records," 22 Am. U. L. Rev. 251, 254 (1973).

19. Trawalter v. Schaefer, 142 Tex. 521, 179 S.W.2d 765 (1944); D. Hagman, *Urban Planning* 245-46 (1971).

20. Boyd & Uelman, "Resurveys and Metes and Bounds Descriptions," 1953 Wisc. L. Rev. 657 (1953).

21. Davis v. Mason, 21 Mass. (4 Peck.) 156 (1826).

22. Wagner v. Thompson, 163 Kan. 662, 186 P.2d 278 (1947); Grell v. Gonger, 255 Wisc. 381, 39 N.W.2d 397 (1949).

23. Childers v. Hoffer, 177 Kan. 174, 277 P.2d 625 (1954).

24. J. Grimes, *Clark on Surveying and Boundaries* 899 (3d ed., 1959).

25. *Cf.* Van Amburgh v. Hitt, 115 Mo. 607, 22 S.W. 636 (1893).

26. Wunderlich, "Public Costs of Land Records," 22 Am. U. L. Rev. 333, 359 (1973). The survey of South Dakota counties shows that the budgets of the various recording offices can be positively correlated with the population of the county.

27. *See* n. 18, *supra.*

28. *See* n. 14, *supra.*

29. *See, e.g.,* Md. Real Property Code § 3-301 (1974) entitled "Record Books; General Duties of Clerks"; a subsequent section describes how the indexes shall be kept, in a grantor-grantee index form. *Id.,* § 3-302; N.M. Stat. § 71-2-1 (1973).

30. *See* Payne, "Continuity and Identity in Land Title Searches—A Perpetual Self-indexing System," 16 Ala. L. Rev. 9 (1963).

31. *Id.,* at 15.

32. *Cf.* Boyer v. Pahvant Mercantile and Inv. Co., 76 Utah 1, 287 P. 188 (1930).

33. Hanson v. Zoller, 187 N.W.2d 47 (N.D., 1971) (subsequent purchasers and encumbrancers not charged with notice when instrument was not correctly indexed under tract index).

34. *See* Jones v. Folks, 149 Va. 140, 140 S.E. 126 (1927).

35. L. Simes, *A Handbook for More Efficient Conveyancing* 60-63 (1961); L. Simes & C. Taylor, *The Improvement of Conveyancing by Legislation* 37-51, 142-51, 183-86 (1960).

36. Parcel indexes may in one sense render titles less certain if automatic exclusion from the record does not follow for facially stale interests filed without the chain of title, although arguably the definition of wild documents, those without the chain of title, should then be narrowed to include only interests that could not convey any interest or estate at common law.

37. Wisconsin Stat. Ann. § 235.60; Douglass v. Ransom, 205 Wisc. 439, 237 N.W. 260 (1931).

38. Home Inv. Fund v. Robertson, 101 Ill. App.2d 840, 295 N.E.2d 85 (1973); Rogers Carl Corp. v. Moran, 103 N.J. Super. 163, 246 A.2d 750 (1968).

39. The idea of a title record purging itself is taken from the civil law. *See* Burke & Fox, "The Notaire in North America," 50 Tulane L. Rev. 318 (1975). *See generally* "A Symposium on Title Recordation," 22 Am. U. L. Rev. 239 (1973).

40. Basye, "A Uniform Land Parcel Identifier—Its Potential for All Our Land Records," 22 Am. U. L. Rev. 251, 258-62 (1973) and notes therein.

41. *E.g.,* "No . . . deed may pass or take effect unless the deed granting it is executed and recorded." Md. Real Property Code § 3-101 (1974). *See also* West v. Pusey, 113 Md. 569, 77 A. 973 (1910). The legislative requirement that a recordable document be acknowledged by the parties or the vendor should be repealed. This would prevent a lack of an acknowledgment or a defective acknowledgment from denying a document already on the record its notice-

giving effect. Requiring an acknowledgment is now a method of permitting vendors to refuse to acknowledge their conveyances and render otherwise recordable documents unrecordable. This refusal to acknowledge is a particular problem with long-term leases and installment land sale contracts. Perhaps a statutory covenant implying in all recordable documents a promise by the vendor that, unless the parties agree to the contrary, the vendor will permit his purchaser to record the document executed by the parties at settlement should also be enacted.

42. The due-process right discussed in this section belongs to both vendors and purchasers as prospective vendors with warranty rights against some or all vendors in their chain of title.

43. *See* text *supra* at n. 33-34.

44. *See* ch. 3, text at n. 22.

45. *See* ch. 3, text at n. 65.

46. 334 U.S. 1 (1948).

47. 334 U.S. at 13.

48. *Id.*

49. Jackson v. Metropolitan Edison Co., 419 U.S. 345 (1974).

50. 419 U.S., at 353-54.

51. 419 U.S., at 351.

52. Note, "The Supreme Court, 1974 Term," 89 Harv. L. Rev. 47, 139, 148 (1975).

53. 4 Am. L. Prop. 528, 538 (Casner ed., 1952). Indeed, the earliest recording acts required a recording to make the transaction valid even as to the vendor and purchaser. Presser, "Introduction to the Legal History of Colonial New Jersey," 7 Rut. Camden L. J. 262, 300 (1976), indicates that all land purchasers had, by statute, to be approved by the proprietor.

54. P. Gates, *Landlords and Tenants on the Prairie Frontier* 48-71 (1973), explains various contexts in which a double sale might occur.

55. Smith v. Burtis, 6 Johns 197 (N.Y., 1810).

56. Marsh v. Stover, 363 Ill. 490, 2 N.E.2d 559 (1936); 4 Am. L. Prop. 542, n. 49-50 (Casner ed., 1952).

57. Evans v. Abney, 396 U.S. 435 (1970) (reverter to heirs under Georgia law could not be the basis of an unconstitutional deprivation of civil rights. However, the common law was "received" by legislative action in many states.) S. Kimball, *Historical Introduction to the Legal System* 280-82 (1966); Seagle, "Reception," 13 *Ency. of the Soc. Sciences* 153 (1934).

58. *But see* Earle v. Fiske, 103 Mass. 491 (1870); Hill v. Meeker, 24 Conn. 211 (1855).

59. 4 Am. L. Prop. 538-41 (Casner ed., 1952).

60. In the case of the recording acts, its major utility from the state's point of view would appear to be that the recording system is self-executing: that is, it depends on private initiative; gaining a statutory priority by recording is usually

sufficient incentive for a purchaser to record his interest. The system of records is designed to minimize government action by encouraging maximum private reliance on it. To achieve a workable system on these premises, the state delegates to private parties a decision-making function over the priorities between conflicting interests. The recording acts delegate resolution of conflicting claims to private parties and adopts the priority which their recordings produce. This delegation and adoption process makes the acts of private parties into "state action."

Second, the exercise of a "governmental function" constitutes "state action." Recording is an indispensable step in the conveyancing process, and the state gives effect to the conveyance by protecting the owners of property against the claims of subsequent parties. Recording is a substitute for a judicial act deciding on a priority between claimants. This arbitral power is an inherent attribute of sovereignty.

A third theory may be argued: Recording is both indispensable to completing a purchase and, later, the purchaser's selling the property. There is, in the language of one Supreme Court opinion on state action, a "symbiotic" relationship between recording and the conveyancing process. Jackson v. Metropolitan Edison Co., 419 U.S. 345 (1974). An owner will later have to prove himself the record owner before his purchaser will accept title. A doubtful title is as bad in this later transaction as an invalid title. Stapylton v. Scott, 16 Vesey 272 (ch. 1809); Marlow v. Smith, 2 P. Will. 198 (1823). Private decisions on title marketability based on public records present a situation in which "the State has so far insinuated itself into a position of interdependence with" private conveyancers that when the findings of the latter deprive an owner of his property right, a due-process claim may be presented. Burton v. Wilmington Parking Authority, 365 U.S. 715 (1961). Burton created a very ad hoc and circumstantial test. *Id.*, at 722. Moose Lodge No. 107 v. Irvis, 407 U.S. 163 (1972) (no state action in liquor license granted to otherwise private club). This private action taken in reliance on public records is the nexus between the supposedly private action and a constitutional right.

So recordation of a claim on public records is arguably "state action" for several reasons. In the future some of these theories might succeed.

61. *See, e.g.,* 49 Pa. Stat. Ann. § 1101 (1975); N. Am. Mfg., Inc., v. Crown Int'l, Inc., N.H. 1975, 335 A.2d 660 (1975).

62. "The right to file a mechanic's lien, as has been uniformly held by all the courts, is of statutory origin. No such right existed at common law." Samango v. Hobbs, 167 Pa. Super. 339, 403, 75 A.2d 17, 20 (1960). *See generally* Cutler & Shapiro, "The Maryland Mechanic's Lien Law—Its Scope and Effect," 28 Md. L. Rev. 225 (1968); Commentary, Uniform Land Transactions Act, Art. 5, Working Draft (Feb., 1975) at 5-1 through 5-5.

63. 3 Am. L. Prop. 521 (Casner ed., 1952).

64. The common-law rights of *lis pendens* remain in force except as

modified by statute. 3 Am. L. Prop. 522 (Casner ed., 1952). As in the case of a mechanic's lien, filing a *lis pendens* before final judgment will make the record relate back to the beginning of the action. Literally, the expression *lis pendens* signifies "pending litigation." At common law, it meant that whoever purchased an interest in property subject to litigation must stand in the shoes of his vendor and so takes the property subject to whatever judgment may be rendered in that litigation. Presidio County v. Noel-Young Bond and Stock Co., 212 U.S. 58 (1909). The operative effect of this doctrine is to hold the subject matter of the litigation in *custodia legis*, i.e., within the jurisdiction and control of the court during the pendency of the litigation, thus preventing third persons from acquiring interests in the property that would preclude the court from granting relief justified under the facts of the case or would serve to vitiate a judgment rendered therein. Massachusetts Bonding and Ins. Co. v. Knox, 220 N.C. 725, 18 S.E.2d 436 (1942). The rule that a purchaser takes subject to judgments issuing out of pending litigation is a rule founded on public policy and necessity and did not at its inception involve the concept of constructive notice. Vicars v. Saylor, 111 Va. 307, 68 S.E. 988 (1910).

The effects of the common-law rule are harsh in that they hold that the pendency of the action is in itself notice to all the world. It presumed that persons who deal with property while it is in litigation have notice of the fact of that litigation and are bound by its results. *Id.* Requisite to the application of the doctrine is a court's having valid jurisdiction of the property that is the subject matter of the litigation. If, for example, a court lacks jurisdiction because the property involved is situated in a county other than the one in which the action was initiated, *pendent lite* transferees of such property will not come within the operation of the doctrine. Lacassayne v. Chapuis, 144 U.S. 119 (1892).

There is general agreement that the doctrine applies to both conveyed and ex parte interests. Terrill v. Allison, 21 U.S. (8 Wheat.) 289 (1823). Persons acquiring their interest in the property by virtue of a lease, purchase, mortgage, descent, marriage, judgment by a court, or assignment in bankruptcy have been included in the class of persons within the definition of the previously mentioned terms. Benton v. Shafer, 47 Ohio 117, 24 N.E. 197 (1890).

Generally, persons who acquire interests in property prior to the commencement of litigation involving it will not be subjected to operation of the doctrine with respect to that interest. The failure to make full payment on a contract for the purchase of land before the doctrine is operative will not subject the *pendent lite* purchaser to that judgment if the contract was entered into before the doctrine was invoked. The doctrine applies to real property and excludes personalty, unless provided otherwise by statute. For this purpose, real property includes water rights, timber, things naturally attached to the soil, and even trees cut while the property was in litigation. Ricken Land and Cattle Co. v. Miller and Lux, 218 U.S. 258 (1910). The doctrine of *lis pendens* has been applied to, among other things, suits for partition, for a specific performance of a contract relating to real property, to quiet title, and to foreclose mortgages and liens. From time to time, it has been applied in actions to compel sale of specific property for the payment of debts, to cancel mortgages, and in caveats to wills. Todd v. Romeu, 217 U.S. 150 (1910).

The courts demand diligence in the prosecution of litigation involving property in order to maintain the doctrine of *lis pendens* against innocent *pendent lite* purchasers.

Finally, with regard to enforcement of a judgment against a *pendent lite* purchaser, the doctrine generally requires such purchaser to convey to the prevailing litigant whatever interests he may have acquired. A writ of assistance is normally recognized as the proper means for ousting a lessee or *pendent lite* purchaser who refuses to surrender possession of the subject premises. Such purchasers who refuse to surrender after judgment have also been held in contempt of court.

65. Note, "Specifying the Procedures Required by Due Process: Toward Limits on Interest Balancing," 88 Harv. L. Rev. 1510, 1511, n. 5 and cases cited therein.

66. Fuentes v. Shevin, 407 U.S. 67, 82 (1972).

67. Burns v. Wilson, 346 U.S. 137, 149 (1953).

68. Baldwin V. Hale, 68 U.S. (8 Wall.) 223, 233 (1863).

69. Mullane v. Cent. Hanover Bank and Trust Co., 339 U.S. 307, 317 (1949).

70. *Id.*, at 318.

71. *Id.*, at 319.

72. *Id.*, at 314-15, 319.

73. Commissioners on Uniform State Laws, Uniform Land Transactions Act, Working Draft, Feb., 1975, at 5-1.

74. Wisconsin v. Constantineau, 400 U.S. 433 (1971) (government publication of person as an excessive drinker).

75. 4 Am. L. Prop. 804 (Casner ed., 1952).

76. Silverside Home Mart v. Hall, Del. Super., 1975, 345 A.2d 427; *cf.*, Tesuro v. Baird, Pa. Super., 1975, 335 A.2d 792; Annot., "Sufficiency of Designation of Owner in Notice, Claim, or Statement of Mechanic's Lien," 48 A.L.R.3d 153 (1973).

77. *See, e.g.,* Md. Code, Real Property, §§ 9-101 through 9-111 (1975).

78. 4 Am. L. Prop. 804 (Casner ed., 1952).

79. Barry Properties, Inc., v. Fick Bros. Roofing Co., 277 Md. 15, 353 A.2d 222 (1976) (mechanic's lien statute held unconstitutional); Roundhouse Const. Corp. v. Telesco Masons Suppliers Co., Docket No. 75-46, Conn. Sup. Ct., Apr. 22, 1975, cert. granted with rem. to Conn. Sup. Ct. to consider whether state or federal constitution involved, 44 U.S.L.W. 3199 (1975).

80. Fuentes v. Shevin, 407 U.S. 67, 82 (1972).

81. *Id; cf.* Lindsey v. Normet, 405 U.S. 56 (1972).

82. Note, "Specifying the Procedures Required by Due Process: Toward Limits on the Use of Interest Balancing," 88 Harv. L. Rev. 1510, 1513 (1975).

83. Fuentes v. Shevin, 407 U.S. 67, 76-7 (1972).

84. 407 U.S. at 86.

85. *Id.*

86. 395 U.S. 337 (1969).

87. 416 U.S. 600 (1974).

88. 419 U.S. 601 (1975).

89. Bonds have long been used to modify the harshness of state replevin statutes for chattel. R. Brown, *Personal Property* 627-29 (3d ed., 1938); *cf.* Beaudreau v. Superior Court, 14 Cal.3d 448, 535 P.2d 713, 121 Cal. Rptr. 585 (1975), noted at 89 Harv. L. Rev. 1006 (1976).

90. *See* text *supra* at n. 26.

91. Smith v. Gale, 155 U.S. 509 (1892).

92. Robinson v. Bierce, 102 Tenn. 428, 52 S.W. 992 (1899).

93. Where property rights are concerned, all adjudication need not take place in one forum. Lindsey v. Normet, 405 U.S. 56 (1972).

Establishing Title Registries

Conveyancing Improvement in the Twentieth Century

In populous jurisdictions a tract index is today one precondition to competition among abstractors, insurers, and attorneys for title business in that it minimizes the advantage of possessing a title plant. It is a cheap, discrete, and proven improvement in many conveyancing patterns and is necessary to preserve them. Further, it may be an important precondition to establishing a title registry, a system for documenting titles, not just title evidence. This is arguably the next step in the evolution of American conveyancing. The seeds of a registration system have already been planted. Two trends reinforce this conclusion. First, the prerequisites for a registry exist in legislative form today; if our recording statutes are viewed as a device for providing information on titles to property, obtaining information on a particular title requires gathering documents scattered throughout the public records. Both marketable-title acts that make only more recent recordings relevant to a title search and curative statutes that eliminate the need for supporting affidavits when documents contain defects in form reduce this effort. A registration certificate, as the only document showing the state of the title, is by this token the ultimate in efficiency, for the searcher would have to locate and read only one document. Second, the impetus toward tract indexes and improved property-related records and toward administrative or judicial control of those records to satisfy the mandates of the due-process clause point in the same direction.

Yet the identification of an impetus toward a registry does not make its advent inevitable. Nor should it. There are other issues of a policy nature to be considered, and a consideration of alternatives too, before a registry can be labeled sound and desirable. To the types of registries in use abroad and to the American experience with the precursor of a registry—the Torrens system—this discussion now turns.

The Registration of Titles

Outside the United States, twentieth-century conveyancing reform has meant either improvement of the land title records or the introduction and modification of the Torrens system of land title registration.[1] The American recording system gives rise to many risks from which the purchaser can achieve little or no protection.[2] A search of the public records will not indicate more than the prima facie validity of instruments in the chain of title,[3] and therefore, a title a purchaser takes is based only on a cumulative compilation of whatever title evidence is available.[4] Under a Torrens system of land titles, the most recent certificate of title on the public record becomes not merely evidence of title, but the title itself,[5] issued and guaranteed by the state.[6] American jurisdictions use certificates of title to transfer ownership in automobiles and ships[7] but not in land transfers.[8] The Torrens system was conceived by Robert Richard Torrens, an Irish immigrant who came to Australia in 1841. While on his way there, he noticed the manner in which ships changed hands.[9] Later when he was a port official in Adelaide, Australia, he came to the conclusion that land titles could be registered in the same fashion as ships and other chattel. When he later became prime minister of one of the Australian states, he got the opportunity to put his ideas into practice.

The Torrens Acts, as adopted and gradually modified,[10] embody three basic principles.[11] The first is the "mirror principle," which holds that public title records should "mirror" the state of the title and that they should declare that the title exists as proclaimed under the authority of the state.[12] The second, "curtain principle," is that no purchaser should have to go further in his inquiry than the last issued certificate of title; no historical search of past registrations of the same property is generally required by his system.[13] Third, land ownership is not perceived as unique or distinguishable from ownership of other things. From this it follows that financial compensation is, in most cases, the equivalent of the ownership right, and the establishment of an assurance fund from fees generated by registrations and transfers assures an adequate compensation to those deprived of rights and interests under his system.[14]

The last chapter discussed the initial restricted role of the recorder and the need to expand his function as title records become more accessible and comprehensive. Outside the United States, the comparable official is the registrar of titles.[15] His job is to maintain records, but in the course of administering a registration act, he also passes on the marketability of a title.[16] Canadian opinions, for instance, take this expanded role as the usual course of events: talking of a "good, safeholding and marketable" (the Canadian phrase for marketable) title, the Supreme Court of British Columbia said:

The Registrar points out that under the [registration] Act his duties are not administrative or clerical only but judicial. There is plenty of authority to support that submission. . . .

Not only do secs. 141 and 156 require the registrar to exercise this judicial function of determining whether the title is a good, safeholding and marketable title, but the whole tenor of the Act, and the whole system of registration of titles, it seems to me indicate that there is a duty cast to so satisfy himself with respect to the registration of any instrument. . . .[17]

In such a capacity the registrar is doing what the purchaser's attorney, assisted by an abstractor, does in the United States. But while the role is similar, the results are not. If the attorney is wrong, the purchaser has remedies against the vendor in damages; or against the attorney, abstractor, or insurance company for professional negligence—but the purchaser loses the property. In a registration system once the purchaser receives a certificate of title from the registrar, he has good title and retains the land.[18] Persons deprived of interests in the property because of the registrar's issuance of a certificate are given a right to compensation out of a fund maintained by the registrar.

Converting Torrens into a Registration System

There are today many variations on Torrens' basic idea. They vary widely in the degrees of similarity to the recording pattern so familiar to American conveyancing. Some are quite compatible. However, the registration system Torrens first developed and used in Australia is the basis for title registration in some thirty political jurisdictions around the world,[19] mostly in countries that were at some time under the influence of the British or were part of the British empire.[20] The original idea proved unworkable in most countries,[21] and indeed, its adaptation in England took well over a hundred years.[22] Modifications in the mirror, curtain, and fund principles and the job of the registrar have been required everywhere.[23] If the purchaser obtains what the certificate states his interest to be "even though an error has been repeated in successive certificates of title,"[24] when may the registrar correct the mistake?[25] Registration laws provide different answers to this problem. Some suggest that he can correct the certificate only before a purchaser with an error-ridden certificate sells his interest to a person entitled, under the mirror and curtain principles, to rely on it.[26] Not only does the certificate here mirror the state of the title as far as the later purchaser is concerned, but that purchaser may not be put on notice of facts "unreflected" on the certificate; the mirror and curtain principles mean, respectively that (1) the purchaser gets what the certificate says, and (2) the doctrine of constructive notice is abolished.[27]

Other jurisdictions provide that the registrar may correct a certificate when moved by an aggrieved party to do so or may on his own motion, correct the certificate at any time.[28] In still other jurisdictions an initial registration of title produces a qualified fee that can be defeated by the holder of a statutorily prescribed interest if the claim is made within a similarly prescribed period of time. In Massachusetts, one of the few states in the United States using the system, a registration decree is subject to open for a period of one year in cases of fraud, provided that during that time no subsequent bona fide purchaser takes the property in question.[29] New South Wales, Australia, gives a qualified fee for six years.[30] After such periods of time, the qualified or defeasible fee becomes indefeasibly vested in the registered owner.[31]

Two consequences follow from the reliance on the title certificate. First, the provisions of the sales contract become even more important to the purchaser since in an action for specific performance a purchaser is more likely to be compelled to take a title based on the certificate.[32] Second, in any transaction for which no certificate is available, fraud by the vendor in selling and by the purchaser in accepting the title is likely to be presumed. The latter result is but one solution of the common-law conveyancing problem discussed in connection with curative acts, of attempting to restrict or codify the powers of equity.[33]

Similar attempts account for some further differences among registration jurisdictions. (1) Some systems insure more than the interests registered on the certificate.[34] In Massachusetts the acreage and description of the registered parcel are insured,[35] but in Alberta and Saskatchewan[36] only the interests described on the certificate are insured. Many jurisdictions found that the bulk of the claims brought against the assurance fund were based on misdescriptions in the physical location of the parcel.[37] Thereafter such descriptions were not guaranteed, and a rule of substantiality was adopted in its place.[38] This is the rule of "general boundaries" which states that the guaranty fund will provide compensation only when the legal description contains substantially more in acreage than was actually conveyed.[39] (2) If someone attempts to register an encumbrance on a registered title, the registrar in British Columbia must decide whether it is registerable either because it relates to the land rather than being a chattel[40] or the statute provides for registration.[41] Varying degrees of discretion are given to the registrar to decide such matters. Some other Canadian provinces, e.g., Manitoba, use a priority of registration rule to determine conflicts when two certificates are issued for the same land.[42] In Ontario the courts are given discretion to decide when a discrepancy in a parcel description is substantial enough to affect the ownership of the registered land.[43]

Torrens' jurisdictions also differ as to whether or not adverse posession, title by prescription, ways of necessity, and other implied easements are eliminated by registration. Manitoba[44] and British Columbia[45] both eliminate adverse possession, as do Hawaii and Massachusetts.[46] British Columbia adds procedures for filing claims of adverse right within a five-year period after registry.[47] Some early established Torrens systems do not provide protection against possessory claims. In England the case of *Hunt* v. *Luck*[48] excepted possessory claims from protection by initial registration. If a grantee cannot take priority over the holder of a possessory right, such rights derogate the mirror and curtain principles and hence the conclusiveness of the certificate in such jurisdictions. Purchasers there must inquire about possessory rights through some inspection of the registered land.[49] There are, depending on the jurisdiction, numerous other interests of which they must inquire as well.[50] Mechanic's liens, the authority of an agent of the vendor to sell, and the identity of the vendor[51] are examples.

The third principle underlying the Torrens system, that an assurance fund will provide adequate compensation for those deprived of rights and interests, has also been diluted.[52] In some areas the fund is a last resort for those deprived;[53] claimants must first pursue private law remedies before suing the state. In addition, statutes of limitations provide a period of approximately six years for suits brought against the fund,[54] and they run from the time the error, omission, or misdescription of the property is made rather than from the time the defect in title is discovered. In addition, certain claims, such as those based on governmental liens, equitable or constructive trusts, special assessments, and defects in grants from the state, may not be brought against the fund.[55]

Some systems, while recognizing only those interests capable of registration, have at the same time accepted the notion that equitable interests may arise from time to time out of either judicial proceedings, unregistered documents, or private dealings. To protect these, notices called *caveats* are filed, without going through the administrative or judicial process of registration.[56] This device is commonly used to protect mortgages, unwritten trusts, and options.[57] They may be filed with the registrar to prevent land from being brought under the registration act, filed by the registrar to correct the register,[58] or filed by third parties to prohibit further dealing in the land without at least notifying the caveator.[59] They can operate much like a recording system within a larger registry system, and to the extent caveats are available the changeover from a recording to registration process can be made easier. In Alberta, a caveat once entered in the register remains there until challenged.[60] This makes it a useful device for protecting the security liens of mortgagees.[61] In British Columbia, however, a caveat automatically expires if the caveator does not proceed to register it within two months of the date on which it is lodged.[62] More types of interests can be "caveated" in British Columbia, however, and the device has the legal effect of a recording.[63]

To be successful, it is often thought that a registry system must be universal and compulsory.[64] Many of the American systems devised at the turn of the century were voluntary[65] and seldom used.[66] Administrative proceedings,[67] less expensive than a full judicial hearing on the state of the title,[68] should also be established and used,[69] with caveats available for equitable interests; such hearings will usually generate a qualified fee, made indefeasible at a future date.[70] A universally applicable administrative proceeding that does not investigate perimeters of parcels sums up the generally conceived preconditions for a successful title registry.

The American Experiment

To the flexibility of registration systems abroad, one need only contrast the rigid Torrens system attempted in this country at the turn of the century, and the stilted debate over it, to realize that the United States lacks any widespread experience with registration. A Torrens system was first discussed in the United States in the early 1880s. Initially the reaction to it was favorable,[71] but this was changed by opposition from the bar, abstractors, and title insurance companies,[72] who characterized it as a foreign system alien to the American legal tradition. Perhaps what really ended the discussions, however, was the poor quality of public information on land.[73] The establishment of a registry system requires that well-organized records be available on which to base the initial title search and subsequent registration; these were lacking in the United States. Originally, a Torrens system was based on the availability of accurate maps, as there had then been no modification of Torrens' original idea of insuring the acreage to the parcel as well as the interests constituting its ownership.[74] In many parts of this country, particularly in the western states and territories, accurate maps were simply not available. In addition, state legislatures would adopt Torrens statutes but make the certificate subject to so many exceptions that in many cases lending and financial institutions decided not to rely on a Torrens certificate and to require a title search.

The existence of the recording acts was another stumbling block to the establishment of an American Torrens system.[75] Title searches were expensive, and the initial cost of registration included them as well as the expense of a judicial[76] or administrative hearing.[77] American courts, with due regard for the then current concepts of due process of law and personal service on adverse claimants, required that the initial registration proceedings be judicial in nature.[78] One jurisdiction that first accepted the Torrens system, i.e., Massachusetts, established a separate court for the purpose[79] since delegation of the duty to find the state of the title to an administrative officer was constitutionally suspect.[80] Even though the initial registration costs are high, a Torrens title is a much less expensive method for subsequent transfers, which compensates for that disadvantage in the long run.[81]

Torrens was widely debated at the time,[82] but the atmosphere in the United States was not very conducive to finding a workable solution. It would have helped to clear up many cloudy titles in uninhabited parts of the United States;[83] by barring claims of adverse possession, absentee owners and landlords would have been provided with secure titles.[84] In areas of the country where public records have been destroyed by fires or earthquakes, a Torrens system would have solved some problems of reestablishing titles after those holocausts.[85]

Twenty states and Puerto Rico have or have had some Torrens legislation,[86] although most of it amounted to little more than legislative exercises[87] since it was voluntary[88] and little used. Those areas that still authorize and use a system of Torrens title registration are: the island of Oahu, Hawaii;[89] the City of Boston, on the south shore, Nantucket, and Martha's Vineyard in the Commonwealth of Massachusetts;[90] Ramsey, Hennepin, and St. Louis Counties in Minnesota;[91] and Cook County, Illinois.[92] Where the system is working in the

United States today, it does so because of the administrative efficiency backing up a judicial registration decree,[93] a light case load,[94] good land surveys,[95] the development of a clientele,[96] and its acceptance by lenders.

Registration in South Dakota

Some typical problems of these experiments with Torrens title registration can be seen in South Dakota's experience. In 1917 without any substantial demand for or knowledge of the idea,[97] the state legislature enacted a law with eithty-three sections,[98] seventy-five of which were taken from the Minnesota statute on title registration.[99] A separate assurance fund was established for each county in the state: The fee was one tenth of 1 percent of the value of the property registered, paid on registration by the owner, his heirs, or devisees.[100] The unpaid balance of any judgments against the fund accrued interest while the fund accumulated enough to pay off the balance.

The procedure for registering title required an application to the circuit court; it was to contain, in part,

1. a "correct description"[101]
2. names of nonowners in possession[102]
3. names and addresses of all parties with any interests in the land.[103]

When the addresses were unknown, a statement was necessary to the effect that "after due and diligent search the applicant has been unable to ascertain" them.[104] Adjoining tracts or those in the same chain of title could be registered together.[105] Separate dockets were required,[106] and once an application was docketed, it had "the force and effect of a *lis pendens*."[107] The caption of the application included "all persons unknown with an interest," and an abstract "satisfactory to the examiner" was required. This examiner acted on the applications referred to him by the court[108] as would a master or referee. He was an attorney appointed by the court but paid by the applicant.[109] If he thought it necessary, he could require a survey of the property, but boundaries were not registered unless a specific request was made.[110] Upon receipt of the report of the examiner, the matter proceeded to a hearing before the circuit court.[111]

Certificates, once decreed by the court, could be opened for sixty days, and actions attacking the certificates had to be brought within six months.[112] If none were,

every decree of registration shall bind the land described therein, and shall forever quiet the title thereto, and shall be forever binding and conclusive upon all persons, whether mentioned by name in the summons, or included in the phrase, "all other persons or parties unknown claiming any right, title," . . . etc.[113]

All lands registered must remain in the system.[114] The recorder was named the "registrar of titles" for the county. He issued the certificates of title and kept the original in the public records, indexed by name and tract number.[115] All later certificates had to refer to the original one.[116]

The registration procedure was seldom used. Powell reports that 2/30 of 0.1 percent of the state's area was registered in the first five years that the system was available.[117] In 1927 Professor Percy Bordwell pronounced the statute "a dead letter,"[118] a fact admitted by another commentator but attributed to the low rate of property turnover and public ignorance of the system.[119] It was used mostly in Beadle and Roberts Counties.[120] Powell reported thirty-seven registrations as of 1938 in Roberts County,[121] which lies in the extreme northeastern part of the state, near the Minnesota border; perhaps its use there is attributable to that fact alone. Beadle County, the chief user, surrounds the town of Huron in the east river country where the need to consolidate small land-holdings probably played a big role in making landowners there use the system.[122] In the western portions of the state where it could have been used to defeat claims of adverse possession, no use was ever reported.

Little modification was made in the legislation during the twenty-one-year period from 1917-1938,[123] nor were there any appellate decisions concerning it during that period.

Several potential defects appear in this system: The county basis for the assurance fund seems too limited, and its liability for misdescriptions too broad; the judicial nature of registration was too cumbersome and expensive, and the limitation on actions attacking a certificate was too short. Its procedures for diligent search, notice for claimants, and the use of attorney-examiners seems a workable enlistment of existing expertise, though the use of deed recorders as registrars seems less so. A similar system succeeded in Minnesota, so it is safe to say that this system foundered on apathy and disuse, not on its own demerits.

Registration in Virginia

Elsewhere, debate over the costs and the organizational features of a registration system was protracted[124]—the decade-long debate in Virginia illustrates the exaggerated debate over a Torrens law.[125] In that Commonwealth a legislative committee to consider the enactment of Torrens legislation was established in 1901.[126] A year later the constitutional convention of the state gave the legislature power to establish a court of land registration, which the opponents represented as an immense bureaucracy established to perform functions the private sector had previously done. In 1902 an abstract review cost Virginians $5 in rural areas and as much as $10 in cities.[127] (South Dakotans also paid $5 at the time.) It was estimated that the total cost of registering the 400,000-odd parcels in Virginia would be in the neighborhood of $22.7 million;[128] 230 officials would be necessary to maintain the system.[129] The initial cost of registering title provided the opponents of the system with their strongest argument.[130] Proponents replied that this $22 million, assuming it was a correct figure, represented only 6.2 percent of the value of the land in Virginia, then placed at $343.8 million.[131] Virginia attorneys charged approximately 1 percent of the value of the parcel for examining the title; thus the initial cost of registration would have been only six times the cost of one review and would have resulted in a guaranteed title as well.[132] In one year (1904) proponents of the system estimated that Virginians spent $421.8 thousand on title searches and examinations.[133] In any event, proponents argued, the state spent far more than $22 million to eliminate rodents and pests from farms; since acreages were to be insured, they made the further point that it would cost $50 million to fence all the land parcels in the state. Over the next several years Torrens acts were introduced in the general assembly but failed to pass, sometimes by only narrow margins. One was finally enacted in 1916 and is on the books today. Except in the southeastern portion of Virginia, the registry was never extensively used.[134] This debate was not over the substantive benefits or procedures of the system but rather centered on the initial costs of registration.[135] Quoting from Judge Dillon's lectures at Yale Law School in 1891-92, proponents had taken the following as their theme:

Real property does not serve with us as the foundation for personal distinction or family grandeur, and is invested with no peculiar sanctity. Its uses are those of property simply. It is an article of commerce, and its free circulation is encouraged. . . . I insist that the law of real property in this country ought to be assimilated as near as possible to the law of personal property. . . .[136]

This goal seems clearly lost in the ensuing debate.

The End of the Experiment

One important reason why the Torrens system did not grow or prosper in the United States is related to the growing need for uniform lending practices. Title insurance was the ready handmaiden of this trend, and the debate over Torrens was fought largely in banking and financial journals from 1900 to 1920.[137] Inconsistent state court opinions giving Torrens certificates differing degrees of conclusiveness required lenders to become specialists in local Torrens laws, whereas a title insurance policy issued in standard form negated the need for such expertise. Many owners who had Torrenized their titles were required to purchase abstracts or title insurance as a precondition to financing their land or improvements on it. Variations on the conclusiveness of the certificate also rendered Torrens laws impractical as a basis for a national market in mortgages and trust deeds; local banks in areas where registration was prevalent usually accepted the certificate in lieu of title insurance but would often encounter reluctance in the national secondary market because of limitations on the negotiability of that mortgage.[138] It has been forcefully argued that modern non-Torrens registration is still a viable means of title protection,[139] but many feel that a need for any type of registration is obviated when a title insurance company promises to defend a title in litigation. Relying on this promise, title insurance has been accepted and allowed to supplant alternative forms of title delivery.[140]

During the 1920s Torrens titles were impeached for many reasons by state courts.[141] The intellectual *coupe de grace* came in 1938 when Richard Powell, a law professor at the height of his prestige, published *The Registration of Title to Land in the State of New York.*[142] The book provoked bitter controversy at the time,[143] and it effectively ended the Torrens debate in this country.[144] Although Powell later retracted his opposition, legal literature on the registration system has been sporatic ever since that time.[145] Powell found no fault with land registration itself. He was satisfied to conclude that no amendment short of making it compulsory could induce wider use, and he saw no justification for making it compulsory.[146] He explored the case law on registration in several states and found that Torrens certificates had been rendered inconclusive by judicial interpretation.[147] Instead of suggesting the reexamination of these decisions, he vaguely proposed amendment of the recording laws and stricter regulation of title insurance as sufficient to answer demands for improving New York conveyancing patterns.[148] Critics suggested that his conclusions did not follow from his study and that the last chapter of his book bore little relation to his analysis.[149] Powell devoted little time to the litigiousness of the principles involved in both common-law conveyancing and registration;[150] his arguments would have been stronger if such comparisons had been added for balance.

The book's conclusions may be outdated and criticized in several other ways. It is, after all, to registration systems moulded by a century of experience, that prudent legislators would look for guidance in drafting new conveyancing principles. The use of administrative proceedings, the implementation of a general-boundaries rule for title guarantees, and the enactment of a universal system of title registries are elsewhere preconditions for a successful land-registration system.[151] Accurate mapping and engineering standards are necessary only if the rule of general boundaries is not maintained,[152] and, in any event, only accurate land title information and records need underlie a registry. (Whether accurate information systems can exist without a registry is today a point of some debate.)[153] In this regard, Powell's one precondition for the introduction of a registry was a drastic reform of our system of landed estates,[154] comprising both present and future interests. Whether ownership is to be certified in one or several names, even existing title information arranged by owner's name can be automated and become quickly available to the registrar and the public. Curative acts and marketable-title legislation are the only legislative steps necessary to clean up those records before automation increases their accessibility and a registry is introduced.[155]

It is time for renewed experimentation with title registration. After the 1930s constitutional law removed many of the constraints on administrative functions in government.[156] Foreign countries have developed a body of practical knowledge of and flexible rules for registration systems and how information and data-retrieval systems make a changeover practical;[157] indeed, so many countries now use some type of registry that the United States appears underdeveloped in this regard. Demography also supports the change: Our population, increasingly mobile[158] and urban, regards housing as a nondepreciating consumer good,[159] as is indicated by the way in which housing is merchandized;[160] short-term ownership requires a fungible title,[161] secure enough to be sold quickly if need be, and a registry would provide title negotiability as well as security. The problems of training personnel to run a registry have been reduced by automation: Form filling is the chief characteristic of registry practices in other countries.[162] The initially high costs of registration can be eliminated by establishing systems that are prospective only in legal effect,[163] which do not guarantee boundaries[164] and which provide a qualified or possessory title certificate for a period of time after registration.[165] A bare-bones registration system along these lines would provide the basis for an adequate assurance fund.[166]

A Registry for Urbanizing Land

Once the outline of an initial registration system is clear, the next problem is to choose a jurisdiction in which to put it into operation. A registry should have the advantage of widespread availability and an appeal to particular constituencies who can marshall support for it. Its least-costly introduction would be prospective, and in the context of American urban development, this feature has a special geographic aspect, not present when discussing the need for tract indexes and title legislation. Widespread geographic use will engender financial stability for the registry, but experience in Torrens jurisdictions and South Dakota shows that owners of unimproved land undergoing urbanization or suburbanization[167] will be the likely users of this legislation. Title examination on their behalf results in a lucrative abstract and title review; attorneys, abstractors, and insurers jockey to get "on" the title at this point because their familiarity with one title at this stage will mean an expertise with the title to every parcel carved out of it in the future.[168] In dollars the value of this expertise is multiplied by the number of subdivided lots. Further, there is no special professional hazard involved in this especially rewarding task since the liability of the searcher, reviewer, or insurer is limited by the purchase price of the land paid by the developer, prorated to each parcel.[169]

The urbanization of a title produces the most difficult problems in setting fees for title-related conveyancing. Developers pay some of these fees directly, but some part is often paid by consumers. The competition to obtain this work induces the use of referral fees and kickbacks. Public intervention to control such sharp practices is most desirable at this point in a title's history,[170] and public assurance of titles is also justifiable because the risk of a title loss can be minimized (and title losses most widely distributed) before the developer's one title becomes the basis for many small holdings. Public assurance can then take advantage of the title-quieting effect of the passage of time during the construction process and the user fees generated by subdivision. At this juncture, too, some title information has just been assembled and passed into public hands for disclosure to consumers—and so a program instituted at this point can take advantage of this work.[171] Then aside from the problem of allocating start-up costs between landowners and taxpayers generally and the fact that any registry could be made self-liquidating through high enough user fees,[172] in all probability a registry for urbanizing counties could pay for itself if designed to heed the experience of existing registration systems in use elsewhere in the world.

This important statement needs support and domestic empirical analysis. The system of fees for a registry may be based on the costs of maintaining the register, the value of the property transferred, or when a registration gives rise to an event taxable under applicable codes, tax revenues.[173] Although the state may be disposed to levy realty-transfer taxes if the registry proves efficient, this last basis for assessing registry fees will not be considered further. The ad valorem principle has the advantage of familiarity—many charges discussed in Chapter 1 are levied in this way—but it may also be subject to abuse if the registrar does not have valuation and appraisal skills at his disposal. The most desirable basis for setting registry fees is therefore administrative costs.[174] These fees are simpler to calculate and less prone to fraud. Insofar as the registry fee includes an indemnity payment into an assurance fund, surpluses in this fund can be used to pay for capital improvements to the registry as needed. Experience with assurance funds in England and New South Wales suggests that such surpluses can in fact be anticipated. England collects £12 million per year for its assurance fund and has paid out less than £4,000 in claims over the average year from 1958-72.[175] New South Wales has had three claims, totaling less than $15,000, against its fund since 1940.[176] The nature of further analysis is suggested by the profitability of title insurance issued for residential property in which the purchaser has little built-up equity and so typically overinsures the premises, as well as the one area in which title insurers do compete for business—on urbanizing land just undergoing subdivision.

Indeed, the experience of registrars in Great Britain suggests that where the process of registration is compulsory but available only in certain areas of the country, it is nonetheless worthwhile to allow the registration of title to large subdivisions, no matter where they are located.[177] English experience suggests that this is true in two senses: First, it builds a constituency for the registration services with the home builders involved, and second, it reduces title risks in advance of the improvement of a parcel.

Elsewhere the same experience is reflected in registration statutes. In Canada the British Columbia act provides:

no person shall subdivide land . . . in smaller parcels than that of which he is the registered owner, except upon compliance with the provisions [of this act]. . . .[178]

Thereafter follow conditions on subdivision that are very much like the provisions of American subdivision ordinances, including requirements for lot access[179] and land descriptions referencing a common development plan.[180] Similar provisions are in effect in other Canadian provinces.[181] Three Australian states have enacted legislation requiring subdivided land to be brought under the operation of the registration acts.[182]

For the United States, evaluation of proposals for such a registry must be considered in light of the reasons Torrens failed,[183] as well as the domestic experience with Torrens and registration systems, and past mistakes must be avoided. The first basic characteristic of a modern registry would include *a voidable defeasible title certificate*, resulting in a state guarantee but qualified by the fact that it may be defeated for a fixed period of time after issuance of the new certificate if forgery or fraud in procuring the certificate or a superior interest is shown. The idea of granting a title defeasible for a stated number of years—say, two to six—places the holder of the registration certificate in the position of the adverse possessor at common law. He is running a statute of limitations by holding the certificate. Indeed, the statutes and rules of law governing adverse user should conform to the registry requirements. In the interim while the title holder's certificate is gradually shedding its defeasible feature, if this feature of the certificate turns out to hold up major land development until the period has run, private title insurers can issue policies covering the risk of defeasance, although subdivision developers might be permitted to shorten the period by a sale to a *bona fide* purchaser of their housing.

Since the certificate holder is already in the position of an adverse possessor, a claim resting on adverse user after the certificate is issued should not run against him. As the prior claimant, the holder should have the opportunity to mature his rights before any later claim puts an end to them. This is a major advantage of a registry in many jurisdictions where adverse possession is barred in cases of registered property. For registered land, the law of adverse possession would remain intact if the question of law were unresolved or unsettled by the registry act; thus if questions involving boundaries and acreage disputes were unresolved by registration, the doctrine of adverse user would remain available to do what it does best, to quiet titles through actual use of the property.

Another advantage of this feature of a registry is to provide a time during which a claim of fraud and an encumbrance may be brought against the certificate holder. Thus holding the certificate as a matter of public record has the legal effect of barring the claims of third parties while at the same time maturing the claim of the holder.

This statute-of-limitations feature of a registry might even toll against parties unknown after a diligent search. South Dakota's Torrens law[184] provided that the registration application state the names and addresses of all known persons with an interest in the land or a statement that

after due and diligent search the applicant has been unable to ascertain the same.[185]

This requirement comports fully with the due-process requirement of notice. In a case where an appellant, a property owner and a seasonal resident, was on the tax rolls, New York City's attempt to divert water from a river flowing through her land after giving notice only by publication was deemed unconstitutional. The city was held to have a constitutional duty to tell the defendant of its diversion and her rights to compensation.

That was the information which the city was constitutionally obliged to make at least a good faith effort to give personally to the appellant—an obligation which the mailing of a single letter would have discharged.[186]

But with the requirement of due diligence satisfied, in an action to settle a trust account, the Supreme Court noted the interest of the state in settling trust and fiduciary matters, the likelihood that interested parties will or should keep themselves informed of such matters and said:

Thus it has been recognized that in the case of persons missing or unknown, employment of an indirect and even a probably futile means of notification is all that the situation permits and creates no constitutional bar to a final decree foreclosing their rights.

Those beneficiaries represented by appellant whose interests or whereabouts could not with due diligence be ascertained come clearly within this category.[187]

The rule emerging from these cases is that where the public records will yield the names and whereabouts of parties with an interest in property, they must be given written notice and personal service.[188] Failure to use the public records will result in a lack of due process fatal to any proceedings, and, conversely, their use reflects a reasonable effort to ascertain the parties' whereabouts.

The second basic characteristic of a registry should be *a guarantee of the interests existing in those persons named on the face of the certificate but not of the precise acreage or the legal description* (unless, perhaps, such a guarantee is expressly requested and undertaken). This merely continues present practice. Matters of acreage and legal descriptions—having to do with boundaries—are seldom covered by an attorney's certificate or title insurance, which customarily excepts from coverage "what an accurate survey would reveal." To some extent, the legal description on the certificate must be guaranteed; if nothing is described thereon (an unlikely event), of course nothing is guaranteed. If, however, the certificate holder cannot reduce the property described in the legal description to possession, he may invoke the guarantee of the description. A rule of substantial variation between the description and the property actually obtained should leave to the registrar and the courts the determination of whether that guarantee is properly invoked. As to covenants, neighbors' rights under them are not always investigated through a search of public records; they might be discovered through overlapping descriptions either recorded or registered on the public records, but not all courts formulate search rules requiring a search of neighboring titles. Registering only named interests will also permit the registry to operate, at least initially, without an engineering or surveying department. Private surveyors could provide any services needed in the course of registration. Where surveying is provided, there is some evidence that (in Massachusetts) the availability of such services is one of the major attractions of the registry. However, any registry will still provide a rudimentary description of the parcel registered, in the form of the registry number assigned during the course of the proceedings. The registry would operate more smoothly if the registry number were identical to the number given the parcel in the tract index. Ideally, the tract index and the registry should be incorporated into one set of records.

A third characteristic of a model registry is *an administrative process for proving title, reviewable by the judiciary.* The constitutionality of providing such a service is scarcely debatable today; strong precedent exists in legislative reform of real property actions and interests,[189] and historical evidence that public recorders were the first abstractors is emotionally comforting, even if too removed to be a logical genesis of this reform.[190]

As a practical matter, such a system must provide a role for existing conveyancing experts.[191] After a state decides which interests must be reflected on a title certificate and which not, attorneys, abstractors, and insurers regulated by the state can be assigned by statute the role of title searchers in initial registrations and subsequent transfers. It was in this way that earlier changes in the law (e.g., Torrens' and workmen's compensation) were made acceptable.[192] The role of the attorney will of course survive into any registration system, as it is unlikely that such a complex statute as registration systems require in other countries can work without the ministrations of the bar. Title insurers can provide coverage for the period during which the certificate holder has a defeasible title and after that period might also insure against forgery in the use of the certificate. To the extent that existing policies of title insurance are not fees for abstracting but are really litigation insurance policies, title insurance counsel will merely shift their practice before the registrar and the courts, with some adjustment in the premiums to reflect this new type of work. Likewise, public recorders would also become registrars, whose records would include title certificates that, unlike recorded deeds, are valid forever.

Probable Effects of Establishing a Registry
on Present Patterns

What effect would the establishment of a title registry have on present conveyancing patterns? The answer depends on the scope of the new system. If it were used only prospectively, then existing abstracts and title insurance policies could become the basis for the future searches needed to guarantee a title. Second, if it were designed for urbanizing, merchant-built subdivisions, it could take advantage of the builders' need for easy transfer of title to housing consumers. It is this that induces South Dakota builders to turn abstracts in for title insurance policies. Third, the builders' trade associations might become a significant constituency for the new system; their industry could absorb, recoup, and spread the initial costs to purchasers, just as they do today for a far less accessible type of title information.

A title registry prospective in nature and designed for raw or urbanizing land will help to shorten the executory period and will make the closing itself less important. Title searches would be eliminated, except for specialized searches (e.g., judgment and tax lien searches where the operations of the courts and government would be hindered otherwise). Abstractors and title insurance companies would still have a role to play in searching records not required to be reflected on the certificate and reported after the date of the last title registration. Title insurers might also insure against unknown defects arising during the period the guarantee is qualified and against known but unasserted encumbrances appearing on a title certificate. They might also perform full sixty- to eighty-year searches for highly valued commercial properties.

A registry first certifying a qualified fee, not insuring acreages and boundaries, and assuring purchasers that their record title is as stated on their certificate, in fact only formalizes present urban conveyancing practices. Title insurers rarely search past the last date on which a title insurance policy was issued, require a survey if boundaries are insured, and even limit their liability for off-record risks through the insurance contract. The certificate of title would assure the title described and supplement coverage of the standard title insurance policy.

The focus of attorneys' activity would no longer be the review of title evidence and the organization of the closing but would in all probability shift forward in time to drafting the sales contract and perhaps to police power restrictions in effect and being violated at the time of settlement. Normally the purchaser takes the risk that the premises he buys may violate public restrictions on occupancy or use, unless enforcement procedures have already begun and brought the matter to the vendor's attention. However, when a public restriction has been held by the courts to imply a covenant made by the transferor, as has now often been the case for urban residential rental properties and newly constructed housing, the question of whether these implied covenants "run" with the leased or alienated properties raises an important title question; this is particularly likely where recently constructed housing is transferred, for in such transfers, a covenant of merchantability for workmanlike construction is increasingly being implied by the courts to run for the benefit of the first, and perhaps later purchasers. This has already occurred in Great Britain. Attorneys might even shift their attention so far forward as to become real estate brokers—as is possible in South Dakota and other states. Attorneys and their clients could but benefit from the legal profession's shifting its attention from the conveyance to the whole conveyancing process.

Conclusion

In suggesting changes whose legal effects are carefully prescribed, the author is not advocating adoption of such proposals in every situation. More sweeping changes may somewhere be appropriate. There is no one type of tract index or registry suitable for every state in the country. The fact that limited proposals are possible indicates that workable compromises with existing conveyancing interests are negotiable without abandoning the goal of making basic changes in our conveyancing patterns. One group to be bargained with are the recorders of deeds. It is always possible that improvements in record keeping, by themselves, will encourage increased reliance on record searches of titles and so encourage the filing of virtually every type of interest in realty. Whether the implementation of a tract index or the establishment of a registry is at issue, some increase in the discretion granted this official will accompany any of these changes in our conveyancing patterns. Here this writer has argued that the inclusion of ex parte documents in a tract index is state action and will require administrative review of filings by the recorder in order to safeguard existing interests and satisfy the due-process clause of the federal Constitution. Once this administrative machinery for a comprehensive tract index is in place, a registry—particularly one that permits a registrable fee simple and freely allows the recording of encumbrances on it—is but a short step away.

A major issue at hand is whether tract indexes and registries can be implemented so as to become an integral part of the conveyancing pattern already in existence or whether they will merely supplement existing patterns. Integration is the aim of the proposals made here. This objective means that we should study carefully proposals to include all types of land-related records in tract indexes since we want the indexes' initial use to be heaviest among the country's conveyancers. So also with registries—we should first consider registries limited in their legal effect since those types would be closest to the present, familiar system of recording. This means that some combination of registration and recording systems will best meet our needs in the immediate future. A residual familiarity with the workings of the system will also permit the present skills of attorneys, abstractors and title insurers to remain useful under any new system. The issuance of limited registration certificates—defeasible for a period after their issuance, without a guarantee of acreages and implemented by administrative action—will serve the citizen's needs by eliminating duplicative title searches on successive transfers. As Lewis Simes once pointed out, defects in titles rarely mean forfeiture of property, but they often do mean a lost opportunity to finance or sell property. The ability to see at a glance on one piece of paper the state of a title will go far toward enhancing its transferability.

Notes

1. A. Axelrod, C. Berger, & Q. Johnstone, *Land Transfer and Finance* 683 (1971); B. Burke & N. Kittrie, *The Real Estate Settlement Process and Its Costs,* II-A-1 (1972).

2. *See, e.g.,* Horton v. Kyburz, 53 Col.2d 59, 346 P.2d 399 (1959); Osin v. Johnson, 243 F.2d 653 (D.D.C., 1957); Cross, "The Record 'Chain of Title' Hypocrisy," 57 Col. L. Rev. 787 (1957); Straw, "Off-record Risks for Bona-fide Purchasers of Interests in Real Property," 72 Dick. L. Rev. 35 (1967).

3. Fiflis, "Land Transfer Improvement: The Basic Facts and Two Hypotheses for Reform," 38 U. Colo. L. Rev. 431, 452 (1966), contains a summary list.

4. M. Friedman, *Contracts and Conveyances of Real Property* 138 (2d ed., 1963).

5. *Id.,* at 151; *see* Risk, "The Records of Title to Land: A Plea for Reform," U. Tor. L. J. 465, 469 (1971).

6. *Id.,* at 475.

7. That is, the title certificate to an American car must be produced and assigned upon a transfer of ownership in most states. All States Title Book Co., Inc., *Summary of Motor Vehicle Laws and Regulations,* pt. IV (1970, looseleaf); Polk's *Motor Vehicle Registration Manual* 1 (1959, loose-leaf), lists "title" and nontitle states. On ownership and transfer of ships, *see* Healy and Sharpe, *Admiralty* 260-264 (1974).

8. The volume of consumer credit extended in the United States is testimony to this familiarity. In 1965 it stood at $87 billion, and over one half of it financed automobiles. 7 Ency. Americana, "Consumer Credit," at 682 (1970).

9. S. Simpson, *Land Law and Registration* 68 (1976); V. Di Castri, *Thom's Canadian Torrens System* 17 (1962); E. Dowson & V. Shepherd, *Land Registration* (2d ed., 1956); A. Axelrod, C. Berger & Q. Johnstone, *op. cit.,* n. 1, at 683, n. 26 (1971).

10. D. Hayton, *Registered Land* 13-17 (1973). The modifications taken together are arguably more important than the original idea of Torrens' since the working out of the system in practice is an important part of its acceptability. Fiflis, "English Registered Conveyancing: A Study in Effective Land Transfer," 59 N.W.U. L. Rev. 468, 469-70 (1964). Indeed, the English today do not perceive their system for title delivery as a "Torrens" system. R. Ruoff, *An Englishman Looks at the Torrens System* (1958). *See also* Risk, *op. cit.,* n. 5, at n. 26.

11. 4 Am. L. Prop. 638-39, 646-48 (Casner ed., 1952).

12. S. Simpson, *Land Law and Registration* 22 (1976); D. Hayton, *Registered Land* 27 (1973).

13. S. Simpson, *Land Law and Registration* 22 (1976). This rule has exceptions, as where mineral rights are being transferred. *See* Alberta Land Titles Act § 155 (1974).

14. D. Hayton, *Registered Land* 144 (1973).

15. Some United States jurisdictions refer to a registrar of deeds to denote what this writer has referred to as the recorder of deeds. Outside the United States, a registrar of deeds administers the recordation of deeds and other documents evidencing title to real property and a registrar of titles administers a Torrens-like or title-registration office.

16. S. Simpson, *Land Law and Registration* 19-20 (1976).

17. *In re* Land Registry Act, Re Evan's Application (1960), 31 W.W.R. 665 (B.C. Sup. Ct.), reprinted in E. Todd & A. McClean, *Property* 11-6 (1968).

18. E. Todd & A. McClean, *Property* 11-6, -7 (1968).

19. S. Simpson, *Land Law and Registration* 76-86 (1976).

20. 4 Am. L. Prop. 637-38 (Casner ed., 1952). Dowson & Shepherd, *op. cit.,* n. 9.

21. *See* S. Simpson, *Land Law and Registration* 76-86 (1976).

22. *See* Fiflis, *op. cit.,* n. 10, at 469-83.

23. *Id.,* at 482; *see also* E.A. Francis, *Moss' Sale of Land in New South Wales* 203, 308 (5th ed., 1973); D. Hayton, *Registered Land* 36 (1973).

24. *In re* Land Registry Act, Re Evan's Application (1960), 31 W.W.R. 665 (B.C. Sup. Ct.), reprinted in E. Todd & A. McClean, *Property* 11-6 (1968).

25. S. Simpson, *Land Law and Registration* 178-79, 283-84 (1976).

26. *Id.,* at 179; Ontario Land Titles Act, § 177 (1974); Saskatchewan Land

Titles Act § 79 (1974) (correction valid "so far as practical without prejudicing rights obtained in good faith for value.")

27. British Columbia Land Registry Act § 44(1) (1974).

28. Canadian Pacific Railroad V. Turta (1952), 5 W.W.R. (N.S.) 529 (1953), 8 W.W.R. 609 (Alberta Sup. Ct., App. Div.), (1954) 12 W.W.R. (N.S.) 97 (Sup. Ct. Canada).

29. Mass. Gen. L. Ann., ch. 185, § 45 (1936); Davis, *Mass. Conveyancer's Handbook* 196 (2d ed. 1967), and *id.*, at 23 (1973 Supp.); *see also* 7 Haw. Rev. Stat. § 501-71 (1968).

30. E.A. Francis, *Moss' Sale of Land in New South Wales* 278 (5th ed., 1973).

31. *Id.,* at 280.

32. British Columbia Land Registry Act § § 26-30 (1974); Saskatchewan Land Titles Act § 58 (1974).

33. S. Simpson, *Land Law and Registration* 33-36 (1976).

34. *Id.,* at 125-58.

35. Mass. Gen. L. Ann., ch. 185, § 47 (1936); *see also* 7 Haw. Rev. Stat. § 501-51 (1968).

36. Alberta Land Titles Act § 178 (1973); Sask. Land Titles Act § 213(C) (1974).

37. *See* text *supra* at n. 99-100; *cf.* Mass. Gen. L. Ann. § 47 (1936), which does insure acreage. The Massachusetts system of title registration is based on precise engineering and surveying standards. Land Ct., Comm. of Mass., *Manual of Instructions for the Survey of Lands and Preparation of Plats* (1971).

38. Fiflis, *op. cit.,* n. 10 at 478-79.

39. S. Simpson, *Land Law and Registration* 136-43 (1976).

40. Carlson v. Duncan (1931), D.L.R. 570, 2 W.W.R. 34 (B.C. Ct. App.) (contract to cut timber held registrable according to the words of the agreement).

41. British Columbia Land Registry Act § § 2, 128, 165, 182 (1974).

42. Manitoba Real Property Act § 59 (1974).

43. Ontario Land Titles Act § § 18, 23 (1974).

44. Manitoba Real Property Act § 61(2) (1974).

45. British Columbia Land Registry Act § 38A(1)-(2) (1974).

46. Mass. Gen. L. Ann., ch. 185, § 53 (1936); 7 Haw. Rev. Stat. § 501-87 (1968); *contra* Alberta Land Titles Act § 42 (1973).

47. British Columbia Land Registry Act § 38A(1)-(2) (1974).

48. (1902) ch. 428, discussed in Farrand, *Contract and Conveyance* 170, 176, 179 (1968).

49. This is commonly supposed a defect in the recording system. Miller v. Green, 264 Wis. 159, 58 N.W.2d 704 (1953), held a duty to inquire binding on a later purchaser. *See generally* 4 Am. L. Prop. 607-08 (Casner ed., 1952).

50. British Columbia Land Registry Act § 38(1) (1974) lists exceptions

and reservations in Crown grants, state and local tax liens, leases of less than three years' duration, public highway or water easements, condemnation rights, *lis pendens* or mechanic's liens, charges noted on the certificate, and the "right of any person" to show fraudulent registration or a misdescription of the property on the certificate. *See also* 7 Haw. Rev. Stat. § 501-82 (1968).

51. Gibbs v. Messer (1891) A.C. 248 (P.C. from Aust.).

52. S. Simpson, *Land Law and Registration* 175-87 (1976).

53. Mass. Gen. L. Ann., ch. 185, § § 99-108 (1936); *accord,* British Columbia Land Registry Act § 222(3) (1974).

54. Alberta Land Titles Act § 175(1) (1973); British Columbia Land Registry Act § 222(6) (1974); Saskatchewan Land Titles Act § 104 (1974).

55. Alberta Land Titles Act § 178 (1973); Saskatchewan Land Titles Act § 207 (1974); *see also* British Columbia Land Registry Act § 229 (1974); M. Friedman, *Contracts and Conveyances of Real Property* 152-53 (2d ed., 1963).

56. Alberta Land Titles Act § 136 (1973); British Columbia Land Registry Act § 269 (1974); *see generally* V. DiCastri, *Thom's Canadian Torrens System* 601-28 (2d ed., 1962).

57. *Id.,* at 609-11.

58. *See, e.g.,* British Columbia Land Registry Act § 212 (1974).

59. Alberta Land Titles Act § 136 (1973).

60. *Id.*

61. Interview with Mr. Ian Dickins, Registrar, Northern Registry District, Province of Alberta, Edmonton, Alberta, Dec. 2, 1975, at 2 p.m.

62. British Columbia Land Registry Act § 212 (1974).

63. Interview with D.H. Storche, Registrar, Vancouver Land Registry District, Vancouver, British Columbia, Dec. 5, 1975, at 10 a.m.

64. Fiflis, *op. cit.,* n. 10, at 475-77.

65. Jones v. York County, 47 F.2d 837 (CCA 7, 1931); *e.g.,* Va. P.L. 1916, ch. 62; *contra* Mass. Gen. L. Ann., ch. 185, § 52.

66. Fiflis, *op. cit.,* n. 10, at 468, n. 1.

67. *Id.,* at 477-78.

68. Illinois Rev. Stat. Ann., ch. 30, § 45-152 (1961).

69. Fiflis, *op. cit.,* n. 10, at 477-78.

70. *See* text *supra* at n. 28.

71. For an early summary of argument in favor of title registration, *see* Beale, "Registration of Title to Land," 6 Harv. L. Rev. 369 (1893), and a reply, Balch, "Land Transfer—A Different Point of View," 6 Harv. L. Rev. 410 (1893). Beale finds comforting precedent for the registry system in the old English copyhold. M. Yeakle (ed.), *Torrens System of Registration and Transfer of the Title to Real Estate* (1894). Burke & Kittrie, *op. cit.,* n. 1, at II-A-3 (1972).

72. Cushan, "Torrens Titles and Title Insurance," 85 U. Pa. L. Rev. 589 (1937); "Common Sense and the Torrens Fallacy," 26 Law and Banking 236 (1933) (no author listed); Burke & Kittrie, *op. cit.,* n. 1, at II-A-3.

73. Chaplin, "Record Title to Land," 6 Harv. L. Rev. 302 (1893).

74. Indeed, R. Torrens, on his return to England in the 1870s, did not register his land under the 1862 Registry Act. In 1875 he said: "It was my intention to have put my land under Lord Cairn's Act, until I found out that it gave no title as regards boundaries." Niblack, *The Torrens System* 19 (1903).

75. England, on the other hand, never had this stumbling block; recording acts had been proposed as early as 1529 when public "enrollment" of transfers of certain types was proposed. This change was successfully resisted by the gentry. D. Hayton, *Registered Land* 9-10 (1973). It was accepted in the United States in the form of the recording acts. S. Simpson, *Land Law and Registration* 86 (1976).

76. State ex rel. Atty. Gen. v. Guilbert, 56 Ohio St. 575, 47 N.E. 551 (1897).

77. Peo. v. Simon, 176 Ill. 165, 52 N.W. 910, 44 L.R.A. 801 (1898).

78. With this, opponents were able to argue that a quiet-title action was the common-law equivalent of a registry. Balch, *op. cit.,* n. 63, citing Arndt v. Griggs, 134 U.S. 316 (1890) (authorizing service to nonresident by publication, in a suit involving title to land); *see also* Comment, "Modernizing the Quiet Title Action," 68 Yale L. J. 1245 (1959).

79. Mass. Gen. L. Ann., ch. 185 (1974), but first enacted in 1898, establishing a land-registration court.

80. People v. Chase, 165 Ill. 527, 46 N.E. 454 (1896); *cf.* State v. Westfall, 85 Minn. 437, 89 N.W. 175 (1902). *Cf.* Uniform Land Registration Act, 9 U.L. Ann. 217 (1917) for the generally approved form of a registry statute. Annot., 11 A.L.R. 772 (1911). It had been adopted by the Am. Bar Assn. in 1916 in its "judicial" form.

81. Burke & Kittrie, *op. cit.,* n. 1, at II-A-6, -7, III-B-8, -9, III-C-9 (1972).

82. A. Axelrod, C. Berger, & Q. Johnstone, *Land Transfer and Finance* 684 (1971).

83. The principal treatise on registration during these years was Niblack, *An Analysis of the Torrens System of Conveying Land* (1912) (the author was affiliated with the Chicago Title and Trust Company, a title insurer). *Cf.* McCall, "The Torrens System after Thirty-Five Years," 10 N.C. L. Rev. 329 (1932); Note, "Impeachment of Torrens Titles," 42 Harv. L. Rev. 945 (1929).

84. Mass. Gen. L. Ann., ch. 185, § 53 (1936).

85. American Land Co. v. Zeiss, 219 U.S. 47 (1911).

86. A. Axelrod, C. Berger, & Q. Johnstone, *Land Transfer and Finance* 684 (1971).

87. Fiflis, *op. cit.,* n. 10.

88. *Id.*

89. Hawaii Rev. Stat. §§ 501-1 thru 501-218 (1968).

90. Mass. Gen. L. Ann., ch. 185, §§ 1 through 108 (1974); Burke & Kittrie, *op. cit.,* n. 1 at III-B-8.

91. 29 Minn. Stat. Ann. § 508 (1974).

92. Illinois Rev. Stat. Ann., ch. 30, §§ 45-152 (1974). (The Illinois registration system operates on a local option basis, and Cook County, alone, adopted it by a substantial margin of votes in 1898).

93. Eliason v. Wilborn, 281 U.S. 457 (1930). As is the case where a special office or court is empowered to hear and decide registration cases.

94. As is the case in Massachusetts.

95. *E.g.,* R.L. Woodbury, *Manual of Instructions for the Survey of Lands and Preparation of Plans to be Filed in the Land Court* (1971).

96. In Massachusetts, this clientele seems to be land developers who encounter title problems during the acquisition of large tracts of land. Burke & Kittrie, *op. cit.,* n. 1.

97. The Torrens law was enacted amid a series of progressive-era legislative efforts of the incoming governor Peter Norbeck, an owner of a well-drilling business. Schell, *History of South Dakota* 265-66 (1961). In 1917 the legislature enacted 376 bills of the 576 brought before it. Most of the important bills were for establishing public enterprises of various sorts—a cement plant, electric projects, a state bank, rural credits, and bank-deposit guarantees. *Id.* Norbeck in his address to the legislature (J. S.D. House, Jan. 2, 1917, at 69, 97) said Torrens "seems to supply a remedy" for the problem of expensive, cumbersome abstracts.

The Torrens legislation was introduced by a young legislator, J. Reeves (b. 1886), a graduate of the U. Minn. L. School, just elected to the legislature. S.D. Ann. 1917, at 641. *See* Sen. Bill No. 53, "An Act Governing the Registration of Land and the Title Thereto, Known as the Torrens System," whose legislative progress may be followed: J. S.D. Sen. 1917, 175 (Jan. 16, 1917), 274 (Feb. 1, 1917), 317 (Feb. 3, 1917) and 442 (Feb. 10, 1917). The Senate passed the bill 37-3.

But the system's introduction by a freshman legislator was not its sole weakness, for its heartiest supporter was outgoing Governor Burne, who addressed the legislature (J. S.D. Sen., Jan. 2, 1917, at 9, 24-25) as follows:

The present custom of indiscriminately recording, without method or system or limit, any instrument offered affecting the title to real property, and then, on the occasion of each new transfer or encumbrance, listing up or abstracting each and all of such instruments or entries, from the beginning of time down to each respective date, hiring lawyers to tell us what they think it all means and to overrule other lawyers who formerly told some one else what they thought it meant, is cumbersome, archaic, and absurd. Its only virtue is that it is ponderous and mysterious. . . . [I]t has nothing to commend it except its complexity and expense.

Still, the legislation passed at a time when attorneys charged $5 for examining abstracts of twenty entries or less; $10 if a probate or foreclosure proceeding was disclosed. S.D. Bar Repts. 1918, at 35; *id.* at 85, the president of the Bar Association made no reference to the Torrens system in his address to his organization.

Companion bills to make uniform transfer documents with blanks failed of passage. Sen. Bill. No. 71, 72. S.D. Sen. J. 1917, at 201, 211, 227, 339.

98. S.D. L. 1917, ch. 368 (1917); *see* S.D. Comp. L. § § 3060-3134 (1929).

99. R. Powell, *Registration of Title to Land in the State of New York* 259 (1938).

100. *Id.,* at 260.

101. S.D. L. 1917, § 6(3).

102. *Id.,* § 6(6).

103. *Id.,* § 6(5).

104. *Id.,* § 6(10).

105. *Id.,* § 8.

106. *Id.,* § 11.

107. *Id.*

108. *Id.,* § § 12-13.

109. *Id.,* § 12.

110. *Id.,* § 11.

111. *Id.,* § 13.

112. *Id.,* § § 25-27.

113. *Id.,* § 21.

114. *Id.,* § 23.

115. *Id.,* § 36.

116. *Id.,* § 34.

117. Powell, *supra* n. 99, at 260.

118. Bordwell, "Registration to Title of Land," 12 Ia. L. Rev. 114, 128 (1927).

119. McCall, "The Torrens System—After Thirty-five Years," 10 N.C. L. Rev. 342, 344, n. 50; *id.,* at 348.

120. Powell, *supra* n. 99, at 260.

121. *Id.* These thirty-seven registrations were the result of one subdivision, Laswell's Addition, built in Orkley, South Dakota, by an attorney-developer. The certificates are all canceled today, but some are still on record in the courthouse. Interview with Gladyce Crosby, Register of Deeds, Sisseton, Roberts County, S.D., June 4, 1975 at 3:45 p.m.

122. The presence of the state surveyor in Huron, the county seat, may also have encouraged use. D. Robinson, *Ency. S. Dak.* 717 (1925). No certificates survive on the public records. Interview with Gladys Johnson, Beadle County Register of Deeds, Huron, S.D., June 4, 1975, at 11 a.m.

123. Powell, *supra* n. 99, 260.

124. People ex rel. Kern v. Chase, 165 Ill. 527, 46 N.E. 454 (1897); State ex rel. Monet v. Guilbert, 56 Ohio St. 575, 47 N.E. 551 (1897); Ohio Const.,

Art. II, § 40. *Contra* Tyler v. Court of Registration, 175 Mass. 71, 55 N.E. 812, 51 L.R.A. 433 (1900) (Holmes, C.J.). Some twenty states adopted the registration system.

125. Virginia enacted its law in 1916, the year before North and South Dakota, the last states to do so, and the year in which the American Bar Association adopted a model act on the subject. Va. Pub. L. 1916, ch. 62.

126. Massie, "Reform of Our Land Laws," 11 Va. L. Reg. 359 (1905).

127. *Id.,* at 660.

128. *Id.,* at 581-82.

129. *Id.*

130. Sym., "The Torrens System: An Open Symposium," 11 Va. L. Reg. 570-608 (1905).

131. Massie, "The Torrens System," 11 Va. Bar Reg. 649, 660 (1905).

132. *Id.*

133. *Id.*

134. Note, "The Torrens System of Land Registration in Virginia," 14 Va. L. Rev. 675 (1928).

135. This is not atypical of the debate in other American jurisdictions. *See generally* M. Friedman, *Conveyances and Contracts of Real Property* 152 (2d ed., 1963).

136. Massie, *op. cit.,* n. 126, at 366.

137. Rood, "Registration of Land Titles," 12 Mich. L. Rev. 379 (1914); *cf.* Warren, Book Review, "A Manual of Land Registration," 32 Harv. L. Rev. 297 (1919).

138. *E.g.,* Freeman, "Bankers Refuse Torrens Titles," 15 Law and Bank. 235 (1922).

139. Fiflis, *op. cit.,* n. 10.

140. M. Friedman, *Contracts and Conveyances of Real Property* 154 (2d ed., 1963).

141. Staples, "The Conclusiveness of a Torrens Certificate of Title," 8 Minn. L. Rev. 200 (1924).

142. New York Bar Ass'n (1938).

143. Powell, *Registration of Title to Land in the State of New York* (1938), has been much criticized for its conclusions, which seem detached from the prior body of analysis. For the criticism, *see* Fairchild & Springer, "A Criticism of Professor Richard R. Powell's book Entitled Registration of Title to Land in the State of New York," 24 Corn. L. Q. 557 (1937); Book Review, "Registration of the Title to Land in the State of New York," 16 N.Y.U. L. Q. Rev. 510 (1938); McDougal & Brabner-Smith, "Land Title Transfer: A Regression," 48 Yale L. J. 1125 (1939); Bordwell, "The Resurrection of Registration of Title," 7 U. Chi. L. Rev. 470 (1940) (not a critical analysis, but necessary to see the sequence of debate); McDougal, "Title Registration and Land Reform: A Reply," 8 U. Chi. L. Rev. 63 (1940).

144. "A survey of its experience in the United States and the British Commonwealth . . . is so solid and negatively impressive that its voluntary development outside its present effective areas appears unlikely," M. Friedman, *Contracts and Conveyances of Real Property* 154 (2d ed., 1963).

145. Hudak, "Registration of Land Titles Act: The Ohio Torrens Law," 20 Clev. St. L. Rev. 617 (1971); Quinn, "Registration of Title: A Statutory Comparison," 4 St. Lou. U. L. Rev. 229 (1957); Patton, "Evaluation of Legislation on Proof of Title to Land Registration," 30 Wash. L. Rev. 224 (1955); Comment, "The Case for Land Registration," 6 Mercer L. Rev. 320 (1955).

146. R. Powell, *Registration of the Title to Land in the State of New York* 74 (1938).

147. *Id.,* at 24, 59, 66-67, and Supps. A, G, and Q.

148. *Id.,* at 75.

149. Fiflis, *op. cit.,* n. 10.

150. Powell, *op. cit.,* n. 146, at 28-33, 73.

151. Fiflis, *op. cit.,* n. 10.

152. Powell, *op. cit.,* n. 146, at 68.

153. Canadian Inst. of Surveying, "Cadastral Conference Proceedings," Oct. 24-25, 1974, Ottawa, Canada.

154. Powell, *op. cit.,* n. 146, at 59.

155. Fairness to Powell requires a statement that, in 1938, when he wrote, such legislation had not yet had much impact on conveyancing, but Powell's sense of constitutional law may have prevented his appreciation of their potential from developing. *Id.,* at 24.

156. L. Jaffe & N. Nathanson, *Administrative Law* 33, 81 (1968), points out that aside from two 1935 cases, ". . . the Supreme Court had never invalidated a delegation. . . ." "And since those cases no delegation has been invalidated by the Supreme Court."

157. *E.g.,* E. Dowson & V. Shepherd, *Land Registration* (2d ed., 1956); D. Hayton, *Registered Land* (1973); E.A. Francis, *Moss' Sale of Land in New South Wales* (1973).

158. 12 *Ency. Britannica,* "Migration," at 185-189 (1974).

159. 18 *Ency. Britannica,* "Urbanization," at 1080 (1974).

160. Roberts, "The Case of the Unwary Home Buyer: The Housing Merchant Did It," 51 Corn. L. Q. 835 (1967).

161. Powell, *op. cit.,* n. 146, at 35-40, 65-66, 100, 143, 181, 206, 244 provides the figures: He found that urban or urbanizing areas provided the bulk of registrations.

162. D. Hayton, *Registered Land* (1973).

163. W. Leach, *Property Law Indicted* 67 (1967).

164. *See* text *supra* at n. 35.

165. *See* text *supra* at n. 18.

166. Fiflis, "Land Transfer Improvement: The Basic Facts and Two Hypotheses for Reform," 38 U. Colo. L. Rev. 431, 432-33 (1966), gives his own reasons for reconsidering title registration; some are presented in the body of this text, and all are worth consideration.

167. McBride & Clawson, "Negotiation and Land Conversion," 36 J. Am. Inst. Planners 22 (1970), argues that urbanization is an empirically identifiable happening. Identification is made through (1) rising but elastic land prices for parcels interchangeable in use, and (2) speculative ownership. It subdivides land and historically results in an oversupply of land parcels. R. Bryant, *Private Property and Public Control* 157-61, 164-65 (1972). This in turn means that the contract vendor of land in oversupplied markets becomes a forced purchaser when buyers default on their contracts. Lindeman, "Anatomy of Land Speculation," 42 J. Am. Inst. Planners 142, 149-50:

[A] collapse of a boom . . . can take a long time; in the meanwhile both during and after a market boom this land which has been encumbered with unattractive lien provisions can constitute an effective diminution of the supply of usable land.

In a somewhat related vein, the complicated chain of deals that may develop over a single piece of property can lead to questions of title. . . . *Id.*, at 149.

168. Burke & Kittrie, *op. cit.*, n. 1

169. Lawyer's Title Ins. Co. v. McKee, 354 S.W.2d 401 (Tex. Civ. App. 1962).

170. Kessler, "The Settlement Squeeze," Wash. P., Jan. 9-12, 1972, at A-1.

171. *E.g.,* N.Y. Real Prop. L., § 337-2(8)-(9) (1968).

172. British Columbia Land Registry Act §§ 83-121 (1974).

173. S. Simpson, *Land Law and Registration* 284-85, 300-03 (1976).

174. *Id.,* at 302.

175. *Id.,* at 180.

176. *Id.*

177. Interview with Mr. Brian Kitching, Director of Training, H.M. Land Registry, London, June 17, 1974. H.M. Land Registry, "Registration of Title to Land" 6 (1968). The British legal profession seems in accord: "Where the client has bought the land with a view to development and selling off in plats, the solicitor is clearly failing in his duty if he does not advise registration." "Land Registry Pamphlet," 24 Conv. (N.S.) 338. Lower solicitors' fees are another result of allowing this type of registration: "Conveyancer's Remuneration," 35 Conv. and Prop. Lawyer 69 (1971). *See generally* "Registered Land Conveyancing—Practice Notes—Eighth Series," 36 Conv. (N.S.) and Prop. Lawyer 152, 157 (1972) for the procedure for registering "building estates," subdivisions, in noncompulsory areas. Over 50 percent of all registrations annually are of building estates. *See Reports of the Chief Land Registrar* 1967, at 6; 1965, at 5.

178. British Columbia Land Registry Act § 83(1) (1974).

179. *Id.,* §§ 91-93, 95.

180. *Id.,* § 99.

181. Ontario Land Titles Act, § 161 (1974); Saskatchewan Land Titles Act § 104 (1974).

182. The states, as listed in Sackvill & Neave, *Property* 405, n. 90 (1968) are New South Wales, Tasmania, and Victoria. The same authors report: "Registration facilitates subdivision of large blocks of land" because each purchaser receives a certificate of title which is the legal equivalent of a discrete chain-of-title evidence.

183. *See* Axelrod *et al., supra* n. 86, at 770, n. 130.

184. S.D.L. 1917, ch. 368, §§ 6(5)-(10); *see* text *supra,* at n. 97.

185. S.D.L. 1917, ch. 368, § 6(5).

186. Schroder v. City of New York, 371 U.S. 208, 214 (1962); *see also* Walker v. City of Hutchinson, 352 U.S. 112 (1956), noted in 25 Tenn. L. Rev. 495 (1956); City of New York v. New York, N.H., and H.R.R., 344 U.S. 293 (1953).

187. Mullane v. Central Hanover Bank and Trust Co., 339 U.S. 306, 317 (1950).

188. Brown v. Fed. Nat'l Mortgage Ass'n, Del. Supr., 359 A.2d 661 (1976).

189. Comment, "Enhancing the Marketability of Land: The Suit to Quiet Title," 68 Yale L. J. 1245, 1265-72 (1959).

190. *See* text *supra,* ch. 2.

191. E. Todd & A. McClean, *Property* 11-3 (1968) (land brokers established in N.S.W.); R. Steacy, *Land Titles: Registration in Canada and the U.S.* 3 (1974).

192. W.B. Leach, *Property Law Indicted* 68 (1967).

**Part III
Federal Scrutiny of Our
Conveyancing**

6

Federal Investigations into Conveyancing

This discussion has proceeded on an assumption that regulation of settlement costs alone is not an improvement in the patterns themselves and probably will not produce improvements in the future. Otherwise, one might have proceeded directly from Chapter 1 to this chapter, without acquiring an understanding of the patterns underlying the costs levied on a settlement.

This chapter is intended to demonstrate the validity of this assumption and to reassure the reader that the intervening discussions have been worthwhile. The foregoing suggested changes in conveyancing patterns can be implemented by state government. All (except possibly some forms of title registries) avoid expensive regulatory bureaucracies. Tract indexes and title-search legislation are reforms that the parties to a conveyance are free either to use or reject. Changes without this advantage should be subjected to the closest scrutiny. Most of the changes achieved by the legislative results of the federal activity described here may ultimately fail to be self-administered (i.e., by vendors and purchasers) and may require bureaucracies to police them.

In the future it will be important to devise remedies and sanctions that dovetail with existing patterns rather than place a layer of bureauractic review over them. Moreover, the protracted debate over federal legislation suggests that the initial policy consideration presented in Chapter 3 applies here as well: The wisest policy might have been inaction. It lasts as long as the government remains without a coherent strategy for conveyancing improvements and rests on the premise that regulation might easily become an obstacle to improvement.

Introduction

The first federal attempts to make changes in our conveyancing and settlement practices have involved procedural changes rather than changes in the substantive law governing our conveyancing patterns. Adding steps to the federally regulated conveyance seems more feasible politically because the results of the process remain the same—and no provider of settlement services has his income affected. The traditional emphasis on the local law aspects of each transaction gives such reform a particular appeal because the nonuniform character of conveyancing law makes substantive change that much more difficult to achieve. These themes are illustrated by the federal debate over regulation of the conveyancing process.

The long-term phenomena that have made conveyancing a political issue are discernible in the growth of American suburbs since the 1940s. The "vast preponderance of new housing" built since World War II has come to the suburbs; in 1970, about 38 percent of the population of the United States lived in suburban areas of our SMSAs. Moreover, the growth rate of jobs has recently been greatest in suburbs, far above that of the central city.[1] Economic opportunities were initially controlled by entry into suburban housing markets where ownership, not leaseholds, predominated. Prospects for the growth of other forms of tenure are not bright;[2] indeed, the ownership of apartments increased as rental housing declined. Such ownership in our conveyancing system is treated as a fee-simple purchase. Closing and settlement costs remain high, and closings are likely to be even more complex as the burden of complying with condominium laws is added to normal procedures.[3]

In a time of rising housing costs, tight money, and environmental controls, the volume of construction goes down.[4] When these three factors combine with a near-zero population growth rate, we can see the time ten to twenty years from now when the formation of new households will drop substantially.[5] Henceforth the people whose income depends on producing housing and servicing land transfers will have to maintain their incomes at past levels with a fixed or declining inventory. In the real estate industry one aspect of this process has already been seen: The credit squeeze of 1965-66 forced many servicers of realty transfers to seek new lines of work within their field of expertise; brokers established escrow agencies; exterminators provided general inspection services; title insurers began to charge for preparing documents; attorneys began to charge for title insurance applications. So it went, with the number of charges multiplying.

The importance of access to housing ownership and economic pressures were compelling reasons for the government to give attention to the conveyancing process. It was a political issue that emerged when the middle class was gaining in cohesiveness as well as economic and locational stability in the suburbs.

Past Governmental Attention to Closing Costs

A chronicle of the efforts of the federal government, particularly the Congress, to address itself to the issue of closing and settlement costs moves very slowly. In 1937 the Public Works Administration assembled much data in conducting a study of all laws affecting real estate. Although this project concerned mainly land registration or Torrens acts, it also examined foreclosure proceedings and the allowable costs that could be collected in such proceedings.

In 1954 the government explored the feasibility of insuring its own mortgage loans against fires and hazards rather than continuing to purchase this protection from private companies. The potential savings persuaded Congress to amend the National Housing Act to give the government this power.[6] A decade later the legislative history of the Truth-in-Lending Act also produced some ancillary research into home-loan charges.[7]

In 1965 the Institute of Urban Life of the University of Chicago prepared a report for the Housing and Home Finance Agency on closing costs for single-family homes in Chicago, Indianapolis, Newark, St. Louis, St. Paul, and San Antonio. This report was eventually published, but no action was ever taken with regard to it.[8]

In 1966 the General Accounting Office investigated the propriety of buying title insurance for government property acquired through foreclosure proceedings, under the Veterans' Administration Loan Guarantee Program in Florida. After reviewing 343 selected cases, minor title defects were uncovered in only 15 cases and were easily cured. The GAO report states in part:

In 1960 the St. Petersburg Regional Office commented that it had never found it necessary to refuse to accept the property due to an incurable title defect and that within 15 years there has been no case in which the title has not been acceptable.[9]

The GAO report concluded that potentially $255,000 could be saved by discontinuing the purchase of title insurance on foreclosures in the St. Petersburg region alone.[10] The VA regional office eventually modified its practice of requiring title insurance and adopted a more flexible policy.

In 1969 Congresswoman Lenore Sullivan became chairperson of an ad hoc subcommittee on home financing practices and procedures. She later said:

The serious abuses in the residential real estate field were first brought to the attention of the Banking and Currency Committee in 1969 after Chairman Patman appointed an *Ad Hoc* Subcommittee on Home Financing Practices and Procedures to investigate speculative housing sales activity in inter city housing in the District of Columbia. This investigation grew out of the series of articles in the Washington *Post* on the operations of the Republic Federal Savings and Loan Association which had financed the large number of inner city residential properties purchased and resold at unconscionable prices by real estate speculators victimizing low income families in the District.* * *

In our investigation in addition to alarming instances on the part of lenders in joining with unscrupulous speculators to inflate the value of inner city housing, we uncovered the outlines in the District of Columbia of the FHA 235 scandal on subsidized housing which was later documented in great detail by the full Committee in a comprehensive national investigation.

In the course of our *Ad Hoc* Subcommittee inquiry into real estate abuses in the District of Columbia we also went into the matter of settlement charges and settlement practices. Sec. 701 of the 1970 Emergency Housing Act reflected the disturbing information we developed.[11]

Although this inquiry focused on financial institutions and the manner in which they abetted the phenomenon of central-city real estate speculation and swindling, the committee did not limit itself to this. In fact, it "felt that the time had come for an examination of the whole spectrum of home financing practices and procedures."[12]

Also in 1969 the President's Commission on Mortgage Interest Rates reported to the Congress. It was critical of HUD and VA regulations and procedures enforced at that time, stating:

Some of the present regulations seem unnecessarily restrictive or cumbersome . . . ; this is discouraging many builders, lenders, and individual buyers and sellers from taking maximum advantage of the programs—particularly the special assistance programs.[13]

Its report recommended reducing the mortgage insurance premium by adopting a more realistic way of calculating risks; streamlining rules and regulations for governmental programs; and making uniform and interchangeable HUD and VA credit reports, appraisals, and foreclosure regulations and procedures. The Senate responded with the Mortgage Credit Act of 1970, § 2, a bill introduced by Senator Sparkman to increase the availability of funds for financing housing. In pertinent portions this bill read as follows.

The Secretary of Housing and Urban Development and the Administrator of Veterans Affairs are respectively authorized and directed to prescribe standards governing the amounts of settlement costs allowable in connection with the financing of such housing in any . . . area. . . .
   The Secretary and the Administrator shall undertake a joint study and make recommendations to Congress not later than July 1, 1970, with respect to legislative and administrative actions which should be taken to reduce mortgage settlement costs and to standardize these costs for all geographic areas.[14]

This proposal was clear enough: The Senate felt that the time had come to open a full-scale inquiry into the entire closing transaction and its attendant "high" costs. Ultimately this intent was to be realized by § 701 of the Emergency Home Finance Act of 1970.[15]

The Inquiry Begins

The majority of the closing and settlement costs listed in Chapter 1 are mortgage costs,[16] and it was these that on April 1, 1969, the President's Commission on Mortgage Interest Rates recommended that HUD and the VA study. In their view the lack of predictable costs and the purchaser's inability to anticipate their magnitude before the closing meant that he could not shop around for less expensive alternatives. HUD and the VA were to review such costs in mortgage transactions underwritten by them and to study the feasibility of standardizing or reducing these costs.[17] They were to report in a year.
   The Commission's primary concern, however, was the rapid rise in mortgage

interest rates since 1965 when a two-year period of tight money sharply reduced the amounts available for home mortgages.[18] It was in this context that they called for a study of closing costs. A year later Congress was still enacting the Emergency Home Finance Act of 1970, which would implement the commission's call for a cost study.[19]

HUD and the VA are traditionally involved in mortgage transactions as underwriters. Federal regulations allow HUD to review mortgage transaction costs to see that costs assessed in its underwritten transactions do not exceed those prevailing in the locale.[20] In practice, federal underwriting for a mortgage as well as a title insurance policy had become a precondition to its moving into the secondary national mortgage market. Officially HUD is neutral as to the type of title-delivery system underlying proof of its mortgages and professes by regulation to follow local custom, but as a matter of practice, title insurance is most often used. Both title insurance and HUD underwriting serve as the underpinning for a national mortgage market. Title insurance guarantees the title to the property; federal underwriting guarantees the loan itself; and both enhance the negotiability of these loans.[21] No one knew then whether the market would function in the absence of one or both of these features; their use had evolved in the natural market process of minimizing the risk in the lender's investment, not as the result of a policy. Where conscious choice was possible, however, as in the better-counseled savings banks participating in the market,[22] much title insurance seemed redundant if federal underwriting was present—and vice versa—because a title failure often will eventually affect the value of the property secured by the underwritten loan.[23]

HUD and the VA, whatever their existing administrative power to regulate closing and settlement costs, had long regulated one such cost—the fee for processing applications for federal underwriting. In the 1950s in response to complaints that the fee was too high, the Federal Housing Administration, then part of HUD's predecessor agency, the Housing and Home Finance Agency, had standardized the fee at 1 percent of the mortgage amount.[24] It was thought that this would reduce the fee in some regions, but the mortgage lenders using federal programs accepted it because, overall, some lenders could increase costs, and furthermore, a percentage basis meant that future increases were built into the fee structure, thereby freeing the industry of future administrative review.

Arguably the reliance on a customary-charges rule and past action on only that application fee suggest administrative unwillingness to involve government in closing and settlement cost matters. FHA's involvement as an underwriter in FHHA and then HUD's mortgage programs meant that in most years its activity realized a profit for the Federal Treasury.[25] In its housing-production programs, the department and its predecessors had been concerned with the subsidization of low and moderate-income, new-house production, but the FHA-underwriting program had for the most part never been made a component of those programs.[26] Because of its profitability and underwriting of the mortgage banking industry, which became its constituent and supporter, it became an independent self-supporting organization within HUD after the creation of that department in 1965. It rarely provoked strict congressional scrutiny, and when the FHA was moved intact into the HUD administrative hierarchy, its independent existence was barely challenged. By 1970[27] it was official department policy to downplay its autonomous existence. Its programs were referred to as "HUD-FHA's," but its autonomy within HUD was still great.

A sign of a challenge to this independence came in 1968 when Congress adopted Johnson Administration proposals for a homeownership program for the poor.[28] This shifted federal interest from rental programs to homeownership programs, and since the use of these new subsidies was unprecedently high,[29] more people became interested in the operation of federal programs. When rental housing was the focus of federal concern, the underwriters could deal with the home-building industry on a service basis; federal policy assumed that subsidizing this sector of the construction industry was socially useful. Homeownership programs, however, broadened both the bureaucracy's constituency and also increased congressional interest in protecting the individual users of the programs. What had been dealt with in terms of industry and economics was, with homeownership, now put in consumer terms, personalized, and made into a political issue.

The FHA was reluctant to broaden its supervision of mortgage transactions. First, it was operating a profitable and self-supporting government activity, and closer supervision of its constituency, other than occasional enforcement of the customary-charges rule and supervision of its own processing fee, might endanger the underwriting function it saw as its primary mission. Second, the closing-cost study called for by the 1969 commission could precipitate a change in its role from subsidizer to regulator. Tacit agency policy was to avoid this broadened role, and the agency realized the potential of a shift to publicly supported homeownership. Third, the agency realized that the impact of its programs on settlement costs was greater than was commonly recognized: In the course of attracting investors to their programs, they had allowed lenders to compensate for below-market interest rates with front-end costs paid by the vendor. Thus if FHA mortgages carried a 7 percent interest rate in 1970 and the conventional or unsubsidized mortgage interest rate was 8 ½ percent, the difference was to some extent made up to the private lender through "discount points"; these were paid by the vendor for the lender's extension of a mortgage loan to the purchaser.[30] Federal regulations and sometimes state usury laws prohibited purchasers from paying these so vendors paid them as an inducement to make the loan. The burden on the purchaser was no lighter than in the conventional market if the vendor passed these costs on to the purchaser; if the vendor could not pass these costs on, there was likely to be no sale through the federal program. Fourth, the FHA realized that close supervision of local lenders was, from the administrative point of view, likely to require internal checks and policing its own personnel. The local abuses uncovered at about this time in the 1968 homeownership programs seemed to show this only too clearly.[31]

But federally subsidized and underwritten home building (indeed, all home building) was slowing down during the 1960s.[32] This combined with tight mortgage money heightened political interest, and a search for new forms of federal housing subsidies formed a backdrop that overwhelmed the FHA's reluctance to investigate the mortgage market it traditionally served.

Enabling Legislation

In February 1970 the House of Representatives held hearings on various measures such as providing Treasury obligations and issuing mortgage-backed, federally underwritten securities and certificates[33] designed to alleviate the current shortage of mortgage funds. Closing and settlement costs were alluded to in general terms throughout these hearings, which included mortgage industry representatives, political figures, and federal administrators.[34] There were discussions of discount points and questions as to whether they could be eliminated by market pressure.[35] (The maximum permissible interest rate on FHA-VA mortgages had just risen from 7 ½ percent to 8 ½ percent, but the points had not been eliminated by that.)

As has been mentioned, the Senate inquiry into closing and settlement charges originated with the Mortgage Credit Act of 1970. The hearings framing the mandate for this study were, with two exceptions, cursory in their treatment of its scope and basic methodology.[36] Only Professor John Payne of the University of Alabama Law School and Mr. Thomas Holstein, president of the American Land Title Association, addressed themselves directly to how this study should proceed. Professor Payne urged that an independent agency carried out a comprehensive nation-wide study, which would also study costs in conjunction with the services rendered. He emphasized the need for more information about conventional, as well as governmental, practice in this area, before Congress should act.[37] The American Land Title Association, the trade group for title abstractors and insurers, went on record opposing the study. It objected, understandably, to the fact that the study was premised on the idea that settlement costs were too high. The Association respectfully suggested that such a study be conducted on an "extremely objective basis"[38] and subsequently commenced its own study. It would compile raw data on settlements in HUD's study areas, as well as a few other counties,[39] but draw no conclusions, for it aimed to show the diversity of charges and, therefore, presumably, the difficulty of drafting any legislation on the subject.

All the affected federal agencies endorsed the study, but several recommended an extension of time, to July 1, 1971, which was later granted.[40] Several private-interest groups—the Council of Housing Producers, the National

Association of Home Builders, and the National Housing Conference—endorsed the study but refrained from going into specifics.[41] The response varied for groups within the conveyancing industry itself: The National Association of Real Estate Boards enthusiastically welcomed the inquiry;[42] the Mortgage Banker's Association, more cautious, strongly urged the committee to avoid acting before all the facts were in hand;[43] and the savings and loan association representative had no comment.[44] The American Bar Association was not represented during the course of the hearings and took no position on this matter subsequently, although in the past it had expressed its concern over conveyancing costs, and the American Bar Foundation had financed a study by Professor Payne in this field.[45]

As finally enacted on July 24, 1970, Section 701 of the Emergency Home Finance Act provided:

(a) With respect to housing built, rehabilitated, or sold with assistance provided under the National Housing Act or under chapter 37 of title 38, United States Code, the Secretary of Housing and Urban Development and the Administrator of Veterans Affairs are respectively authorized and directed to prescribe standards governing the amounts of settlement costs allowable in connection with the financing of such housing in any such area. Such standards shall—

(1) be established after consultation between the Secretary and the Administrator;

(2) be consistent in any area for housing assisted under the National Housing Act and housing assisted under chapter 37 of title 38, United States Code; and

(3) be based on the Secretary's and the Administrator's estimates of the reasonable charge for necessary services involved in settlements for particular classes of mortgages and loans.

(b) The Secretary and the Administrator shall undertake a joint study and make recommendations to the Congress not later than one year after the date of enactment of this Act with respect to legislative and administrative actions which should be taken to reduce mortgage settlement costs and to standardize these costs for all geographic areas.

Whether this authorization was needed is open to some doubt; federal agencies had for an indeterminate period been assuming the power to set maxima for mortgage transaction costs on loans for which an FHA or VA commitment was outstanding.[46] How this power, once implied but now explicit, was questioned is a subject for discussion later in this case study.

The HUD-VA Study

In the joint-agency study, HUD assumed the primary task of data collection. Carried out by the FHA statistics branch, it became the responsibility of the chief of the section and one assistant. The data was to include a 10 percent sample of underwritten loans for one month (March 1971) in a dozen regional offices of the department and the VA; the areas selected had field offices of both agencies in each.[47] In smaller offices more than a 10 percent sample was required to insure sufficient volume.[48] Lenders were requested to submit copies of the purchaser's and vendor's closing and settlement sheets; field-office personnel transcribed the data onto standardized coding sheets for computer tabulation. The cases, selected from a special register, all had case numbers ending with the numeral 2. Both the register and the coded sheets were submitted weekly to the Research and Statistics Division, HUD, Washington, D.C.[49]

The Housing Production and Mortgage Credit branch of the FHA reviewed these statistics; the principal assigned the task was on special loan from the General Counsel's Office.[50] His counterpart in the VA was a career civil servant, near retirement, who maintained an office solely to handle the VA's role in the study. He brought various field personnel to initial meetings to review and comment on HUD's data compilations; by summer 1971 HUD officials perceived the study as their own with the VA serving as only a commentator on its work, a relationship that continued thereafter.

Since legislative interest in the study came first and foremost from Senate hearings and since the final language of § 701 had its origins in Senate bills, a close liaison was maintained with that body. The House committees and staffs were quiescent, both on record and in private. A legislative aide to Senator Proxmire conducted a survey in the spring 1971 of the hundred major title insurance companies around the country.[51] From his forty-one replies, he found a pattern of small claims, as opposed to high labor and personnel costs. Along with an economist serving as his senator's liaison to the committee and its staff, these two handled most of the communications with HUD.[52]

In the agency the staffs reviewing the data seldom involved senior agency attorneys or civil servants of more than ten years' standing at the agency. Bimonthly reviews by the assistant commissioner-FHA in charge of policy, programming, and development and sporadic telephone reports to the secretary's office were the extent of staff reporting. Wider departmental meetings were held in June, but they produced little of substance or guidance. The senior officials feigned ignorance of the subject; indeed, staff assigned to the project regarded it as a matter of self-education as the study progressed. The agency finally assigned a full-time supervisory staff to the study in April 1971 after the guidelines for data compilation had been set.

The Preliminary Report

Given the agency's recalcitrance and the one-house congressional interest, the first deadline for the report—July 24, 1971—was allowed to pass with only a preliminary report submitted by HUD. Both sides needed more time to evaluate the data and each other. The supervising attorney at HUD who had been assigned the task of compiling the report had seen as his first task gaining familiarity with past proposed reforms[53] and maintaining contact with Congress and interested trade groups. He also contacted those people (primarily law professors) who had previously done research on settlement practices.[54] The protectionist instincts of the FHA were marshalled on one particular point: In writing the preliminary report, the agency had decided not to address itself to the problem of mortgage discount points,[55] which was, one consultant was told, a "politically hot potato."[56] Although the agency had mixed feelings, universally-based consultants who would report to FHA alone were hired in May 1971[57] and included the author.

The net of agency communications was widened to include the legislative group of attorneys within HUD's general counsel's office and the Office of Management and Budget, once the importance of the project was established. One staffer in OMB said in July that "any type of report can be written, as long as no one gets hurt."[58] After this the staff grew more nervous and started to report lunches and offers of future employment from trade groups.[59] In all of this, talk seldom, if ever, exchanged substantive information; rather, discussants used these occasions to sound each other out on attitudes and approaches of interest groups and individuals.

With the release of the preliminary report, the local press started to write stories that emphasized the unpredictability of costs from the purchaser's point of view, citing the wide variation in costs in the preliminary data; perhaps because conveyancing involved a local angle, it made good wire-service copy.[60] National press reporters specializing in real estate wrote about it too,[61] but little copy appeared in the actual real estate sections of newspapers.[62] This coverage helped to make the study a political item.

After the preliminary report was released, the last links in the communication lines thought necessary for this study were established with four law professors who had previously published in this field. Besides providing advance critiques, they would, the staff thought, most likely be called to testify on the study before Congress.

Interest Groups

The American Land Title Association, representing title insurance and abstract companies and located in Washington, D.C., emerged early as the group most interested in the outcome. Founded in Chicago on August 8, 1907, primarily by 13 state abstractors' associations, 59 companies, and 181 individuals and called the "American Association of Titlemen," it was very successful in lobbying for industry-oriented abstractor laws at the state level. It became the Land Title

Association in the 1930s when it became dominated by the growing mortgage-guaranty and title insurance industry and by its largest corporations.[63] Initially alerted by Senator Proxmire's interest in their rates and claims, they overreacted with a "why-us?" attitude and assumed that they were at the center of the government's investigation, which largely bemused Senate and agency aides.

In Colorado during a conference on economics and real property sponsored by the USDA, the staff encountered representatives of the American Bar Foundation who were working on an ABF-funded project on multifaceted numerical land identifiers for use by government agencies, as well as in conveyancing work.[64] The ABF staff would shortly ask HUD for funding for this study and for conferences arising from it, and afterwards, was regarded as part interest group, part colleague by the attorneys on HUD's staff.

Watchful also of the study was the National Association of Real Estate Boards, now the National Association of Realtors and the national representative of about 1,500 local boards.[65] It was founded in Chicago in 1908 by nineteen local boards and one state board and drafted its first code of ethics in 1913. In 1970-71 local boards in a half-dozen areas of the country were fighting an antitrust attack on their commission scale[66] where fees had recently increased from 5 percent to 7 percent. NAREB declared that this increase was necessary because the industry had to maintain itself on a smaller inventory of unsold housing at a time when the organizational structure of the real estate industry was becoming larger.[67] Because these factors and not greater service caused the increase, the antitrust division of the Justice Department was alerted by the end of the summer of 1971.[68] NAREB was a political opponent to be respected, for it could generate a torrent of telegrams to Congress on short notice. From the first, the Washington, D.C., office of NAREB was uncooperative and kept referring questions to its Chicago counsel. Additionally, HUD was unable to propose an economically justified alternative to the percentage sales commission, which led them finally to deemphasize this phase of the study.[69]

Throughout the summer and early fall 1971, several other government agencies explored the possibility of joining HUD in the study. The Justice Department was in contact with the general counsel's office concerning broker-age commissions and minimum-fee schedules maintained by local bar associations for possible violation of the antitrust laws. The Cost-of-living Council explored the idea of wage and price controls but decided that its mandate did not involve fee regulation aimed at reforming or increasing industry efficiency.

A November Consensus

Throughout the fall of 1971 HUD remained uncommitted to any particular reform or strategy. In November the four professors read and evaluated the draft report, which was also used as a sounding board for a meeting held on November

11-12 at HUD,[70] attended by the four professors, the HUD attorney in charge, study consultants, the statistics branch representatives,[71] and, intermittently, representatives of the HUD general counsel, information systems program officers, and other senior civil servants. The conferees[72] cautiously advised that, should action be taken, it include an item-by-item review of charges, the avoidance of conflict with lenders and mortgage bankers, and amortization of charges as a function of mortgage interest. They stressed the dual nature of these charges—hidden interest to some, mortgage assurance to others.

The consequences for agency policy depended on two arguments. As early as July, it had been argued that costs should not be regulated by imposing maximum levels for charges. They would increase costs in some areas even if the regulation were imposed only in particular states or metropolitan areas. Maxima would quickly become the standard or even the minima, these experts said. A second argument was that the consumer usually ends up paying for changing practices in the market and regulating costs—for computing costs for advance disclosure, for information booklets, and new settlement sheets. Initially imposed on the industry, the costs of reform would only be passed on to the consumer.

The root of the problem, most agreed, was poor public land records.[73] It was impossible to define the short-term benefits of improving these, and the federal government would arguably have to institute a grant program for state and local governments to do it. HUD had pilot programs in six small cities,[74] but these were aimed at gathering data other than land title data for local governments.

Agency staff, particularly those in the statistics branch, had noticed large cost increases in charges when title insurance was added to the title-delivery system.[75] They also found the lowest charges in states where statutes, in restricting the period of time that previously recorded or unrecorded interests in land could be asserted, limited the amount of time a title search must cover.[76] Staff asked for suggestions why this should be, but on both these statistical correlations, the answer came back that title insurance and such statutes were found together in high-cost areas of the country as well.

These arguments, together with the desire to do nothing not based on detailed study of particular charges, inclined agency staff to think that weakly justified charges, not susceptible to regulation, would have to be outlawed. Charges for applying for insurance, preparing documents, and surveys, as well as title insurance charges when a commission was paid, were most suspect.

Congressional Activity

Meanwhile Congress considered several pieces of legislation on the closing and settlement problem. Senator Proxmire's staff's title insurance study and subsequent draft legislation resulted in the introduction, on October 29, 1971, of The Title Charge Reduction Act of 1971,[77] which cast the cost of title abstracts, examination, and insurance—all defined as title-related services[78]—onto the residential mortgage lender. The bill's proponents reasoned that lenders could bargain more effectively than anyone else for lower rates with title insurers, abstractors, and attorneys for title-related services.[79] Opponents said that this was speculative; that massive collusion might as easily result. The bill drew lukewarm support from independent experts,[80] was regarded as a broadside by HUD staff, and, of course, drew the fire of lenders.[81]

In the House, Representative Wright Patman, chairman of the Banking and Currency Committee, was working on The Real Estate Settlement Cost Reform Act.[82] Drafts were available to the HUD staff, who regarded it as the minimum which their report would have to deal with; i.e., outlawing kickbacks and rebates given or accepted in connection with a settlement (§ 101), prohibiting attorney's rebates and commissions on the issuance of title insurance (§ 102), proscribing price and rate discrimination by title insurers (§ 103), and requiring the lender to pay for "any portion of title insurance in residential real property which insures its interest in such property" (§ 105). This last was the Proxmire bill reiterated but was more specific and comprehensive. The draft also provided for information booklets for purchasers, advance disclosure of costs, and a federal title insurance program.[83]

The Final Report

HUD staff wrote their final report during November and December.[84] The proposals were mild and included most of the consumer-protection devices of the House's draft legislation, with a proposal to prohibit kickbacks. On January 9, 1972, the Washington *Post* began publishing a four-part series on settlement costs[85] by an investigative reporter who specialized in real estate. The series, "The Settlement Squeeze," sensationalist in tone, claimed to have uncovered widespread kickbacks based on interviews with suburban Washington attorneys and builders.[86] These kickbacks were actually undisclosed commissions within the widely used but little understood fee structure. The final story compared the high costs of buying a home in Washington to the lower costs in Boston.[87] Its publication had the effect of forcefully bringing the HUD study to the attention of high HUD officials who had known of the impending series and its tone for some time but had failed to foresee its impact. After publication, there was pressure on the agency to "do something." The go-slow strategy of the November consensus dissolved. The intent to focus on a few itemized charges and work on middle- and long-range goals like public land record improvement were deemphasized. The legislative section of the general counsel's office reviewed the draft report, proposed eliminating any requirement for title insurance on FHA- or VA-underwritten mortgages, and criticized the report for being too soft on attorneys and for not emphasizing their role. It was suggested that the report should not have been assigned to attorneys for writing.

Pressure from the secretary's office to emphasize the problem of kickbacks was strong.[88] Secretary George Romney, wanting in no way to be associated in the public's eye with known wrongdoing, had vowed in several speeches during the past fall to fight kickbacks wherever found[89] and inserted notice of antikickback regulations in the Federal Register on October 9, 1971.[90] After a January 14 meeting at which the staff made their final argument for improving title records and prohibiting specific costs, they were told, "You may be right, but you misunderstood our options," by an assistant secretary who decided, with the undersecretary and Romney, that regulation by imposing maximum charges must be proposed and reported, if possible, as administrative action already underway at HUD.[91]

Maxima regulation was appealing for several reasons. Politically, it was thought that there would be less opposition to fee regulation than there would be to structural reform of the industry. One component of the "maximum-standard" argument was that it would freeze the present structure of the industry,[92] and even though this would not improve its efficiency, it would cause some long-range goals for improvements in industry structure to be neglected. Second, regulation of charges avoided a potential confrontation with the title insurance industry. Even though some of these companies were perceived as efficient abstractors,[93] attorneys on the HUD staff came to regard the title insurance contract as worthless[94] because of the many exceptions it contained limiting payments on claims to search errors (which would incur liability at common law anyway[95]). The title insurance industry had been so nervous about congressional action that they became a clear target[96] on the theory that "they must have something to hide." Yet federal regulation of title insurance would require partial repeal of a federal statute granting this regulation to the states[97] and would, it was feared, arouse the whole insurance industry.[98] Third, cost regulation would postpone determinations on which costs were too high and why. What survived of the November staff consensus was that blanket fees, percentages of sales price or loan amount, should be abolished providing an alternative method for computing the worth of the services was found.[99] This continued to leave brokerage fees free of regulation.

The final report was delivered to Congress on February 17, 1972.[100] Besides establishing "maximum allowable charges for all individual settlement cost items paid by both buyer and seller, except loan discount payments" and "state imposed taxes and fees,"[101] it proposed:

Mandatory use of a uniform settlement sheet in FHA and VA transactions,

Detailed estimates of charges,

A limitation on initial escrow deposits,

An audit of origination fees, and

A federally sponsored computerized land parcel recording system in selected jurisdictions.[102]

But the scope of the report's major recommendation for establishing maxima was unclear. It extended either to FHA-VA mortgages only or to the conventional market.[103] A broad reading of it engendered an attempt at rule making during 1972 and much debate, but came to nothing.

Congressional Consideration

The 1972 Housing Bill

Settlement cost legislation was introduced in the House of Representatives on February 23, 1972, six days after the release of the HUD-VA report.[104] Representative Patman, who saw federal settlement cost regulation of some type as "logical since the charges are required as a condition to getting loans,"[105] said that hearings would be held "in the next several weeks."[106] At the outset he saw this legislation being incorporated into the omnibus housing law,[107] which was supposed to be enacted by June 30, 1972.[108]

The House bill (H.R. 13337) was far reaching compared to the Senate bill, which dealt with title-related services and whose principal objective was to control title insurance charges.[109] The House bill applied to any "federally related" loan and

Prohibited any person from accepting or furnishing any thing of value for a referral of business,

Prohibited charging a purchaser for an attorney's settlement services unless the attorney was personally retained by and solely represented the purchaser, and

Prohibited commissions in connection with the issuance of title insurance.[110]

These provisions alone make several judgments worth exploring. "Federally related" mortgage loans included mortgages issued by lending institutions that were regulated or whose deposits were insured by the federal government; that would bring 99 percent of the mortgage-lending industry under the proposed statute.[111] The prohibition against touting was a matter of state law[112] or, for attorneys, canons of ethics[113] enforced by bar associations; here the principle was extended to all other types of settlement businesses.[114] The second feature, like the Senate bill, accepted lender absorption of title-related services when provided by an attorney. However, the bill as law would have had a doubtful impact on costs: Compliance with it may have resulted in separate attorneys for lender and purchaser or else might have made the purchaser rely on the lender's services and presume that his interest was identical with the lender's on many matters.

The House bill also prohibited rate and price discrimination against purchasers (as opposed to lenders).[115] It provided that purchasers should be given HUD-published information booklets outlining, on a "regional or local" basis, the nature and purpose of each charge, the "fair dollar amount" of each, and any "unfair practices and unreasonable or unnecessary charges."[116] It required an itemized disclosure of charges ten days in advance of settlement;[117] it established a self-supporting federal title insurance[118] program for FHA or VA transactions;[119] it required lenders to pay interest on escrow accounts[120] and to disclose to the purchaser the previous selling prices of the property over the past five years at least five days before settlement.[121]

The records of the hearings on the House side began with the insertion of the *Post*'s "The Settlement Squeeze" articles. William Barrett, House subcommittee chairman, said that the articles had "certainly prompted serious congressional interest."[122] Secretary Romney, presenting *et alia* a report on closing costs in the § 235 homeownership program, went back to one of the original concerns of the inquiry: the front-end loading of transaction costs on the poor who must pay without reference to their financial ability or the services rendered.[123] The chairman and the secretary discussed where the responsibility for this rested,[124] and what the effect on "actual costs" the proposed maximum cost regulation would have:

Romney: I think there is always the danger that a maximum may become a minimum; . . . that people may charge up to the maximum simply because you have a maximum.[125]

Both agency and congressional staff became aware of the weakness of HUD's position. Romney continued,

I guess maximums are kind of like taxes; I don't think you can ever achieve perfect equity with them, but the abuses that have crept in here are of such a character that it does seem that people will generally be better off if the Department and VA undertake to identify . . . in each market area . . . a maximum.[126]

Questions were reserved for submission after the hearing[127] and reiterated earlier arguments[128] concerning the implausibility of effective competition and the desirability of a federal title-insuring bureaucracy.

On the second day of hearings, Congressmen Gude and Stephens disagreed as to what impact on costs the "coziness" of settlement businesses had.[129] Actually these hearings were filled with promises of cooperation and mutual concern between industry witnesses and Congress. They struck a balance, as did press coverage, between defining a "national problem"[130] and hearing about local practices.[131] Most public-interest and consumer groups testified by letter; the bulk of the time was devoted to industry spokesmen. Lending-industry spokesmen indicated the necessity for their present charges[132] and said that public transfer taxes were the source of high costs.[133] Builders generally supported closing-cost legislation[134]; the Mortgage Bankers Association followed suit, except that they did not want to pay interest on escrow accounts[135] and wanted mortgage-brokerage fees exempted.[136]

Ten days later Senate committee hearings were held;[137] many of the same witnesses appeared,[138] and there were more public-interest witnesses,[139] but the result was little more than colorful language: One witness called the title insurer the "bailbondsman" of the settlement process and a "leech" on a sickly system of public land records.[140] There was some criticism of the HUD-VA study[141] and little direct support for Senator Proxmire's bill requiring lender payment for title-related services.[142] The results of these hearings were mixed: The Senate committee used the time to vote a statute permitting HUD to set maximum allowable costs,[143] but it did not broaden the coverage of its bill to all federally related transactions covered by the House legislation.[144]

These hearings did, however, generate a general theory for public action: The benefits of cost savings were spread so thin but were in the aggregate so large that individuals could not be relied on to serve the public interest. Romney said, in this regard:

No one appears much interested in competing by cutting costs to the homebuyer since he is not likely to be in the market for another home in the near future. . . .[145]

An analogy to the "benefits" of the public recording laws was also made:[146] The benefits of the recording system are so widely scattered throughout the population that no individual has an interest in its improvement. That cost regulation would "legitimize" the present title-transfer system was also a concern,[147] as well as the problem of not covering a specific settlement-related cost such as brokers' sales commissions and the fear that regulation could not be effective if such loopholes remained.[148] (Amendments to cover realty brokers' commissions were turned down by the chairman.[149])

Senate hearings provided an opportunity for testimony by local[150] as well as national interests and impressed upon the committee the elusive nature of real estate transactions involving national corporations and local laws. Appearing for the American Land Title Association was a title company executive from New England[151] where little title insurance is written; he became the chief representative of his industry over the next two years.[152]

By the time the hearings closed, both houses of Congress saw a quick legislative solution of the settlement issue by making it part of the 1972 housing bill, due for passage in June, which contained a settlements title,[153] and in HUD's administrative action to implement maximum standards on certain charges. Title IX of the 1972 housing bill incorporated the Patman legislation virtually intact and added a demonstration computerized-recordation system[154] and authorized title companies to perform any "title services in connection with the issuance of (title) insurance."[155] This was a bid by the companies to legitimize their services in federally related (or all) transactions. Testifying on June 13, 1972, Romney said that maximum-cost regulations should be limited to FHA-VA transactions and not be applicable to conventional transactions; he also added that HUD would need more than 180 days to complete even this limited job.[156] The American Bar Association held conferences on the subject in Washington, D.C., on May 17-18, 1972, and the next day the ABA Board of Governors adopted a resolution opposing Title IX of the House 1972 housing bill.[157]

Over the summer the 1972 housing bill was filibustered to death in the House committee.[158] Although the committee once voted to repeal HUD's authority to regulate costs,[159] the action failed to pass when the House Rules Committee failed to report the 1972 act in its entirety to the House floor for debate.[160]

Other Bills

Two separate settlement charges bills appeared anew in 1973 and contended for committee favor;[161] it was apparent that the major issue was becoming the scope of HUD's regulatory authority: The bill introduced by Congressman Stephens would repeal § 701 of the 1970 Emergency Home Finance Act;[162] the bill authored by Congresswoman Sullivan would confirm the administrative power to regulate charges.[163]

This issue arose when it became apparent that HUD would not promulgate its 1972 regulations inserted in the Federal Register. (Congress was arguing over whether it should confirm a power that HUD said it had but was reluctant to use.) No action was ever taken on the regulations.

Both House bills retained provisions for:

Uniform settlement statements. The Sullivan bill called for a "single standardized form"[164] while the Stephens measure allowed more than one standard form[165] and provided that its use signify compliance with federal truth-in-lending requirements.[166]

Special information booklets. The Sullivan bill provided for indications of "amounts of the charges which a borrower should be prepared to pay,"[167] while the Stephens bill deleted this requirement (part of the 1972 act). The Sullivan bill added a requirement that these booklets describe how interest is to be calculated on escrow accounts and how a borrower may use these accounts.[168]

Advance disclosure of settlement costs. The Stephens bill added the possibility of a waiver form if the disclosure was not made ten days before closing.[169] The Sullivan legislation provided that if any charge was 5 percent or more above the estimate at closing, a presumption of bad faith arose.[170] The Stephens version threw the burden of showing bad faith by the "preponderance of the evidence" on the borrower.[171]

Prohibiting kickbacks. The Stephens bill was broader than the Sullivan version when it defined who was involved but narrower when defining the value of the kickback.[172] The Stephens version expressly excepted title insurance commissions.[173]

Escrow accounts. The Stephens version provided that no borrower be required to deposit money for taxes and insurance into escrow [174] The Sullivan bill required a borrower's election to escrow these monies.[175] The difference was one of emphasis on continuing customary local practices.

Disclosure of past selling prices. Both bills were substantially the same on this requirement,[176] although the Stephens bill added a clause protecting the lender.[177] The Sullivan version required a history of any improvements.[178] Both bills reduced the time period to two years preceding the present closing.

In addition, both bills barred fees for preparing truth-in-lending statements,[179] established demonstration projects for computerizing title-search data,[180] and legitimized title company services incidental to a closing.[181]

On the Senate side, Senator Proxmire abandoned his emphasis on title-related services and submitted a bill very similar to the Sullivan bill.[182] On introducing it, he said that with its passage he estimated that, nation-wide, home purchasers could save $700 million.[183] He wanted HUD to implement its maximum-charge regulations within six months of passage.[184]

Both the Proxmire bill[185] and a bill[186] sponsored by Senator Brock defined a federally related[187] mortgage in the same way, but where the Proxmire bill applied to "title services,"[188] the Brock bill used the broader term *settlement services*[189] to include most mortgage closing costs plus "services rendered by a realtor, and the handling of the processing, and closing or settlement."[190] But the Proxmire bill went on to mandate HUD to "establish the maximum amounts of the charges to be imposed on the borrower and seller for services incidental to . . . settlement."[191] The maximum levels would be designed to reflect "reasonable charges for necessary services"; this was a stringent standard that would require HUD to evaluate charges and levels of service performance. But most real estate brokerage commissions would not be regulated.[192] No federal action concerning the loan would be undertaken if the maximums were exceeded.[193]

Both Senate bills included provisions for:

Uniform closing statements. Their definitions of these started out to be identical,[194] but the Brock bill added a clause that the sheet "may be used in satisfaction of the disclosure requirements of" the Truth-in-lending Act and shall contain a waiver provision.

Special information booklets. These provisions were identical in each bill.[195] Unfair practices had to be explained in the booklet, which was to be given to the borrower when he filed his application.

Advance disclosure of settlement costs. Both bills required ten days' advance notice,[196] but the Brock bill went on to add disclaimer sections to benefit the lender:[197] If the borrower waives his right in writing to a ten-day notice, the provisions of §§ (a) "shall be deemed to be satisfied."[198]

Prohibiting kickbacks. The Proxmire bill specifically aimed at attorneys' commissions on title insurance;[199] the Brock version did not decide this point.[200]

In addition, neither bill would permit fees for preparing truth-in-lending statements;[201] both would establish computerized land recordation systems on a demonstration basis.[202] Moreover, the Proxmire bill contained prohibitions against certain interlocks and legitimized title company activities,[203] while the Brock bill, which required further study of the matter by HUD,[204] did not.

The major question was whether regulation of charges would improve the efficiency of the conveyancing system.[205] The design of the information booklets would give HUD a chance to develop a knowledge of our conveyancing patterns in detail, and if it did not, Proxmire's legislation requiring "reasonable costs for necessary services"[206] could mean that the efficiency of the conveyancing services themselves would have to be determined before an optimum charge for each could be established. Witnesses fenced with this point, but none faced it directly. Regulation was necessary, some said, to guide the inevitable future economic concentration of conveyancing services in large urban areas.[207]

Administration support for any action was tepid: HUD spokesmen, who said the issue had been studied enough, now openly opposed mandating maximum-charge levels. They maintained that advance disclosure was the key to the problem.[208]

The House held more hearings on its bills in early 1974. Debate proceeded along the same lines:[209] Would regulation rigidify present services, and was regulation necessary? One other issue developed was the idea, originally Senator Proxmire's, that the lender should absorb title-related services.[210] None of the forty consumer groups who testified wanted HUD s authority repealed.[211] The Stephens bill did not survive the House committee;[212] he was prevailed upon to withdraw it and not make it an amendment to the 1974 Housing Act.[213] Congresswoman Sullivan wrote to committee members asking that no repeal be included in any bill. A stalemate resulted, but a month later Stephens tried again and won, 18 to 12, on a committee vote to repeal HUD's authority and to enact his measure.[214]

Initial support for the Brock measure came from committee Democrats, particularly Senators Cranston and Stevenson, and Republican Senator Packwood,[215] who emphasized the bill's reforms and ignored its limitations. The Washington *Post* supported the bill,[216] even after Congresswoman Sullivan, in a letter to the editor, explained their editorial oversight and wrote that repealing HUD's never-used authority was the main question;[217] she contended that it would be better to retain the authority than to enact uniform settlement sheet and advance disclosure requirements, which would emphasize the exorbitant charges exacted. Real estate industry lobbying for the bill was intensive,[218] and in the end, the Brock bill was reported out of committee as the Senate version.[219]

"Dear Colleague" letters were written by five senators in an attempt to defeat the Brock measure on the floor if the repeal was not stricken.[220] On July 23, 1974, the HUD-authority repeal was stricken from the bill by the full Senate[221] in a "healthy" 55 to 37 vote after an hour's debate.[222] The question of HUD's authority was still open for debate. There the matter stood for five months, with both sides arguing over HUD's continuing authority. In a sense the debate in Congress had come full circle in two years.

The Real Estate Settlement Procedures Act of 1974

Final agreement on a bill by a conference committee of both houses came on December 9, 1974.[223] The agreement was approved by the House on December 9 and by the Senate on December 11. The enacted bill was signed by President Ford on December 22, 1974. The law that emerged from the legislative process did not mention any authority in the federal government to set maximums on settlement costs, but neither did it repeal federal authority to do so.[224] Rather, it dealt with four basic areas of lending for residential, federally related mortgages (the broader definition, first appearing in House bills, had prevailed). First, it provided three types of advance disclosure to the purchaser-mortgagor of real property: disclosure of information on the conveyancing process through the distribution of "special information booklets" by lenders; disclosure of settlement costs in advance of closing; and disclosure of selling prices of certain properties.[225] Second, it required that the disclosure of costs be made by the lender on a "uniform settlement sheet" to be devised and administered by HUD.[226] Third, it prohibited certain types of kickbacks and rebates from passing between those servicing the mortgage loan.[227] Fourth, it placed maximum limits on the amounts of money a lender could require a borrower to escrow for taxes and insurance on the secured property.[228]

Each of the four aspects of the act will be discussed in turn. The analysis of each will encompass the language of the act, the regulations issued by HUD under its authority in the act and the amendments made during the summer and fall of 1975. Any unresolved interpretative problems will then be discussed and, finally, the subsequent administrative history of the act will be presented.[229]

Advanced Disclosure

Special Information Booklet. Under the act (§ 4), purchasers of residential property were to receive "special information booklets" with a text prepared by HUD and printed by the government or lenders.[230] Its purpose was "to help persons borrowing money to finance the purchase of residential real estate better to understand the nature and costs of real estate settlement services."[231] In "clear and concise language," the act provided that the booklets "shall include"

> a description and explanation of nature and purpose of each cost incidental to a real estate settlement;

> an explanation of the settlement sheet to be used at closing and of escrow accounts;

> an explanation of the choices available to purchasers in "selecting persons to provide necessary services," and

> an explanation of "unfair practices" or "unreasonable or unnecessary charges" to be avoided by purchasers.[232]

After June 20, 1975, lenders had to provide this booklet to every person submitting an oral or written loan application to buy or mortgage residential property.[233] ("Loan application" was redefined within four months to mean only a written application.) The booklet and application were exchanged, each for the other. These provisions were nothing new or unexpected, for all the major bills had contained similar provisions, but they were watered down in one respect; that is, average costs were not to be included in the booklets.[234] Instead, the secretary of HUD was given two years to report on the "feasibility" of reporting such averages in selected "housing market areas."[235]

One text was to be prepared for nation-wide use.[236] (Regional texts were to follow.) It was prepared by HUD staff and a consultant who was a former employee of the agency.[237] The bulk of the text was devoted to a series of definitions and discussions—much like those contained in Chapter 1—of various settlement charges.[238] So the text aimed at describing the types of charges and the settlement sheet at the same time. This precluded any generalized discussion of the sequence of events leading up to a closing,[239] as well as any discussion of whether these charges were "necessary." The two "unfair practices" explained in the booklet did not reflect actual conveyancing practices, but were instead lifted out of later sections of the act which prohibited kickbacks, defined in the booklet as the "referral of business for gain,"[240] and a vendor's requiring the purchaser to obtain title insurance from a particular title company.[241]

A lengthier discussion in the booklet dealt with the "choices open to the buyer," which advised caution in dealing with the recommendations of real estate brokers; questioning the settlement attorney or officer about matters unclear to the purchaser; how to hire an attorney, select a lender, buy title insurance, and minimize repetitive title searches and surveys as well as unnecessary escrows and settlement agents.[242]

Since the act applies to all federally related mortgages,[243] these booklets would be required in practically all transactions involving a third-party mortgage. They reach a purchaser's hands after the contract of sale is signed[244] and thus arrive after the standards for financing, title, and the details of the closing (date and place) have been fixed. Only in regions of the country where an application for a loan precedes the sales contract (such as Philadelphia, Pennsylvania)[245] can a purchaser evaluate the information and use it meaningfully. Since the lender assigned most of the duties under the act is not a party to the contract of sale, there is little hope of rescinding or reforming it as the result of information provided while procuring the loan. Instead, purchasers as borrowers often rely on the lender's self-interest to protect their own. This practice will doubtless continue, despite the fact that the booklet clearly implies that the loan applicant is to be informed of all services performed for his protection both as a borrower and an owner.[246]

Where no booklet is tendered the borrower-purchaser, no remedy is provided.[247] Presumably the courts are free to fashion one suitable to the transaction. This imposes a good-faith requirement on the purchaser-borrower seeking to reform or avoid the loan contract or damages flowing from a lender's failure to provide the booklet. It must be shown, with the burden of proof on the purchaser, that the lack of booklet information caused him some injury or denied him a choice concerning settlement services; and any purchaser should have the option of waiving his rights. Alternatively, the borrower might be required to show that the lender's failure to provide the booklet was willful. Since Congress did provide remedies and sanctions for violations of other sections of the act, it might also be presumed that silence implies that no legal, equitable, or administrative remedy was intended.[248] In recent tight mortgage markets, borrowers are not likely to seek avoidance of a loan commitment. They may, however, seek damages or reformation of the loan contract.

Advance Disclosure of Costs. In practice, the booklet was provided at the time the "loan application" was filed by the prospective purchaser-borrower with the lender. By regulation, HUD first defined *loan application* to include oral or written applications, thus making some lenders discontinue giving out information on loan costs by telephone or orally for fear of violating this section.[249] The booklet belatedly suggested that the contract be made contingent on the purchaser's approval of the costs of the loan disclosed by the lender.[250]

When the booklet was received, the second type of disclosure required under the act (§ 6)—advance disclosure of the lender's settlement charges—might have been made as well. The legislative choice was otherwise. The act as initially enacted required, as a precondition for extending a federally related loan commitment, an itemized disclosure of each settlement cost sixty to twelve days before closing on the same sheet used at the closing.[251] The provision for making the disclosure on the uniform settlement sheets coordinates this disclosure with the uses the borrower must make of the information given him. The purchaser receives the booklet in exchange for his written loan application, examines the booklet and so familiarizes himself with the costs of the loan and the accounting necessary to close the transaction. This all makes sense, but also injects a new step for the lender into each settlement process—the preparation for disclosure on the disclosure-settlement sheet. If the costs disclosed are identical with those actually charged at settlement, no extra work is incurred. Some lenders might even be encouraged to make identical charges to save paperwork.

However, it might have been better to recognize that no matter when disclosure is made, the basis on which these charges are computed, as well as the number and types of charges, is unlikely to vary over the majority of residential mortgage loans. This would allow the lender to prepare one disclosure statement for a loan of, say, $1,000 and allow the borrower to compute his own costs on this basis. Most charges are computed on a set amount per $1000 or are fixed fees, charged at a flat rate regardless of the loan amount involved.[252] The booklet and the disclosure of costs could have been given at the same time, so long as the settlement was held within ninety days. HUD could accomplish this by regulation: The act requires only that "good-faith" estimates of charges or the "actual costs" of the loan be disclosed. A regulatory definition of *good faith* could have encompassed disclosure for a hypothetical $1,000 mortgage loan.[253] By the same token, this information could also be included in the information booklets today.

HUD did later define the *loan commitment* invoking a § 6 disclosure as a written commitment only. This further alleviated some lenders' fears of violating the section by inadvertent nondisclosure in an oral discussion of other mortgage terms.[254]

Subject to a regulatory definition of the term *days*,[255] the advance disclosure of costs was treated in three ways, depending on the length of the settlement period. First, if the date of settlement was, at the time of the loan commitment, anticipated to be less than sixty days, disclosure was required within seven days after commitment by the delivery or mailing of the disclosure to the borrower. Settlement may occur twelve and fifteen days after the disclosure was delivered or mailed. Strangely, if the disclosure was mailed, but then hand-delivered to save time, the fifteen-day rule still applied.[256]

Second, if the settlement was anticipated to take more than sixty days, disclosure had to be made at least sixty days before settlement. If the parties' plans change and settlement was advanced, disclosure had to be made within seven days of the time the lender knows of the change and settlement can occur twelve or fifteen days after disclosure, depending again on the method used to make the disclosure to the borrower.[257]

Third, where neither disclosure was practical or the parties desired a speedier settlement, the borrower might waive the twelve days minimum requirement[258] in writing up to three business days before the closing.[259] In cases of waiver, three days' actual advance disclosure sufficed.[260] Both the vendor and the purchaser must have signed one (or separate) waiver form(s).[261] Waiver was possible only when the time lapse between the loan application and settlement was twenty-one days or three calendar weeks.[262] By amended regulation, on October 9, 1975, HUD expanded the waiver process. It eliminated the three-week requirement and reduced the three-business-day waiting period to one calendar day.[263] These disclosure requirements, however, remained needlessly complex.

If the objective of the act was to encourage shopping around, disclosure comes belatedly in regions where the contract is signed before the purchaser seeks financing. Ending a contract because of high transaction costs is not recognizable at law; this should be contracted for if needed.[264] If meeting these requirements or a refusal to waive requires a twelve-day postponement of the closing, contracts of sale would have had to provide for this contingency, for the time needed for compliance with a regulatory statute may not extend an otherwise reasonably long executory period. Similarly, disclosure related to the time of a commitment would be more meaningful if the commitment takes the form of an option in the borrower to accept the loan within a reasonable time. Yet this aspect of the commitment contract was not covered in the act or in regulations under it.

Other ambiguities remained to cloud implementation of the Act in 1975. No matter how far in advance disclosure must be made, it must be made for all costs on the uniform settlement sheet to be charged at the closing. The costs must be either the actual charges or good-faith estimates. Precisely whose good faith was at stake—the lender's or the person providing the estimate—was (and is) unclear on the face of the statute, but since the lender is made responsible for the closing, presumably his good faith is at stake.[265] Whether only those costs passed on to the purchaser-borrower or all settlement services must be disclosed, whether or not their cost was passed on, was also an open question. HUD regulations stated that the lender must "reasonably believe (the cost quoted) is a good faith estimate," placing an *e* after every estimate included on the sheet.[266] To be safe, if cumulative records of the lenders' past dealings with servicers were unavailable,[267] the originator of the charge should probably have provided a written estimate to the lender.[268]

If the lender normally held a settlement twelve to fifteen days after the disclosure, the purchaser-borrower had only this much time to shop around for better loan transaction terms and charges. If he found a better deal and wanted to keep to his original timetable for settlement and moving, he had to use the waiver process under § 6. This might have encouraged hasty, incomplete comparisons between lenders.

In its original version of Regulation X, issued May 22, 1975, HUD ruled that once a § 6 disclosure was made, it need not be updated.[269] It was deemed effective when placed in the mails.[270] Also § 6 was ruled by amended regulation (October 1975) not to apply to home-improvement loans secured by a mortgage, refinancings, construction loans, mortgages on unimproved lots, farms over a hundred acres, and properties with between ten to one hundred acres where the land is worth more than the improvements on it.[271]

Intentional violations of the § 6 disclosure provisions were punishable by fine, imprisonment, a $500 judgment against the lender or "actual damages," whichever is greater.[272]

By October 1975 ineffective as the section might have been, nothing in the advance-disclosure requirements need have delayed a settlement. The twelve- to fifteen-day waiting period would in the larger cities be required in any event while the abstractor and attorneys cleared the title. In Washington, D.C., it took three to four weeks to clear an order through one of the city's title plants. On the other hand, South Dakota settlements might have been delayed. The use of one uniform settlement sheet, distributed to both vendor and purchaser, was intended to minimize paperwork. The tendering of the booklet and all disclosures might have been more effectively made at the time of the loan application and still satisfied the requirement of the act. Nonetheless, HUD made a passable attempt to dovetail the use of the booklet and the disclosures. However, all its efforts at providing advance disclosure of longer than one day were halted by statutory amendment in the fall of 1975. (Of this, more later.)

Advance Disclosure of Certain Sales Prices. A third type of disclosure, now totally repealed but formerly a precondition to a loan commitment on used housing, was that some prospective purchasers must know its previous selling price, disclosed in writing, as well as the name and address of the present owner and the date on which he acquired the property. (Only the year was required if his tenure had been longer than two years.)[273] In certain situations where the property was more than one year old and where the vendor had owned the property two years but had not resided there, the lender could not extend the loan commitment unless he confirmed that the seller had disclosed

the date and purchase price of the last arms-length transfer of the property, a list of any subsequent improvements made to the property (excluding maintenance repairs) and the cost of such improvements.

This information was provided by the vendor, with a copy to the lender.[274] Receipt of that copy satisfied this requirement as far as the lender was concerned.[275]

In the context of this act, this section (§ 7) was different in character and purpose from the rest of the statute. Its aim was to reveal information about the vendor's, rather than the lender's, costs. The legislative history of the act shows that its intent was to single out those situations in which the vendor was seeking capital gains on property he had owned a short time and not used as a residence. In a general way then, § 7 was aimed at the speculator in housing. It was drafted at the insistence of congressmen familiar with the scandals in the homeowner-ship programs for low-income people, particularly the § 235 program.[276] In 1969-70 congressional investigation of this program provided one of the main vehicles for investigation of settlement costs.

However legitimate the aim of § 7, it remained overbroad. The drafters of the act never did come up with wording that limited the applicability of the section to speculators.[277] The types of vendors covered included merchant-builders who kept homes for one year in their unsold inventory. Possibly included were executors of estates selling real property of a decedent; a trustee selling property that is the *res* of a long-established trust; the trustee under a deed of trust; trustee in bankruptcy; receiver; official selling at a tax sale; installment land contract sale vendor where the contract's executory period is over two years; and donative vendors who may be engaged in intrafamily transactions.[278] As to each, the statutory overbreadth of the section is apparent; so is the difficulty of defining "the last arm's length transaction" affecting the property.

HUD attempted to contain the reach of § 7 in a legal opinion issued by its general counsel.[279] If any one of many vendors had resided on the property, the opinion ruled the price-disclosure provisions of the section inapplicable.[280] Where multiple parties were involved on both sides of the § 7 transaction, only one vendor need make disclosure to only one purchaser. Good-faith estimates of the home-improvement costs disclosed satisfied the requirements of the section, and in lieu of disclosure each purchaser could provide the lender with an affidavit detailing his attempts to obtain the required disclosure. This affidavit satisfied the lenders' duty under § 7. Finally, assumptions and foreclosures of an existing loan, purchase of a property at a public foreclosure, a judgment levy and sale, a tax sale, and a bankruptcy sale were exempted from the disclosure requirements of the section. Similarly, sale by the executor of an estate whose decedent had owned and resided on the property for at least two years prior to the loan application was exempt.[281]

Satisfaction of § 7 disclosures might usefully have been made in the agreement of sale, which could then have been presented to the lender as proof of compliance with the section.[282] The information generated would also have provided an abstractor with a means of starting to uncover the chain of title.

Past regulatory efforts such as provisions for disclosing information during the course of interstate land sales for recreation and second-home communities have imposed duties on one party to the sales contract.[283] In this act no such direct regulation was attempted; only lending without the disclosure was interdicted, on the theory that the prior sales price is of interest even after contract negotiations end. Besides the purchaser's interest (really his legal rights, to be discussed shortly), the lender is interested later so that he may judge whether the property purchased is overfinanced; he is presumably not interested in financing speculatively leveraged sales of housing.

If the law had been enacted in a state legislature rather than the Congress, there is a good possibility that inclusion of § 7 would violate the "one-subject" rule for state legislation.[284] Congress, however, does not have such a rule,[285] but if mortgage costs are the subject of the act and if lenders finance properties bought cheaply, cosmetically repaired, and sold at inflated prices, they are buying undersecured mortgages at overinflated prices. In turn, these prices are often used to compute some costs of settling the loan.[286] So the justification of § 7 related back, albeit indirectly, to the main subject of the act.

A failure to disclose the owner and prior selling prices for housing more than one year old might have also affected the substantive law of conveyancing and nullified the sale. Recently, disclosure of "the name and address of the present owner"[287] and the price of "the last arm's length transfer of the property"[288] on public records has required special statutory authority.[289] In the case of a developer caught with unsold inventory in a tight financial market lasting one to two years, what would the last arm's length sale be? No previous "owner" should also mean no previous transfer is available and no definition of an owner was given for this section: It might have meant the person with any beneficial interest in the unsold property as well as the legal title holder. In consonance with the disclosure provisions in the act as a whole, it might arguably have included both so that all real parties in interest might be disclosed. When a builder is the vendor and the home is unsold after one or two years, costs should have been disclosed if the lack of a sale implies poor-quality housing and not just a slow market. State courts have highly-developed case law to determine whether the undisclosed principal (vendor or purchaser) was a harmless and socially permissible device[290] or whether it affected the transaction financially to one party's detriment.[291] A strict reading of a section like this could have brought this case law into play, implying a statutory duty to annul loan commitments in which the purchaser-borrower does not know his opposite number, is injured financially by the lack of information on past selling price, and so has a basis for rescinding the contract.

The statute was silent on purchasers' remedies but was explicit on lender's duties and sanctions.[292] As is often done with the sales contract,[293] lenders would probably have asked that purchasers have the prior sales price before they file a loan application. After all is said and done, this type of disclosure can be made more efficaciously before execution of the contract of sale. Moreover, in housing markets where intensive renovations and large capital gains occur, vendors might be reluctant to disclose past selling prices or be unable to show the value of their improvements.[294] In such situations vendor (rather than lender) financing was a likely result of this section. This would avoid the requirements of the section altogether. For the future legislative reconsideration of this problem will be necessary, both for speculative sales and in cases of vendor-financed purchases where the vendor is a large merchant-builder. In the latter situation some vendors had already begun to advertise that "no closing costs" would be charged and absorbed these costs themselves.[295] As to some developer vendors, this might have been found a commercial sale, and so beyond the reach of the act in any event.

In general, it is doubtful whether the parties would, in situations where the property value was rising, be willing to postpone the execution of a contract until the information in the booklets was received and the two types of disclosures were made. It is unlikely that the lender's failure to provide the information would void the loan commitment and have left the purchaser without a loan, unable to close, and worse off than he would have been without the act. In a backhand way, the lender's nonperformance of these statutory duties could postpone the mortgage closing and cause the entire transaction to fall through—hardly a consumer-oriented result; this was an especially doubtful result in the case of the provisions for disclosing the sales price, for the remedy was explicit, criminal in nature, and related solely to the mortgage closing and the lender.[296] However, if the contract of sale ever becomes susceptible to recission because of noncompliance with these statutory provisions, any true advance disclosure might move American conveyancing toward a system of two contracts—one binding the purchaser to seek financing, but not working an equitable conversion; and another signed when the loan application is made and a commitment extended, utilizing or incorporating the information provided and disclosed under the auspices of the lender and, in most respects, "selling" the property as of its execution date. If this was indeed the direction the disclosure provisions of the act moved American conveyancing, these sections would have put us on the same path as English conveyancers.[297]

Others might argue that these sections set out in quite another direction— and that disclosing and providing information is only the first step toward "requiring lenders of federally-related mortgage loans to bear the costs of particular real estate settlement services that would otherwise be paid for by borrowers."[298] This is the wording of a later section of the act: "the Secretary of HUD is, within three to five years, to report on whether lenders should bear such costs."[299]

The Uniform Disclosure-Settlement Sheet

The important point about what remains of loan-cost disclosures is that they are made on the settlement sheet. This is HUD Form 1. Its use in the implementation of the act demonstrates the broad scope of the act itself. In many respects it aims at lending practices, but the information required of the lender in the course of disclosing the costs of the loan deals with many charges beyond the lender's control. Taxes, for example, are generally prorated between vendor and purchaser as of the date of settlement. They are, however, not within the lender's control; the same may be said of brokers' commissions, recording fees and utility charges. HUD ruled in 1975 that the lender, in filling out the disclosure form, may assume that the taxes are not in default and subject to delinquency charges, but later regulations were silent on this matter.[300]

Certain other charges for services not performed directly by the lender are nonetheless subject to his control. As a volume purchaser of appraisals, credit reports, termite-inspection reports, and title insurance, he may be able to buy at a discount.[301] So it makes some sense to require disclosure of these charges by lenders even when the charges are in fact "passed through" to the person providing the service. Besides this justification, the lender has a legitimate interest in informing a borrower of all costs of the loan so the latter will not overcommit himself to take out a loan he cannot afford. Likewise, the borrower has a similar interest in realistic financial planning for himself. So the act's reach in the disclosure-settlement statement serves both lender and consumer goals.

Another use of the statement is to allow HUD to monitor settlement costs through use of a uniform form.[302] Experience over the first six months of use indicated that deletions of some items were necessary for different areas of the country.[303] HUD regulations and later the act itself permitted two statements to be prepared, one handed to each party to the transaction,[304] presumably in the name of financial privacy. By regulation also, HUD for a time ruled that a lender need not make a § 6 disclosure of attorneys' fees and title insurance premiums where the borrower selects the provider.[305] (HUD admitted the act did not expressly provide for these latter exceptions but had inferred their validity from the intent of the act.)[306]

Uniformity among lenders' settlement statements is desirable from the borrower's standpoint. Critics of the form cited its inappropriateness in some regions but gave no specific examples. In such instances a "not applicable" insertion or a single-line deletion on the form should suffice as a good-faith disclosure of costs under the act.[307]

The act states that no fee may be charged for the provision of this form to the parties.[308]

Kickbacks and Rebates

Two provisions of the original act survive today and are worth an extended discussion. All services detailed on the closing sheet must "actually be performed" (§ 8): No kickbacks are permitted.[309] Vendors are prohibited from selecting the title abstractor or insurer (§ 9),[310] which would have the effect of prohibiting a contract call such as "the title to be insurable by X title company." By inference, a call for an insurable title with a filled-in blank following on a binder form used by a broker as the vendor's agent is prohibited as well. A better call for quality of title in the sales contract would be "title shall be marketable and insured by a reputable insurer of titles," although a similar standard might be inferred from a call for "X title company" if X in fact lives up to those standards.[311]

The legislative history of § 9 suggests that it is aimed at the developer-vendor who requires his purchasers to insure their titles with particular insurers.[312] This prohibition on any vendor's selection of a title insurer may disrupt a well-established settlement practice in the Midwest where the vendor pays for the cost of title abstracting, review, and title insurance policy.[313] (In other midwestern areas, the vendor may present only the old abstract to the buyer.) Where in accordance with custom the vendor has selected an abstractor, attorney, or insurer and later the purchaser selects a different one at a higher price, the vendor is out of pocket and inconvenienced. In cases where the purchaser refuses to deal with an insurer who has previously insured the title and so will issue a new policy at a lower "reissue" rate, similar results obtain.

Clearly, amending § 9 to allow for local practice is in order. In lieu of this, the section can be interpreted to apply only when the purchaser is supposed (when his contract is silent) to purchase title insurance under prevailing local custom; but for this purpose the section should encompass developers as vendors; they arguably should remain covered by the section because a tie-in between a developer and an insurer may result in sloppy search practices in some instances. However, such a tie-in can benefit the borrower because the developer can bargain for discounted rates on the subdivision sales, and his purchaser can in any event obtain title insurance at a reissue rate reflecting "services actually performed."

Section 9 is overly broad and should be amended to encompass developers as vendors without casting its net more broadly over all vendors and purchasers. Even as to developers, however, there are good arguments on both sides of the question of whether to prohibit developer-vendors from specifying a particular insurer. Perhaps this explains the lack of regulations under this section. So long as the specified insurer is reputable, requiring the purchaser to procure title insurance is distinguishable from the situation in which the developer-vendor recommends purchase of insurance from an insurer with whom the vendor has previously dealt to his satisfaction if the insurer offers the developers' purchasers a substantially lower rate. Amendment of § 9 to reflect this distinction is in order.

One major issue of the debate touched off by press reports of payoffs and kickbacks involved payments to attorneys by title companies. This was left in doubt by the act.[314] Section 8 provides:

(a) No person shall give and no person shall accept any fee, kickback, or thing of value pursuant to any agreement or understanding, oral or otherwise, that business incidental to or a part of a real estate settlement service involving a federally related mortgage loan shall be referred to any person.

(b) No person shall give and no person shall accept any portion, split, or percentage of any charge made or received for the rendering of a real estate settlement service in connection with a transaction involving a federally related mortgage loan other than for services actually performed.

(c) Nothing in this section shall be construed as prohibiting (1) the payment of a fee (A) to attorneys at law for services actually rendered or (B) by a title company to its duly appointed agent for services actually performed in the issuance of a policy of title insurance or (C) by a lender to its duly appointed agent for services actually performed in the making of a loan, or (2) the payment to any person of a bona fide salary or compensation or other payment for goods or facilities actually furnished or for services actually performed. . . .[315]

Subsection c attempts to leave some existing practices unimpaired. The principal question for future interpretation is whether commissions, computed as a percentage of the value of a title insurance premium, are for "services actually rendered" or "performed" by a title attorney submitting his title opinion to a national title insurer to obtain insurance for a client. In this situation the specificity and breadth of subsection b apparently sweep subsection c-1-B before it, but the ambiguity is indicative of the heated debate that preceded enactment of this section. Subsection a prohibits kickbacks, b prohibits fee splitting, and both subsections are qualified by c, but not to the extent that attorney agents may accept referral fees. Regulations have so far left the status of payments to attorney agents unclarified.[316] When a title insurer hires salespersons who solicit business and who are paid on a commission basis, depending on the fact amount of the policies written as a result of their efforts,[317] subsection b might arguably, but should not, apply. Solicitation of business is a separate function of the insurance industry, and the salesperson's salary is a cost of doing business. If an insurer can establish a tradition of conducting his business in this way and it is not a means of avoiding the penalties of noncompliance with the act, that solicitation should continue without penalty. Fee splitting by salespersons in violation of attorney's canons of ethics and brokerage-licensing laws would continue in force. The problem of solicitation by salespersons working on a commission basis will have to be resolved by their employment relationship with the title insurance company. If found to be that of an employee whose principal business is solicitation and whose work is perhaps the subject of regulation by the insurance commission, § 8a or b would presumably not be violated. Where the thing of value or fee splitting benefits one (e.g., an attorney or broker) whose principal service is not given in exchange for the fee, then the sections are violated.

The interpretive questions under § 8 generally involve compartmentalizing conveyancing patterns into separate business functions. A kickback or the splitting of fees between the functionally separate units would likely involve a violation of § 8. A title insurer furnishing entertainment, meals, or gifts to brokers, lenders, or attorneys violates § 8a.[318] The "thing of value" is there unrelated to the common interest of both in conveyancing. On the other hand, the provision of forms, abstracts, land descriptions, or conveyancing documents by insurers or abstractors to attorneys is incidental to the business of both, and so no violation of § 8a occurs because both donor and donee have an interest in smoothly run conveyances.[319] The various units within a conveyancing pattern may share expertise, but should not share anything extraneous to their common line of work. On this question, the final regulations are somewhat more flexible, although they confirm the general rule. Free seminars on title matters or a reception by a title company "not directly conditioned on the referral of business" and not involving "the defraying of expenses of persons in a position to refer settlement business" are ruled generally to be "normal promotional and educational activity" exempted from § 8.[320]

What then of the special rates given by abstractors and insurers to subdivision and condominium developers? The developer will typically agree to refer business to the abstractor or insurer in return for the special rate.[321] The same rules apply. If he agrees only to refer his business to the title assurer, no violation of § 8a or b occurs. However, if he agrees to refer another's business to the title searcher, their agreement involves more than their mutual interest, and a violation would occur. When a merchant-builder sells his housing, he may therefore refer business to the title searcher where he is the vendor and responsible for the title search. If the purchaser has this responsibility, the developer's reference should be legal under § 8a only where the vendor recommends the title assurer to the purchaser who is offered a substantially lower rate for abstracting or insurance. Again, to prohibit an arrangement benefiting the purchaser and developer mutually would seem contrary to the intent of the law.

Title assurers may finally wish to assure the parties to a transaction that they or their agents have engaged in no negligent conduct, taken no bribes to ignore a visible easement on the property, or violated this act. Such assurances, in certificate or letter form, are not a "thing of value" because they would be incidental to their business and no violation of § 8a. They merely represent an improvement in their product or service that gives them a competitive edge, rather than aiming to exclude competitors from the market.[322] The same result obtains when a title insurer offers broader policy coverage.

One obvious interest that Congress had in the passage of these sections is in asserting jurisdictional authority over the proscribed activities; i.e., Congress here asserts that conveyancing patterns, insofar as they are related to federally underwritten or insured mortgages or mortgage funds, are part of interstate commerce and so a permissible subject for federal regulation.[323] The drafters of these sections, particularly § 8, may have hesitated to limit the scope of the statutes in detail because of then pending antitrust litigation, which they surely followed with interest. In that litigation, the facts were as follows.

In 1971 Ruth and Lewis Goldfarb signed a contract of sale to purchase a home in Reston, Virginia, a suburb of Washington, D.C.;[324] they sent thirty-six letters to local attorneys asking what they would charge for settlement services; nineteen responded, and all of them said that they charged the 1 percent of the purchase price allowable under the minimum-fee schedule promulgated by the local and state bar associations.[325] The Goldfarbs closed on their house and then sued the bar under Section 1 of the Sherman Antitrust Act, which forbids combinations or conspiracies in restraint of interstate trade or commerce.[326] They ultimately prevailed, but only after an appeal to the United States Supreme Court. The Court said that the provision of settlement services by the bar was a price-fixing action affecting interstate commerce[327] and so reachable under the Sherman Act. Many housing lenders and the source of mortgage funds were located outside of Virginia, and these lenders protected their funds with a lien on the property arising as a result of the title examination. It rejected the argument that attorneys were exempt from the antitrust laws because of their professional status, at least as to their providing conveyancing services, which the Court viewed as the business side of law practice.[328] In dicta the Court indicated that in future cases it would balance the need of the bar for self-regulation as against the needs of consumers to subject the bar to the discipline of price competition.[329] In rejecting the arguments of the bar that the Commonwealth of Virginia preempted the field of attorney regulation by delegating regulatory power to the state supreme court, the Court left open the possibility that the bar might still escape the antitrust laws in the business-related aspects of law practice by submitting to state regulation as would a public utility. This is hardly desirable from the bar's perspective, but if it is to be avoided, attorneys must find ways of making the one business aspect of law practice now subject to the Sherman Act (i.e., settlement services) more competitive.

Section 8a is one tool for achieving this objective in the field of convey-ancing. The broadest phrase used there, a "thing of value," is an invitation to the courts to balance the need for competition against the need to use standardized practices. A broad interpretation of a "thing of value" will include the benefits of a combination or conspiracy to fix the prices of conveyancing services by brokers, lenders, and attorneys and deprive the purchaser of better service.[330] The phrase might arguably also include the benefits of tying arrangements by lenders, saying "I'll extend a mortgage loan to A if he buys the following settlement services—e.g., appraisals, surveys, credit checks, escrow accounts," whether or not the service is appropriate for the loan to be extended.[331] Section 8a and the penalties in section 8d suggest that much of the tort aspects of the antitrust laws are incorporated by reference. Section 8d provides for specific penalties, fines up to $10,000 or up to one year in jail for violators, but also provides for a more open-ended tort liability. Persons violating § 8a are

jointly and severally liable to the person whose business is referred in an amount equal to three times the value or amount of the fee or thing of value.[332]

Not only is a thing of value distinguished from a fee but this section places no limit on the number of persons who may be named as defendants; presumably as many defendants as the combination or conspiracy includes can be named, including providers of settlement services who have not had personal dealings with the plaintiff but who are nonetheless included with a number of others who have had such dealings. All may be defendants in a class action. Indeed, to make suits under § 8a of practical value, class actions will likely be necessary[333] and, toward this end, the joint and several liability language of § 8d anticipates their use.

The conveyancing patterns challenged in such suits may be the use of uniform mortgage forms, escrows, and settlement services. Two theories, both suggested above, may be used: first, that the practice is the product of a combination or conspiracy to fix prices or restrain trade, and, second, that the imposition of settlement services is a tying arrangement restraining trade. Both of these theories will require evidence of conscious parallel practices in extending mortgage money to consumers.[334] Studies of those practices that are customary in a region will be necessary to establish what parallels presently exist but may also be important to establish a conspiracy arising when and if those patterns are changed. Under a competitive model of business conduct, uniform practices are not in the self-interest of the broker, lender, or attorney since breaking with standard practice may bring more business. So uniformity is illogical (under the logic of competition) and is unlikely to be the result of competition. Defendants are likely to respond that the uniformity is only a like-minded reaction of reasonable, prudent businessmen to the need to protect their interests. For lenders, this reaction means boilerplated mortgage forms and extensive proof of collateral security, whether the contract protection or the collateral is called for;[335] for title insurers, it means limitations and exceptions to title policy coverage, and for attorneys, issuance of limited title certificates. After passage of this statute, these responses must also rebut the contention that, no matter what uniform safeguards the marketplace permits, it cannot also be reasonable to violate this statute. Thus § 8a should aid antitrust plaintiffs seeking to establish a combination or conspiracy based on the parallel use of customary conveyancing forms or services of little benefit to the consumer.

Membership in the bar or conveyancing trade associations can also show a conspiracy to fix prices. Assuming that Congress intended to proscribe § 8 and 9 activity but leave the measure of damages suffered because of the conspiracy or tying arrangements to the course of proof usual in antitrust cases, the remedy provided in the *Goldfarb* case raises the question of whether trade associations can be forced to assess members for violations when they are defendants themselves.[336] In the context of *Goldfarb*, not every member of the state bar is a conveyancer who used the minimum-fee schedule, but determining which attorneys used the minimum-fee schedule is a difficult task for a court fashioning a remedy. After the final opinion in that case, many attorneys protested the imposition of higher dues to satisfy the judgment issued against the bar.[337]

Maximum Escrow Amounts

Section 10 of the act controls the lender's escrow of taxes and insurance premiums. It was substantially rewritten in the fall of 1975. Originally it limited the amounts a lender may require a purchaser to escrow at settlement to all amounts due as of that date plus one twelfth of the current year's taxes and premiums.[338] After settlement the lender could not require more than one twelfth of the taxes and premiums then estimated to become payable during the upcoming twelve-month period.[339] Amendments in 1975 changed the one-twelfth limitation to one sixth, payable at or after the settlement.[340]

The purpose of this section is to prevent the lender requiring more than the statutory amounts of these charges to be escrowed as a reserve against the borrower's default in later escrow payments. However, it does not prohibit a lender in the ninth month of the tax year from requiring the escrow of nine months' worth of taxes. What the lender may not do at settlement is require that more than two months' worth of additional, future tax obligations be paid in advance. He may, however, maintain the one-sixth cushion in his reserves throughout the ensuing year. The lender is implicitly responsible for showing that his estimates are reasonable and not designed to increase his reserves out of proportion with his needs to clear the mortgaged properties of superior liens. Good record keeping and data gathering will be particularly important for this showing in jurisdictions with steeply rising tax rates and erratic reassessments; in the case of newly constructed housing not yet assessed or in jurisdictions where reassessment is triggered by a resale of the property, similar problems will arise. A proviso in the 1975 version of § 10 took these problems into account.[341] No penalties were set out for a § 10 violation so presumably only "willful" violators would be liable in damages.[342]

Title Information System Improvement

Other aspects of this bill deal with procedures by which information is provided to purchasers during the executory period. The executory interval between the contract and the closing is used by the purchaser to discover the state of the title. Section 13 provides:

The Secretary shall establish and place in operation on a demonstration basis, in representative political subdivisions (selected by him) in various areas of the United States, a model system or systems for the recordation of land title information in a manner and form calculated to facilitate and simplify land transfers and mortgage transactions and reduce the cost thereof, with a view to the possible development (utilizing the information and experience gained under this section) of a nationally uniform system of land parcel recordation.[343]

The next section requests the secretary of HUD to recommend whether financial assistance should be provided to communities that seek to adopt the "model system or systems."[344]

Earlier versions of § 13 had required that these demonstration projects be computerized, but since the final version stated only that these demonstrations should be established in "representative political subdivisions . . . in various areas of the United States," this is no longer a requirement. Many rural jurisdictions need assistance with recorded data but do not have the volume of conveyancing to warrant a computerized system unless the computer were maintained for other governmental purposes as well. For example, an alphabetized name index of vendors and purchasers could be automated by land parcel, or longhand or typewritten records could be automated. Chapter 3 argued that land records receiving legislative attention will make computerization more feasible, although some consider immediate computerization worth the extremely high front-end costs because of its long-range benefits. In any event, preparative legislation in the form of marketable-title laws, curative acts, and tract indexes will certainly reduce the initial costs of automation or computerization. Such legislation already exists in enough states to assure that HUD's choice of "representative political subdivisions" for demonstration projects include jurisdictions with none, some, or all of these legislative devices. In the long run, this section might also encourage adoption of title registries. HUD is to study "ways in which the Federal Government can assist and encourage local governments to modernize their methods for the recordation of land title information," including financial assistance,[345] and will report further to Congress on this.

Aside from establishing this regulatory framework and pattern of disclosures for federally related mortgage conveyancing, Congress has yet to give a direction to its interest in this area. The 1974 act is a reactive statute. After all this time Congress still wants further reports on whether federal regulation of settlement costs is "necessary and desirable."[346] The legislative history of the Real Estate Settlement Procedures Act through mid-1975 suggests only a peripheral concern with systematic changes in our conveyancing patterns. It does manifest a great concern for HUD's authority to control settlement charges, however, and the final outcome might encourage HUD to exercise the authority to regulate settlement costs, a power carefully preserved for it by the legislative history of the Real Estate Settlement Procedures Act of 1974. While experience in Great Britain suggests that its exercise will not immediately improve conveyancing patterns, any level of allowable fees will presuppose a hypothetical conveyancing firm capable of rendering services at this level. Indirectly, then, maximum-fee levels might encourage better use of existing procedures or, still more indirectly, systematic changes in the patterns of conveyancing. This spectre may account for the debate engendered by the implementation of the act in 1975.

The Backlash

The Real Estate Settlement Procedures Act of 1974 went into effect on July 1, 1975. In the spring of that year HUD drafted its first regulations under the act. These were issued on June 20, 1975.[347] Local conveyancing groups and bar associations held meetings to inform their members of its requirements,[348] but these engendered insufficient understanding, particularly among the bar, to quell hostility to the act. This hostility turned into an intensive lobbying effort to repeal those sections of the act dealing with the uniform settlement sheet, advance cost disclosures, and disclosure of the previous selling price of a property, and to amend its sections dealing with the information booklets and the limitations on escrow accounts.[349] Joining in this "high-pressure campaign" were attorneys, brokers, and lenders' trade associations.[350]

The last two groups lobbied vigorously for the repealers and amendments to the act.[351] Passed in response to a congressionally perceived need, first opposed by abstractors and title insurers but later accepted by the largest title insurance corporations, the act was substantially redrawn in response to the lobbying of the American Bankers Association. The commercial banks had been inattentive and uninterested in the three years of the act's legislative passage. Furthermore, one of the principal staff activities of the American Banker's Association was education of its member organizations, and that function was proceeding apace during May, June, and July of 1975. Their seminars on compliance with the act left the impression that the organized bankers intended to comply with it. By the fall of 1975, however, they let their members forget their supportive role as educator and urged a repeal of several sections of the act.

Real estate brokers' fees were included as a disclosable item on HUD's uniform disclosure and settlement form. The breadth of the language of § 8 suggested that cooperative-brokerage and multiple-listing agreements would be prohibited. This was an unlikely but possible interpretation, heightening brokers' hostility.

If the act was promoted by the consumer advocates and congressional committee chairmen, with some limited support from large title insurers, it was gutted by the bankers and brokers; this shift in the coalition in opposition to the act brought it down because the title insurers could not put themselves in visible opposition to the bankers—and there is no evidence of their tacit support of the act in the fall of 1975.

HUD and some large banks counseled giving the act a longer period of time to prove itself,[352] but when it had been in effect for four months, both houses of Congress conducted several days of hearings on bills to repeal § 4, 6, and 7 of the act and modify § 3 and § 10. In September the Senate held three days of hearings, focusing on a bill to suspend three sections,[353] i.e., those involving

complicated uniform settlement procedures statement, a 12 day advance disclosure of settlement costs by lenders, and a requirement, in some instances, of the disclosure of the previous selling price of existing real property.[354]

The House of Representatives held similar hearings in October under a special congressional rule to consider the Senate bill. Its Committee on Banking, Currency, and Housing reported:

When enacting the Real Estate Settlement Procedures Act last year, your committee was attempting to provide the prospective homebuyer with adequate protection against unscrupulous practices that were causing homebuyers to pay unconscionable fees in closing costs and to provide homebuyers with adequate advance disclosure of what the cost of settlement would be.[355]

However laudable their aim was, the committee continued, variations in settlement procedures around the country made the uniformity required in the act impractical.[356]

Although there is little to support the latter conclusion, the record of these hearings is a balanced one. Consumer groups argued that the law should be kept intact for a longer period before amendments were made. Many trade groups argued for a repeal of the advance-disclosure provisions (§ 6 and § 7) and its vehicle, the uniform disclosure-settlement statement.[357] Some favored retention of the statement as a data-gathering device.[358]

One consumer group's representative was

decidedly unenthusiastic about RESPA when it was introduced, promoted and finally sold to Congress in the name of consumerism. The political and settlement industry-related background of that coup is hardly a secret. Recognizing RESPA's inherent inability to significantly lower settlement costs, many consumer representatives and enlightened members of Congress expressed deep dissatisfaction with the bill's failure to attack the major flaw in the overall settlement cost structure; namely, that the structure is uncompetitive and archaic.[359]

Another consumer witness said his "experience suggests that real estate transactions are encrusted with costly and unproductive industry procedures."[360] Trade groups, on the other hand, talked only about the delays incurred because of the act.[361] To many congressmen, the issue was whether the act or the industry was responsible for the long executory period complained of.

The amendments enacted and signed into law by the president on January 2, 1976, either suspended, replaced, or modified parts of the original law.[362] Two of the definitions in the preliminary sections of the act were narrowed. Excluded from the definition of a "federally related mortgage" were second mortgages or deeds of trust, "construction loans," and other types of "temporary financing."[363] HUD had previously exempted many of these by regulation,[364] but HUD provided further exemptions in June, 1976. Regulations issued then exempted loans "to finance the purchase or transfer of a property of 25 or more acres"; home-improvement loans; loans on vacant lots; "assumption, novation, or sale . . . subject to a pre-existing loan"; and installment land sale contracts under which title is not transferred to the purchaser upon execution.[365] Construction loans were also exempted, except where converted into permanent financing by a purchaser of the improved realty, not for resale; where the borrower "already owned" the land for which he sought a construction loan, that loan was exempted as well.[366] Thus a developer's or broker's financing was exempted by regulation.

Also mortgages "eligible for purchase by" (e.g.) the Federal National Mortgage Association and the Government National Mortgage Association covered by the original act were now excluded unless originally "intended to be sold by the originating lender to" these two entities.[367] Thus two secondary-market buyers of large blocks of mortgages may be denied the benefits of RESPA-induced uniformity. Finally, state agencies and instrumentalities were exempted from the definition of "creditor" in the act.[368]

A new section on uniform settlement statements allowed variations in the form to take account of "local laws or customs" as long as the "numerical code prescribed by the Secretary" was maintained for each itemized charge.[369] If administered properly, retention of the numerical code would allow HUD to monitor cost levels in the future. Regulations under this modified version of § 4 permitted flexibility in the size, style, and interlineations that lenders might introduce when they reproduced the form for their own stocks.[370] The commentary on the June 1976 regulations said that many lenders had complained that not enough space was available to them on HUD Form 1 as originally designed.[371] While complaining that HUD Form 1 was burdensome paperwork, they were asking HUD to expand the form to meet local requirements. The inconsistency may be more apparent than real, and suggests that the burden of their own paperwork is substantial even without the use of the uniform statement.

By regulation also, two types of transactions were exempted from the requirement that HUD Form 1 be used: (1) those in which the purchaser is "not required to pay any settlement charges or adjustments"; and (2) those in which the purchaser-borrower "is required to pay a fixed amount for all charges imposed at settlement and . . . is informed of the fixed amount at the time of the loan application."[372] This aspect of the regulations should be used by lenders or developers offering "no closing costs" or a package of services at a fixed price.

Lenders were also allowed to furnish separate statements to the borrower and the vendor.[373] No explanation was provided for this, but the confidentiality of the finances of each is a plausible reason for the change.[374] By regulation, the lender was to retain the form used at settlement for two years from the date of settlement unless he sold his interest in the loan and did not continue to service it during that time.[375]

Most importantly, what remained of the twelve-day advance disclosure was a right in the borrower to be able to inspect the uniform statement one business day prior to settlement.[376] Even this requirement may be waived by the purchaser-borrower,[377] and HUD may exempt lenders from this requirement in localities where the settlement sheet is not customarily made available or it is impractical to do so. HUD regulations make clear that this is the case where an escrow agent handles the transaction.[378]

In the six months during which the original act was in effect, lenders argued that the provisions requiring advance disclosure of settlement costs at the time of the loan application was overbroad. Without a written application to trigger the act, lenders reported that they were not giving out information over the telephone. They required a written application before they provided any information, and then they presented the borrower with the special information booklet required.[379] Under the amendments the lender is then also to make

a good faith estimate of the amount or range of charges for specific settlement services the borrower is likely to incur.[380]

The regulations require a more objective measure of good faith in that each estimate has to bear a "reasonable relationship to the charge a borrower is likely to be required to pay at settlement and must be based upon experience in the locality" of the property and the lender's knowledge of charges made by the provider of a settlement service.[381] In making the estimates, lenders "are encouraged, but not required" to use the numerical code on HUD Form 1.[382]

The terminology used for the estimate must be "identical, so far as practicable, to the terms used in" the form.[383] The estimates must be delivered at the time of a written loan application, along with the special information booklet, or mailed within three business days if the application is not delivered in person by the purchaser.[384]

In June 1976 a rewritten § 3 (now § 5) booklet was issued. It is required to be given separately to the borrower at the time he makes a written loan application, in the form prescribed by the secretary, without additions or deletions.[385] By regulation, it may also be dropped in the mail within three business days of the date the lender receives the application (again, for situations in which the application is not personally delivered to the lender).[386] Presumably the costs of a $1,000 loan could be the basis for good-faith estimates. Permitting the purchaser to review a copy of the uniform settlement sheet, itemized for his settlement, one business day in advance of the settlement is hardly time enough for a borrower to shop around for better loan terms. Advance disclosure seems now intended only to facilitate the closing, and not to foster competition between lenders.

The original provisions for a minimum twelve-day advance disclosure of settlement costs (§ 6) and certain prior sales prices of properties (§ 7) were repealed.[387] Congressional reports called the twelve-day advance disclosure unnecessary since the disclosure provided in the booklets was sufficient. "Completion is what the parties want," Congress' report stated.[388] The disclosure of past selling prices was "unworkable."[389] Its objective was admittedly to curtail "unscrupulous speculators," but it had "ensnared honest vendors too and discouraged loans in the inner city."[390] Indeed, this section in the original bill aimed at disclosing capital gains on (1) housing bought for speculation and held only a short time, as well as (2) housing held as unsold inventory by a merchant-builder. The latter type of vendor is presumably one type of honest seller ensnared by the provision. Moreover, since the disclosure was permissible after the contract of sale was signed, the report realistically concluded that the purchaser might be forced to give up the deposit or buy a home at a price above its fair market value. Earlier disclosure might have provided a remedy less drastic than repeal, but since the past selling price was now deemed not directly related to the objective of the law as a whole, repeal of the section followed.[391]

Certain arrangements, "payments pursuant to cooperative brokerage and referral arrangements or agreements between real estate agents and brokers," were excluded from the kickbacks section (§ 8) in the amended law.[392]

The amendments required use of HUD's settlement form at a closing, and no fee could be imposed for its preparation.[393] Nor could a lender require establishment of an escrow account in an amount greater than that needed to meet payments for taxes and insurance on the secured property under prudent lending practice, plus one sixth.

Only a very little of the § 6 disclosures and no § 7 disclosures of past sales prices remained. Sections 8 and 9 remain, only slightly amended, and § 10 was amended to permit a two-month reserve to be escrowed for taxes and insurance.

Future Use of the Act

Little remains of the original act, and what does remain (§ 8-9) is now administered solely by HUD in consultation with the Department of Justice.[394] These sections can be expected to be most effective when functioning as limited-purpose antitrust laws in fluid situations, e.g., for brokers and independent escrow agents caught in tying arrangements with lenders. However, it will require careful industry monitoring to determine whether formerly separate conveyancing businesses merge or spin off subsidiaries to avoid the § 8-9 interdictions on tie-ins. One difficulty in using the sections will arise when their enforcers, charging that tie-ins and interlocking relationships prohibited by § 8 or § 9 exist, are unable to delineate precisely the functions the defendants perform. The dependencies of one set of personnel on the work of others makes the conveyancing process hard to define as one "industry" or as a discrete number of separate businesses. For example, the dependence of attorneys on abstracts and insurance policies, of surveyors on recorded land descriptions in deeds, of lenders on attorneys, and of escrow agents on others to prepare documents, suggests that the fragmented series of services, which together lead to a conveyance of real property, will be hard to sort out. Close studies of particular regions will be necessary before enforcement is possible.

Politically, this fragmentation means that real estate settlements are conducted in a way capable of generating a great deal of political pressure to preserve the status quo, even when the changes are as modest as those contained in the act initially. The provisions of the act were never onerous, but they provided too many people with a chance to use it as a scapegoat. For its advocates, one political lesson is, "next time, single out one aspect of the industry and legislate separately for it." It would, for example, make sense to administer any disclosure of past sales prices through statutory covenants incorporated by operation of law into the sales contract calling for federally related financing; other disclosures of probable settlement costs could be administered through regulation of real estate brokers.

Several other lessons are taught as well by the rise and fall of federal regulation of closings. HUD proved a weak spokesman and rulemaker for the law. The agency did not enlist its traditional clientele—the home-building industry—in the service of the act, although it exempted many of their activities from its provisions. Not only did the act fail to pinpoint those sectors of the industry that need regulation, it also failed to build a clientele for the act and dealt instead with a hostile lending industry, which eventually engineered the repeal of the sections at the core of its regulatory aspects. With hindsight, it is doubtful that the whole banking industry should have been taken on at once. Lenders apparently preferred the relative certainty of dealing with the already much interpreted Regulation Z of the Federal Reserve Board to a (relatively) uncertain future in dealing with HUD as the new lead agency in the field of residential consumer credit.

HUD is not likely to have to deal with further amendments to the act in the next several years. Monitoring of costs is, however, an on-going potential role for the agency, which should be written into the act. In the course of the long debate over settlement costs, HUD developed much information on the need and utility of tract indexes and title legislation. Continued use of the uniform settlement sheet should facilitate the up-dating of cost information and provide purchasers with a worksheet on which to plan for a settlement. Congress should encourage its use, but in a way that will, given the diversity of American conveyancing patterns, involve the federal government less directly. To date, Congress has appropriated $3 million for implementing § 13 of the act—demonstration projects to improve "the recordation of land title information in a manner and form calculated to facilitate and simplify land transfers."[395] If the word *recordation* is not a limitation on the scope of the projects that may be undertaken, the "facilitate and simplify" language permits experimentation with title registration in the jurisdictions which HUD selects.

In making the selection of jurisdictions, HUD should select:

1. jurisdictions that have, through marketable-title and curative acts, prepared their land records for modernization and reduced the costs of automating or updating them; and
2. integrated as many as possible records and offices to facilitate title searches and allow them to be conducted in one location.

In selecting jurisdictions, HUD will also have some choices to make that will require amending § 13 in the future.[396] It will have to decide how multifaceted a data base it will encourage in its improved recordation systems. In the past comprehensive, multi-use data collection has been encouraged by commentators. In a cost-benefit analysis, multipurpose data appears to have greater benefits than single-use data, and so "title information" may be redefined to provide a legally sufficient description of the property as well as land-use data made available to city planners, fire and police departments, and other governmental agencies. Initially, holding to a more traditional definition of title information may be desirable because wide experience with more comprehensive data-banks in the public sector is lacking, and additional important questions are raised.

One such issue is the decrease in the privacy of assets afforded owners of realty as title information becomes more accessible. A second basic issue is whether a good base of title information is necessary for improvement in the recording system; without any change in title information systems, registration systems might be achievable in some jurisdictions.

Issues involved in any wider grant-making process must be resolved as well: a federal contribution to total project costs must be set; evaluation criteria must be predetermined so that grantee jurisdictions will know how to measure the success of their project; and projects will have to be set in the context of continuous improvements in recording but be at the same time discrete enough to be funded separately.

In the long term, Congress might provide underwriting by the federal government of state and local bonds to improve the indexes for land records and the records themselves. Several factors suggest that this is a proper role for the federal government. First, this is the role which HUD-FHA knows best, for the FHA has been underwriting residential mortgage loans for forty years. Its programs required no congressional monies and have over most of their years in operation been self-liquidating. There is no reason not to underwrite the system that provides the loans it has long guaranteed. Second, states could be given incentives to modernize their title laws by allowing federal underwriting for larger percentages of the costs to states that will enact marketable-title, curative laws and statutes of limitations, and title registries. Tract indexing and record keeping need not be mentioned because conversion to such indexes, or their automation, would be the initial aim of many applications for federal underwriting. Finally, grantee jurisdictions with accessible and comprehensive land title data in any form might be forgiven remaining federal regulatory controls.

With the shortcomings of the 1974 act, it is doubtful that its provisions would ever have materially aided borrowers. Outside of the general counsel's office, HUD has never devoted much staff time to the act and knows little of its practical effects on borrowers. And after repeal and modifications of so many of its sections, Congress has made clear its residual interest in changing the patterns of conveyancing rather than the patterns of borrowing mortgage money. Whether this interest will abide remains to be seen.

Notes

1. A. Downs, *Opening Up the Suburbs* 17-25 (1973).
2. D. Mandelker, *Housing Subsidies in the United States and England* 219 (1973).
3. P. Rohan & R. Riskind, *Condominium Law and Practice,* ch. 13 (1965).
4. Task Force and the Use of Land and Urban Growth, *The Use of Land* 50 (1973).
5. *Id.,* at 84.
6. Act of August 2, 1954, P.L. 560, 68 Statutes 590, 591 (Housing Act of 1954, § 8(a), § 203(h) and (i).)

7. *See* United States Senate, Committee on Banking and Currency, Production and Stabilization Subcommittee, *Truth in Lending 1963-64*, Part 2, 1191-1253 (1964).

8. Ducey, McMullen, & Berliant, "Loan Closing Costs on Single Family Homes in Six Metropolitan Areas" (May 1965).

9. General Accounting Office, "Review of the Purchase of Title Insurance on Property Acquired in the State of Florida under the Loan Guarantee Program, Veterans' Administration," (June 1966) 10.

10. *Id.,* at 15.

11. *Congressional Record* (Oct. 26, 1973) E8319.

12. United States House of Representatives, Ad Hoc Subcommittee on Home Financing Practices and Procedures, Committee on Banking and Currency, *Report and Recommendations*, 91st Cong., 2d Sess., 1 (1970).

13. Commission on Mortgage Interest Rates, *Report to the President and to the Congress* 109 (1969).

14. S.3442, Mortgage Credit Act of 1970, § 2.

15. P.L. 91-350, § 701.

16. *See infra* text at n. 33-46.

17. *Report of the President's Commission on Mortgage Interest Rates* 69 (1969); United States Senate, Committee on Banking and Currency, 91st Cong., 1st Sess., "Hearings" (Sept. 25-6, 29-30, Oct. 1, 1969).

18. *Id.,* at 32.

19. P.L. 91-351, § 701(b).

20. 24 C.F.R. § 203.387 (1973).

21. B. Burke & N. Kittrie, *The Mortgage Settlement Process and Its Costs* III-E-49 (1972).

22. Q. Johnstone & D. Hopson, *Lawyers and Their Work* 243 (1966); Cardinali, First Letter to Local Counsel, "Clearing a New State," in Real Estate Financing 205 (K. Lore, ed., 1971).

23. Fiflis, "Land Transfer Improvement," 38 U. Colo. L. Rev. 431 (1967).

24. *See* ch. 1, n. 25.

25. Schussheim, "Housing in Perspective," The Public Interest (Spg., 1970) at 18.

26. HUD, Fifth Ann. Rept. 39 (1969).

27. *Id.,* at 33.

28. Carnegie, "Homeownership for the Poor: Running the Washington Gauntlet," Am. Inst. Planners J. (May 1970) at 160.

29. Edson, "Sections 235 and 236—The First Year," 1 The Urban Lawyer 14 (1969).

30. Payne, "The Typical Home Purchase Transaction in the United States," Conv. and Prop. Law 190 (1967).

31. Committee on Banking and Currency, United States House of Representatives, 91st Cong., 2d Sess., "Investigation and Hearing of Abuses in Federal

Low- and Moderate-income Housing Programs" (1970); Shah, "Housing Mess," Nat. Observer (June 24, 1972) at 1, col. 6; Raspberry, "FHA Checks are No Guarantee," Wash. P. (Oct. 24, 1970) at A19.

32. United States Savings and Loan League, *Fact Book 1971*, Table 7, p. 20 (1971); in the first quarter of 1971, housing was economically sluggish, but 1971 statistics finished with between 1.6-1.9 million starts that year. Slevin, "Home Builders Gearing Up; Buyer Response in Question," Wash. P. (Jan. 2, 1971) at D2, col. 1.

33. Committee on Banking and Currency, House of Representatives, 91st Cong., 2d Sess., "Emergency Home Financing" at 3 (1970).

34. *Id.,* at 533.

35. *Id.,* at 227.

36. S.3442, § 2, 91st Cong., 1st Sess., Subcomm. on Hsg. and Urban Affairs, United States Senate, Committee on Banking, Housing and Urban Affairs, 91st Cong., 1st Sess., "Hearings on S.3442," at 41, 42 (1970); *Id.*, "Secondary Mortgage Market and Mortgage Credit Hearings on S.2953, 3508, and 3442" (March 1970); Senate interest in discount points has a long history post-World War II. *See* HUD, "Mortgage Discounts," United States Senate, Committee on Banking and Currency, 90th Cong., 1st Sess. (1967).

37. *Id.,* at 297-304.

38. *Id.,* at 347.

39. American Land Title Ass'n, Research Committee, "Closing Cost Project" (1971, undated).

40. 1970 Hearings on S.3442, at 50, 51, 53-4 (1970).

41. *Id.,* at 174, 228, and 263.

42. *Id.,* at 188-89.

43. *Id.,* at 214-15.

44. *Id.,* at 210.

45. *E.g.,* Payne, "Ancillary Costs in the Purchase of Homes," 35 Mo. L. Rev. 455 (1970).

46. *See* FHA Regulations, 24 C.F.R. Part 203, § § 203.12, 203.27, and 203.100 (1969).

47. Selected were the following urban counties:

Area Surveyed	Principal City
Bexar County, Texas	San Antonio
Cook County, Illinois	Chicago
Denver County, Colorado	Denver
Duval County, Florida	Jacksonville
Essex County, New Jersey	Newark
King County, Washington	Seattle
Los Angeles County, California	Los Angeles
Marion County, Indiana	Indianapolis
Ramsey County, Minnesota	St. Paul

Area Surveyed	Principal City
St. Louis County, Missouri	St. Louis
Suffolk County, Massachusetts	Boston
Washington, D.C.	Washington, D.C.

Field offices in some cities were more helpful and responsive than others. The Newark office was slow in responding, and attorneys reported a system of "preferred" attorneys there who inflated costs. Memorandum of telephone conversation between author and R.J. Horn, H.U.D. Washington, D.C., July 8, 1971.

48. HUD-VA, "Preliminary Report on Mortgage Settlement Costs," 3-5 (July 1971). In draft and final version, this report emphasized the wide variation between costs in each of the twelve counties. For example, total settlement costs ranged from $2,845 in Newark, Essex County, New Jersey, to $1,320 in San Antonio, Bexar County, Texas. Of $15,000-$20,000 homes, closing costs ranged from $847 in Newark to $332 in Boston, Suffolk County, Massachusetts. Among all transactions reported, title-examination costs varied between $269 and $6; attorneys' fees between $18 and $475; escrow fees from $6 to $184. *Id.,* at 12-15.

49. *Id.,* at App. A., p. 3.

50. Unpublished memorandum, Burke "Congress Regulates the Conveyancing Industry" (1972).

51. Questionnaire, "Operating Statistics" (unpublished) sent to major title insurers by the office of Sen. Wm. Proxmire (1971).

52. *Id.*

53. HUD, "Bibliography prepared for HUD-VA Closing Cost Study" (May 26, 1971).

54. Unpublished memorandum, on file with author, *supra* n. 50, at p. 20.

55. HUD, "Preliminary Report on Mortgage Settlement Costs" 8 (1971); draft #2 (July 13, 1971) of this report also contained summaries of § 235 closing-cost data, then a congressional topic of interest, but this reference was eliminated from the final draft of the report.

56. Unpublished memorandum on file with author, *supra,* no. 50.

57. "HUD-VA Set Study on High Closing Costs," Wash. P. (July 17, 1971) at D10, col. 4.

58. Although OMB was established to examine and set budgetary priorities, it came in 1969 to serve as a clearinghouse for executive branch policy matters as well.

59. One staff member was offered future clients in any practice later established.

60. *See infra* n. 156.

61. Paulson, "Kickbacks and Fees Raise Home Costs," Nat. Observer (Oct. 29, 1971), at 8, col. 1; "HUD survey finds home seller pays four times as much

closing cost as buyer," House and Home (Sept., 1971); "House Buying: The Cost of Closing the Deal," Changing Times (Nov., 1971), at 15; Jones, "The Extras Mount in Home Buying," Balt. Sun, (Aug. 15, 1971) § F, p. 102; "Insurance—A Bite of Homebuyer's Apple," *Id.* (Aug. 22, 1971) § F, p. 1; "Settlement Costs: Cause and Cure," *Id.* (Aug. 29, 1971) § F, p. 1; Willmann, "Costs of Home Ownership Scrutinized," Wash. P. (Nov. 20, 1971) at C13.

62. *See, e.g.*, Willmann, *supra*, n. 61.

63. *See* "Am. Land Title Ass'n Answers Some Important Questions about the Title to Your Home," 2-3 (undated booklet).

64. D. Moyer & K. Fisher, "Land Parcel Identifiers for Information Systems" 11 (1973).

65. National Ass'n Real Est. Bds., "Superior Equipment of the Realtor" 9 (1970).

66. *E.g.*, United States v. Prince George's County Board of Realtors, Inc., U.S.D.C., D. Md., Civ. No. 21545 (order entered Dec. 28, 1970).

67. This was largely speculation by government officials involved in the study: They saw no way of proving it beyond a study of new data, which they did not have the time to collect.

68. Willmann, "Brokers' Fee Structure Facing Legal Challenge," Wash. P. (June 5, 1971) at El, col. 1; Meltzer, "Agents' Fees: Is Sharp Hike 'Outrageous'," Phila. Sun. Bulletin (July 18, 1971), § 1, p. 1, col. 1.

69. Unpublished memorandum on file with author, *supra* n. 50.

70. "Agenda, HUD/VA Settlements Costs Workshop" (mimeo.).

71. *Id.*, "List of Invitees": Included were Allison Dunham (Univ. Chic.), Ted Fiflis (U. Colo.), Quintin Johnstone (Yale), and John Payne (U. Ala.).

72. The sessions were taped, and the tapes are in the offices of Program and Policy Development-FHA in Washington, D.C.

73. *See* "Symposium on Title Recordation," 22 Am. U.L. Rev. 239 (1973) for a collection of the citations.

74. R.J. Horn, "Computerization of Land Parcel Records: A Proposed Federally Sponsored Program" (draft memorandum, dated Nov. 8, 1971).

75. HUD-VA, "Report on Mortgage Settlement Costs" 47 (1972), reprint by United States Senate, Committee on Banking, Housing, and Urban Affairs (March 1972).

76. *Id.*, at 47-8.

77. S.2275, Oct. 29, 1971, 92d Cong., 1st Sess.

78. *Id.*, § 3(a).

79. Interview with M. Lobel, legislative assistant to Senator Proxmire, Washington, D.C., July 1971.

80. United States Senate, Subcomm. on Hsg. and Urban Affairs, Committee on Banking, Housing and Urban Affairs, 92d Cong., 2d Sess., "Mortgage Settlement Costs" 116, 130, 213.

81. *Id.*, at 158.

82. H.R. 13337, Feb. 23, 1971, 92 Cong., 2d Sess.

83. *Id.,* at § 201(a)-303(c).

84. Unpublished memorandum on file with author, *supra,* no. 50.

85. Kessler, "The Settlement Squeeze," Wash. P. (Jan. 9-12, 1971) at Al; *see also id.,* "The Second Mortgage Nightmare," Wash. P. (Oct. 17, 1971), at Al for the origins of the reporter's interest. "It (The Settlement Squeeze) has certainly prompted serious Congressional interest," Congressman Barrett would say in opening hearings in 1972. *See* text *infra* at n. 122-125.

86. *Id.,* (Jan. 11, 1971) at Al, col. 1-2.

87. *Id.,* (Jan. 12, 1971) at Al, col. 1-3.

88. Throughout the fall 1971 settlement charges and points for § 235 homeownership programs for the poor had been a subject of press and congressional interest. Jonès, "Battle Looms on Housing Policy," Balt. Sun (Oct. 3, 1971) p. 1, col. 1; Anderson, "Skinning the Poor," Wash. P. (Oct. 19, 1971) at B13; Carson, "Some Tips in Shopping for a Mortgage on Your House," Wash. P. (Dec. 4, 1971) at D6, col. 1.

89. "Romney to Fight Kickbacks," Wash. P. (Oct. 16, 1971) at C4, col. 1.

90. *Id.*

91. The report in final form did not phrase it this way.

92. B. Burke & N. Kittrie, *The Real Estate Settlement Process and Its Costs* III-E-56 (1972).

93. Q. Johnstone & D. Hopson, *Lawyers and Their Work* 276 (1967).

94. A. Axelrod, C. Berger, & Q. Johnstone, *Land Transfer and Finance* 628 (1969); Interview with Carl Coon, Jr., Nat'l Ass'n of Homebuilders, by N. Sirak, Washington, D.C., July 1971.

95. Comment, "The Duty to Search," 68 Yale L. J. 1245 (1959).

96. *E.g.,* Mintz, "Title Insurance Firms Yield on No-fee N.Y. Bill," Wash. P. (Aug. 3, 1971) at A9; Report of the Joint Legislative Committee on Insurance Rates, Regulation and Recodification of the Insurance Law and Related Statutes, State of N.Y., Legis. Document No. 12 (1970). The unofficial monopoly of much urban conveyancing is probably the source of their nervousness. *See* "Statement of Principles Relating to Real Estate Transaction," Joint Am.L.T.A.-Am. Bar Ass'n resolution (1969).

97. 15 U.S.C. §§ 1011-1015 (the McCarran-Fergusen Act), enacted after United States v. South-Eastern Underwriters Ass'n 322 U.S. 533 (1946); *see also* Burke & Kittrie, *supra,* n. 92 at Appendix 2.

98. Telephone conversation of author with M. Lobel, legislative assistant to Senator Proxmire, Washington, D.C., Nov. 2, 1971.

99. HUD-VA, *Report on Mortgage Settlement Costs, supra,* n. 75, at 33.

100. *Id.,* at v.

101. *Id.,* at 3.

102. *Id.,* at 3-4.

103. *Id.,* at 3; *see also* United States Senate, Hearings at 23-27 *infra* at n. 137.

104. H.R. 13337, Feb. 23, 1972, 92d Cong., 2d Sess.

105. Kessler, "Laws Urged to Cut Home Buying Costs," Wash. P. (Jan. 19, 1972) at C2, col. 1.

106. *Id.*

107. *Id.*, at col. 2.

108. Kessler, *supra,* n. 105, col. 2.

109. Kessler, "Senate Unit Votes Settlement Ceiling," Wash. P. (March 14, 1971) at C1.

110. H.R. 13337, Feb. 23, 1971, 92d Cong., 2d Sess., §§ 101, 102, 103.

111. Kessler, *supra,* n. 109.

112. *E.g.,* Va. Code 1950 §§ 54-78, 54-83 (1973).

113. American Bar Ass'n, Code of Professional Responsibility, DR 2-103(B)-(D) (1969). In advance of hearings in either houses of Congress, the Washington *Post* ran a story in which American Bar Association officers denounced the practice of accepting commissions for placing title insurance as unethical. The lead quote read, "Any lawyer who takes a commission from a title insurance company without crediting it to his client's account (or giving it to his client) is stealing." Kessler, "Settlement Kickbacks Here Decried by ABA," Wash. P. (Feb. 11, 1972) at A1, col. 3. In many transactions the client may be the lender as often as the purchaser, with the lender billing the purchaser. So the purchaser may think he has employed an attorney when in fact he is only paying the lender for services, including the attorney's. The statement is misleadingly strong. It was, however, followed by others, terming the acceptance of such commissions, even when permitted by state statute, unethical. Kessler, *op. cit.*

In advance of hearings, the American Bar Association appointed a special committee from its real property section to investigate the matter. *Id.* State probes in Maryland and Virginia, the states on which the *Post* stories concentrated, were also launched in advance of the hearings. *Id.* Kessler, "Va. Probes Realty Settlement Costs," Wash. P. (Jan. 25, 1972) at A19, col. 4; Kessler, "Home Buyers are Misled at Settlement," Wash. P. (Feb. 6, 1972) at A1, col 4; Kessler, "Settlement Bill Killed in Maryland," Wash. P. (Feb. 12, 1972) at A1, col. 1. The Washington *Post* continued to run much news about local settlement practices. One suburban Washington attorney, testifying before a Maryland legislative committee, said he would raise his fees if forced to return title insurance commissions. Kessler, *op. cit.*, n. 23, Wash. P. (Feb. 12, 1972) at A1, col. 1. This publicity build-up used quotations from bar officials, and occurred in the context of impending revelations of corruption in some housing-subsidy programs. "Romney hits hard at subsidy scandals," Busin. Wk. (Feb. 19, 1972) at 28, col. 3. Prepublication leaks of some of the HUD-VA report conclusions were reported alongside an announcement by Senator Sparkman to hold hearings on the question in March. Kessler, "HUD to Set Ceilings on Settlements," Wash. P. (Feb. 19, 1972) at A1, col. 3.

114. HUD staff had found evidence of interlocking businesses in the

settlement field, and this had also been the subject of past federal investigations. *See* B. Burke & N. Kittrie, *The Real Estate Settlement Process and Its Costs* (1972); E.S. Herman, "Conflict of Interest in the Savings and Loan Industry" in *Study of the Savings and Loan Industry* at 771, 928 (1969). *See* H.R. 13337, § 601(a), (b).

115. H.R. 13337, § 104(a).

116. *Id.,* at § 201(a)-(c). The aim was to sensitize HUD and to keep the matter before HUD as well as to benefit borrowers. *See also* Comp. Gen. of the United States, "Review of the Purchase of Title Insurance on Properties Acquired in the State of Florida under the Loan Guaranty Program—Veterans' Administration" (June 1966).

117. H.R. 13337, § 202. Kessler, "2 Bills to Reduce Settlements Costs Move Ahead on Hill," Wash. P. (Feb. 18, 1972) at B2, col. 1.

118. H.R. 13337, § 301(a).

119. *Id.,* at § 301(b)(1). *See op. cit.,* n. 116; the federal government thought title insurance not worth buying for its own properties. *See also* Fed. Nat'l Mtge. Ass'n, "Public Meeting on Conventional Mortgage Forms" 89, 111 (1971).

120. H.R. 13337, § 401. The rate was 1 percent below current savings bank rates.

121. *Id.,* at § 501.

122. United States House of Representatives, Committee on Banking and Currency, 92d Cong., 2d Sess., "Hearings on H.R. 13337: Real Estate Settlement Costs, FHA Mortgage Foreclosures, Housing Abandonment and Site Selection Policies," Part I, at 1 (1972).

123. *Id.,* at § 101; *see also id.,* at 18. Congressional questioning implied a perception of the same source of interest. *Id.,* at 233, 245, 259 (questions of Congress members Sullivan, Blackburn, and St. Germain). Another saw tight money as the cause of the problem. *Id.* at 261.

124. *Id.,* at 229.

125. *Id.,* at 231 (direct testimony), 298 (in response to a written question submitted by Congressman St. Germain).

126. *Id.,* at 232.

127. *Id.,* at 238.

128. *Id.,* at 240-41.

129. *Id.,* at 310-12.

130. *Id.,* at 426.

131. *Id.,* at 559.

132. *Id.,* at 313.

133. *Id.,* at 323.

134. *Id.,* at 330.

135. *Id.,* at 333.

136. *Id.,* at 339.

137. United States Senate, Committee on Banking, Housing, and Urban Affairs, 92d Cong., 2d Sess., "Mortgage Settlement Costs," (Mar. 1-3, 1972).

138. *Id.,* at 12, 53, 146, 158; Kessler, "Excessive Settling Fees Paid," Wash. P. (Mar. 2, 1972) at C1, col. 8.

139. *Id.,* at 38, 45.

140. *Id.,* at 39.

141. *Id.,* at 213, the testimony of Prof. J. Payne, and the release of his earlier memorandum to HUD consultants; *id.,* at 216, 228.

142. *Id.,* at 45; *cf. id.,* at 228.

143. Kessler, "Senate Unit Votes Settlement Ceiling," Wash. P. (Feb. 18, 1972).

144. Kessler, *supra,* n. 138.

145. Hearings, *supra,* n. 137 at 14.

146. *Id.,* at 19.

147. *Id.,* at 21.

148. *Id.,* at 137-8.

149. Kessler, *supra* n. 143.

150. Hearings, *supra,* n. 137 at 89, 235.

151. *Id.,* at 68.

152. This witness (*id.,* at 71) was not the first to question introducing a title-registration system in place of title insurance, but this replacement was supported by others. *Id.,* at 43, 138. *See also* Jones, "Settlement Costs Unsettled," Balt. Sun (Mar. 5, 1972).

153. H.R. 13337 (Committee Print), May 11, 1972, 92 Cong., 2d Sess., title IX, p. 206, reprinted in United States House of Representatives, Committee on Banking and Currency, 92d Cong., 2d Sess., "Housing and Urban Development Act of 1972," (hearings on June 8, 9, 12, 13, 1972). *See* testimony at 468, 473, 574.

154. *Id.,* at § 911.

155. *Id.,* at § 912; *see* Hearings, *supra,* n. 153, at 587 for supporting judicial opinions inserted in the record.

156. Hearings, *supra,* no. 153, at 618, 710, 712-14, and letters inserted in the record at 723-25, 757-64 (these letters are mostly from attorneys), 786.

From February to mid-June, 1972, agency staff at HUD worked on draft regulations for maximum closing costs. "New Rule Aids Borrower; Closing Cost Control Set," Wash. P. (May 13, 1972) at D9. In the same period meetings with trade and bar groups were held with many HUD officials at every level of the agency, ("New Committee Studying Closing Cost Limits of FHA, VA Sales," 17 Am. Bar News (May, 1972) at 2.) some quite stormy. One state bar representative demanded issuance of proposals for regulation charges be postponed, making his demand to no less than Secretary Romney. That was to be the last interview the secretary would permit on the subject. "Fresh Drive to Cut Home Buying Costs," U.S. News and World Report (Mar 6, 1972); "Costs Vary Widely on Home Settlements," Phila. Inquirer (Feb. 23. 1972) at 3, col. 4; "Cite Attorney Fee Setting," Des Moines Register. (Mar. 26, 1972); "Closing Fees of Attorneys under Attack," J. Commerce and Commercial New York (Mar. 28,

1972); "Buyers and Sellers of American Homes Unwittingly Finance Kickbacks, Payoffs with 'Closing Costs,' " Dubuque Telegraph-Herald (Apr. 17, 1972), *id.,* Fargo Forum; *id.,* Anniston Star; *id.,* Towanda Review (Apr. 20, 1972).

    The regulations were released by insertion in the Federal Register for July 4, 1972. (37 Fed. Reg. 13186 (1972).) To be regulated were settlement charges in six metropolitan areas around the country. In each, maximum levels were established for between four to six charges, less than half of the customary charges levied in the regions around Cleveland, Newark, San Francisco, Seattle, and St. Louis.

    The following costs were regulated for Washington, D.C.

1. Credit report	The charges for a credit report are to be in accordance with the HUD contracts in the SMSA covering credit-report fees.
2. Field survey	$55.
3. Title examination	
District of Columbia	$90.
Maryland & Virginia	$130.
4. Title insurance	$2 per $1,000 of coverage for lender's policy. $3 per $1,000 of coverage for owner's policy. $3 per $1,000 plus $10 for a lender's and owner's policy issued simultaneously.
5. Closing fee	$50.
6. Pest & fungus inspection	$15.

    In the Washington, D.C., area, reactions to these regulations were mixed: Attorneys would be "forced out of the business altogether"; those attorneys who "don't do the work" will "keep on not doing the work"; "Shocking! They don't appear to be realistic at all in terms of the cost of doing business." Kessler, "HUD to Propose Slash in Realty Fees," Wash. P. (July 2, 1972) at A16, col. 1. There was some recognition here that while marginal-quality work would not be affected, it was the low-volume attorney's conveyancing practice that would be reduced in profitability. One lawyer said it was possible that "less cumbersome" methods of title search could be developed. Attorneys' fees in one of the Virginia suburbs could be cut by 68 percent on a $40,000 purchase, 75 percent on a $60,000 one. Maryland attorneys would have had their fees reduced by 66 percent in one county and 53 percent in another on similar home purchases. *Id.*, at A1, col. 5. The period for comment on these regulations was initially to be forty-five days; this was extended by the secretary for an additional thirty days, and through November 11, 1972, 854 responses were logged by the HUD Docket Clerk's office, which was an unusually high number. Burke, "Conveyancing in the National Capital Region: Local Reform with National Implications," 22 Am. U. L. Rev. 527, 569-71 (1973). Most of these responses were from the conveyancing bar in the regions to be regulated. *Id.*, at 571, n. 172; *see also* N.Y. State Land Title Ass'n, *Fifty-first Annual Meeting and Convention* 85 (1972) (speech by D.A. Whitman). The more detailed responses were drafted by Washington attorneys for the bar associations in the regulated areas, and they made a threshold argument that HUD lacked the statutory power to set settlement charge maximum levels. *See* Hearn, "Comments of the Northern Virginia Lawyers Ass'n on Proposed HUD Regulation: Revision of 24 CFR Part 203 § 203.67," 3.7 (1972).

Section 701(a) of the Act [the 1970 Emergency Home Finance Act] authorizes the Secretary to *continue* HUD's current practice of reviewing closing costs to see that they conform to local area standards. (*Id.*, at 3.)

Congressional history was cited in support of this contention: Congress' requiring the HUD-VA study in § 701(b) is "strong evidence that Congress intended to obtain additional information prior to instituting any basic changes in closing practices." The secretary's directive to "study and recommend" was inconsistent with his present action. *Id.*, at 7; *see also* Hourihan, "Comments of the Prince George's County, Maryland, Bar Ass'n," at 3 (1972); Am. Bar Ass'n, "Comments on Proposed Federal Regulation of Residential Settlement Costs" at 1 (1972), noted at 17 Am. Bar News (Nov., 1972) p. 4. Due-process objections were raised as well. Fitzpatrick, "Proposed Settlement Cost Regulations, Comments of the Montgomery County Lawyers Association," 3-16 (1972). Pre-1970 powers were not discussed.

 Few attorneys attacked the statistical methods utilized by HUD. *But see id.*, at 17. Consultants were, in the main, hired to do this. Arthur D. Little, Inc., "An Exploratory Overview of the HUD/VA Analysis of Title Related Costs" 1 (1972); Arthur Anderson and Co., "Report on Review of the Analytic Methods and Procedures Used by the U.S. Department of Housing and Urban Development to Establish Maximum FHA and VA Mortgage Settlement Charges" (1972); F. Benson, Letter to HUD Docket Clerk, dated October 13, 1972, for St. Paul Title Insurance Corp., Troy, Michigan. Several other state bar associations began studies of this problem, (Pa. Bar Assn. Q., *Legislative Bulletin* (Nov. 21, 1972); "Bar Officers Confer with HUD on Closing Costs Rule," N.J. L. J. (Aug. 10, 1972), p. 1, col. 3; *see also id.*, col. 4.), and some local jurisdictions as well. Report of the Temporary Housing Settlement Review Council, Fairfax Co., Va., (1972); Committee on Home Purchase Costs, Report to the Montgomery County Council (1972). The former were aimed at disputing HUD's figures; the latter were mainly aimed at improving the jurisdiction's public land records.

In some jurisdictions bar associations took steps to clarify for the purchaser the position of the attorney and to require advance disclosure of costs. Walsh, "Reforms Urged in Land Sales," Wash. P. (Aug. 4, 1972) at C1, col. 8; Kessler, "Settlement Rules Urged for Lawyers," Wash. P. (July 7, 1972) at C1, col. 7. National press coverage continued. Katz, "Home Buyers Who Pay Lawyer May Not Call Tune at Closing," Nat'l Observer (July 22, 1972) at 8, col. 3, recognized the issue of the attorney's divided loyalties.

157. "New Committee Studying Closing Cost Limits of FHA, VA Sales," 17 Am. Bar News (May 1972) at 2.

158. Evans & Novak, "Tyranny on Capitol Hill" Wash. P. (Aug. 10, 1972) at A23, col. 1. In the Senate, hearings were delayed by the reelection campaign of Senator Sparkman. Anderson, "Fatcats Show Sparkman They Care," Wash. P. (Oct. 7, 1972) at B11, col. 5; Herbers, "Federal Housing Reform Unlikely Despite Scandals," N.Y. Times (Sept. 20, 1972) p. 1, col. 6.

159. Kessler, "House Panel Sets Vote on Settlements," Wash. P. (Sept. 10, 1972) at D1, col. 7; id., "Panel Clears Settlement Kickbacks," Wash. P. (Sept. 14, 1972) at A1, col. 4. Both the chairman and Rep. Stephens introduced this legislation, and the vote to repeal § 701(a) was 28 to 8. Id.

160. Braestrup, "$10.6 Billion Housing Bill is Rejected," Wash. P. (Sept. 29, 1972) at A1, col. 4, indicates the rejection was on grounds other than the settlements issue. Existing programs were continued at the same time, in place. Braestrup & Kessler, "Hill Panel Backs Extension of Housing Programs," Wash. P. (Sept. 29, 1972) at A19, col. 1. Staffs on both sides of Congress considered a separate settlement cost bill at this stage, but since HUD's authority was left intact, there was little reform pressure generated for this idea, particularly in view of the successful last-minute attempts in committee to repeal this authority. Braestrup & Kessler, op. cit. Local mayors were generally for the 1972 Omnibus Housing Bill, with its "block grants" to cities; civil rights groups and the home builders opposed restriction on suburban low-income housing, and real estate groups opposed settlement regulation.

In the executive branch, however, news of Secretary Romney's retirement made hopes dimmer. "Why Romney decided to quit," Busin. Wk. (Aug. 19, 1972) at 19. At a farewell party at the agency, he said that the opening up of the settlement issue was, he considered, one of the biggest accomplishments of his Cabinet tenure. Cf. Karmin, "No Joy in HUDville," Wall St. J. (Dec. 29, 1971) p. 1, col. 6. Romney had at last been waging a losing battle to retain present housing programs. See Braestrup, "Romney Barred Housing Cuts," Wash. P. (Jan. 1, 1973) at D1, col. 1; he failed. Willmann, "U.S. Freezes Subsidies for Housing," Wash. P. (Jan. 9, 1973) at A1, col. 4.

161. H.R. 9989, Aug. 3, 1973, 93d Cong., 1st Sess.; H.R. 12066, Dec. 20, 1973, 93d Cong., 1st Sess.

162. H.R. 9989, § 4(d).

163. H.R. 12066, § 4(a)(1); Cong. Rec. (Dec. 26, 1973) at E8319; *see also* H.R. 11460, Nov. 14, 1973, 93d Cong., 1st Sess., dealing with escrow accounts exclusively.

164. H.R. 12066, § 5.

165. H.R. 9989, § 103.

166. *Id.*; HUD, "Disclosure Statement of Loan and Settlement Costs" (undated, 1972).

167. H.R. 12066, § 6(b)(2).

168. *Id.,* at § 6(b)(4), (5).

169. H.R. 9989, § 105(c) and (d).

170. H.R. 12066, § 7(b).

171. H.R. 9989, § 105(b).

172. H.R. 9989, § 106(a); H.R. 12066, § 8, 9, 10, 11.

173. H.R. 9989, § 106(c).

174. H.R. 9989, § 107.

175. H.R. 12066, § 12(a).

176. H.R. 9989, § 108(a); H.R. 12066, § 13(a).

177. H.R. 9989, § 108(b).

178. H.R. 12066, § 13(c).

179. H.R. 9989, § 109; H.R. 12066, § 14.

180. H.R. 9989, § 110; H.R. 12066, § 15.

181. H.R. 9989, § 111; H.R. 12066, § 16, which also prohibited certain interlocking relationships by title companies. *Id.,* § § (b), (d).

182. S.2288, July 30, 1973, 93d Cong., 1st Sess., introduced in the House as H.R. 11183, Oct. 30, 1973, 93d Cong., 1st Sess.

183. 119 Cong. Rec. 26548 (July 30, 1973).

184. *Id.*

185. S.2288, July 30, 1973, 93d Cong., 1st Sess.

186. S.3164, Mar. 13, 1974 (on this date, it was essentially the Stephens bill as introduced in the House), 93d Cong., 1st Sess.; amended May 22, 1974.

187. S.2288, § 3(1); S.3164, § 3.

188. S.2288, § 3(3).

189. S.3164, § 3(3).

190. *Id.*

191. S.2288, § 4(a)(1).

192. *Id.,* § 4(a)(4).

193. *Id.,* §4(b). After penalties are set out in § § (c), § 701 of the 1970 Emergency Home Finance Act is repealed. *Id.,* § § (d).

194. S.2288, § 5; S.3164, § 4.

195. S.2288, § 6, S.3164, § 5.

196. S.2288, § 7(a); S.3164, § 6(a).

197. S.3164, § 6(c).

198. *Id.,* at § 6(d); *see* 15 U.S.C., § 1640(a), in substantive conflict with the present legislation, though § § (c) and (d) are not.

200. S.3164, § 7(a); *cf.* S.2288, § 8; *see also id.,* at §§ (c); S.2288, § 8.

201. S.2288, § 10; S.3164, § 11.

202. S.2288, § 11; S.3164, § 9.

203. S.2288, § 12.

204. S.3164, § 10(a), (b). Hearings were a part of the hearings on administration housing proposals. United States Senate, Committee on Banking, Housing and Urban Affairs, 93d Cong., 1st Sess., "Administration's 1973 Housing Proposals," Oct. 2, 3, and 4, 1973. The Administration witness did not testify on settlement issues.

205. *Id., see also* "Capital Comment," 18 Am. Bar News (Sept., 1973) at 9.

206. *See supra* text at n. 77.

207. United States Senate, Committee on Banking, Housing and Urban Affairs, 93d Cong., 1st Sess., "Administration's 1973 Housing Proposals," (Oct. 2, 3, and 4, 1973) at 119.

208. United States House of Representatives, Committee on Banking and Currency, Subcommittee on Housing, 93d Cong., 1st and 2d Sess., "Real Estate Settlement Costs" (Dec. 4, 5, 1973, and Jan. 29 and 30, 1974) at 58.

209. *Id.,* at 697.

210. *Id.,* at 673, 706, *cf.* 731.

211. Mintz, "High Settlement Costs Spark Debate," Wash. P. (July 22, 1973) at C7, col. 4.

212. "Housing Bill Gets OK," Providence J. (June 13, 1974), p. 2, col. 7.

213. *Id.*

214. Simpson, "Panel Votes Down U.S. Policing of Settlements," Wash. P. (June 29, 1974) p. E3, col. 1.

215. Anderson, "President Believes Worst is Over," Wash. P. (May 24, 1974) at B19, col. 5.

216. "The Systematic Fleecing of Homebuyers," Wash. P. (June 2, 1974) at C6, col. 1; "More on Real Estate Settlements," *id.* (June 12, 1974) at A28, col. 1; Bowman, "Senate Set to Vote on Home-loan Bill," Wash. P. (June 9, 1974) at E6, col. 1; Wash. P. (June 12, 1974) at A29, col. 5.

217. *Id.; see also* Mills, "Settlement Cost Fight Continues," Wash. P. (June 22, 1974) at E2, col. 1.

218. Mintz, *supra* n. 11.

219. United States Senate, Rept. No. 93-866 (May 22, 1973); Mills, *op. cit.,* n. 53.

220. Mintz, *supra* n. 11.

221. "Congressional Report: Senate Passes Bill to Force Speedy Trial," Wash. P. (July 24, 1974) at A5, col. 1.

222. Telephone interview with Senate staff member, July 24, 1974, Washington, D.C.

223. 93d Cong., 2d Sess., House of Representatives, "Real Estate Settlement Costs," Rept. No. 93-1526 (Dec. 9, 1974) (hereafter 1974 House Report).

224. *Id.,* at 11.

225. *See* text at n. 30-99, *infra.*

226. *See* text at n. 100-108, *infra.*

227. *See* text at n. 109-137, *infra.*

228. *See* text at n. 139-142, *infra.*

229. *See* text at n. 143-194, *infra.*

230. 1974 House Report, § 5 at 3; 12 U.S.C. § 2604 (1977 supp.); 88 Stat. 1724.

231. 1974 House Report, § 5(a) at 3; 12 U.S.C. § 2604(a) (1977 supp.).

232. *Id.,* § 5(b) 3-4; 12 U.S.C. § 2604(b)(1)-(5) (1977 supp.).

233. *Id.,* § 5(c) at 4; 12 U.S.C. § 2604(d) (1977 supp.).

234. *Id.,* at 12.

235. *Id.,* § 15 at 9; 12 U.S.C. § 2613 (1977 supp.).

236. *Cf.* 12 U.S.C. § 2604(b) (1977 supp.): "Such booklets shall take into consideration the differences in real estate settlement procedures which may exist among the several states and territories and among separate political subdivisions within the same state or territory."

237. This was Dale A. Whitman, Professor of Law, J. Reuben Clark Law School, Brigham Young University, Provo, Utah. Today changes in the booklet's text require the written approval of the HUD Secretary. 24 C.F.R. § 3500.6(c) (1977).

238. HUD, "Settlement Costs and You: A Guide for Homebuyers" 5-9 (Gov. Printing Office, Washington, D.C.) (1975).

239. *Id.,* at 4-5.

240. *Id.,* at 14.

241. *Id.*

242. *Id.,* at 14-15.

243. 1974 House Report, § 2(b)(4)(1) at 2; 12 U.S.C. § 2602(1) (1977 supp.).

244. *Id.,* § 5(d) at 4; 12 U.S.C. § 2604(d) (1977 supp.).

245. Roberts, "Urban Conveyancing in the United States," 35 Conv. (N.S.) 190 (1963).

246. Real Estate Settlement Procedures Act of 1974 (hereafter RESPA), § 5(b) (1)-(5); 12 U.S.C. § 2604(b) (1977 supp.), which refers to the booklet's description of "settlement services," defined (in § 2602(3)) as including "any service provided in connection with a real estate settlement including, but not limited to, the following: title searches, title examinations, the provision of title certificates, title insurance, services rendered by an attorney, the preparation of documents, property surveys, the rendering of credit reports or appraisals, pest and fungus inspections, services rendered by a real estate agent or broker, and the handling of the processing, and closing or settlement." Debate over whether or not to include loan assumptions brought HUD very close to the question of whether it might regulate assumption fees and prepayment penalties under the act and so also close to regulating the form of the mortgage agreement.

247. *Id.,* § 5 at 3-4; 12 U.S.C. § 2604 (1977 supp.); 24 C.F.R. § 3500.6 (1977).

248. If no legal remedies are provided, no equitable ones may be implied. K. York & J. Bauman, *Remedies* 1061-67 (2d ed., 1973). *See also* text *infra* at n. 142.

249. "Real Estate Settlement Procedures," 40 Fed. Register 22449 (May 22, 1975) (contains the original regulations, in which "loan application" might have been "oral or written" application for a mortgage or assumption approval); 24 C.F.R. para. 82 (1975), (hereafter cited as Regulation X), was amended Oct. 9, 1975). *See* 40 Fed. Register 47792 (Oct. 9, 1975). Subcommittee on Housing and Community Development, Committee on Banking, Currency and Housing, U.S. House of Representatives, "Hearings on H.R. 5352, S.2327 and H.R. 10283" (Oct. 28-30, 1975) at 14 (testimony of Robert Elliot) (hereafter 1975 House Hearings).

250. HUD, "Settlement Costs and You: A Guide for Homebuyers" 12 (1975).

251. *See* 1974 House Rept. at 4; RESPA § 6(a); Act of Dec. 22, 1974, P.L. 93-533, § 6(a), 88 Stat. 1726.

252. *See* ch. 1, *supra.*

253. Regulation X, para. 82.7(f) (1975); the same would be argued under present regulations. *See* 24 C.F.R. § 3500.7 (1977).

254. *See supra* n. 49.

255. Regulation X, para. 82.2(c) (1975).

256. *Id.,* para. 82.7(b) (1975).

257. *Id.,* para. 82.7(c) (1975).

258. *Id.,* para. 82.7(d) (1975).

259. RESPA, § 6(c); Act of Dec. 22, 1974, P.L. 93-533, § 6(c), 88 Stat. 1726; 1974 House Report at 4.

260. RESPA, § 6(a); Act of Dec. 22, 1974, P.L. 93-533, § 6(a), 88 Stat. 1726; 1974 House Report at 4.

261. The form is prescribed in Regulation X, Appendix A, 41 Fed. Register 22710 (June 4, 1976) superseding Regulation X, para. 82.7(d) (1975) (hereafter Regulation X).

262. *Id.*

263. 1975 House Hearings at 14, 35-36.

264. RESPA, § 18; 12 U.S.C. § 2616 (1977 supp.).

265. RESPA, § 6; Act of Dec. 22, 1974, P.L. 93-533, § 6(a), 88 Stat. 1726.

266. Regulation X, para. 82.7(f) (1975).

267. *Id.,* para. 82.7(m) requires that disclosure forms be retained for two years by lenders. Presumably these records would suffice to show "good faith."

268. P. Barron, *Federal Regulation of Real Estate: The Real Estate Settlement Procedures Act: A Practical Guide with Forms* 35 (1975).

269. Regulation X, para. 82.7(1) (1975).

270. *Id.,* para. 82.9 (1975).

271. Regulation X, para. 82.4(b), amended June 23, 1975, 40 Fed. Register 26251 (June 23, 1975).

272. RESPA, § 6(b); Act of Dec. 22, 1974, P.L. 93-533, § 6(b), 88 Stat. 1726.

273. RESPA, § 7(a)(1)-(3); Act of Dec. 22, 1974, P.L. 93-533, § 7(a)(1)-(3), 88 Stat. 1727; 1974 House Report at 5.

274. RESPA, § 7(b); Act of Dec. 22, 1974, P.L. 93-533, § 7(b), 88 Stat. 1727; 1974 House Report at 5.

275. *Id.*

276. *See* text *supra* at n. 11.

277. The section talked in terms of "sellers" of housing completed more than twelve months prior to the date of the loan commitment; disclosure in writing of the "name and address of the present owner" and the date he acquired his interest had to be made. Act of Dec. 22, 1974, P.L. 93-533, § 7(a)(1)-(2), 88 Stat. 1727. In addition, disclosure of his acquisition price was required when the present owner had owned the property for less than two years and had not resided there. *Id.*

278. 1975 House Hearings, at 55-58.

279. Office of the General Counsel, HUD, "RESPA Legal Opinion No. 2" (1975), reprinted at 1975 House Hearings 49-52.

280. *Id.* When one of several owners does reside on the property, the ruling that no price disclosure need be made implied that the interests in the property constituting "present ownership" include only possessory interests whose holders are popularly known as "owners" and would exclude mortgagees and security-interest holders, possibly even excluding land sale contract vendors as well. This point, however, was never resolved by HUD.

281. *Id.*

282. Repealed § 7(a) seemingly referred, however, to a separate writing: "Disclosure must be confirmed that the following information has been disclosed in writing by the seller or his agent to the buyer. . . ."

283. 15 U.S.C. § 1705(3) (Federal Interstate Land Sales Act of 1968, as amended).

284. Rudd, "The 'One-Subject' Rule in State Legislatures," 42 Minn. L. Rev. 389 (1958), reviews this matter comprehensively.

285. *Cf.* 1 U.S.C. § 104 (each section of an act shall have "a single proposition of enactment"). However, the one-subject rule may also have a constitutional basis in the protection of an effective executive veto power.

286. The purpose clause of the act contains no reference to speculation. 12 U.S.C. § 2601 (1977 supp.).

287. RESPA, § 7(a)(1); Act of Dec. 22, 1974, P.L. 93-533, § 7(a)(1), 88 Stat. 1727; 1974 House Report at 5.

288. RESPA, § 7(a)(3); Act of Dec. 22, 1974, P.L. 93-533, § 7(a)(3), 88 Stat. 1727; 1974 House Report at 5.

289. *See, e.g.,* Neb. Rev. Stat. § 76-214 (1976).

290. *See, e.g.,* Houtz v. Hellman, 228 Mo. 655, 128 S.W. 1001 (1910); Brett v. Cooney, 75 Conn. 388, 53 A. 729 (1902).

291. Hersch v. Silberstein, 424 Pa. 486, 227 A.2d 638 (1967).

292. RESPA, § 7(c); Act of Dec. 22, 1974, P.L. 93-533, § 7(c), 88 Stat. 1927; 1974 House Report at 5. The lack of a specific penalty, plus the unanswered questions posed *supra,* and the difficulty of defining one other statutory phrase in subsection (a)(3), make it arguable that § 2606 was "void for vagueness." International Harvester Co. v. Ky., 234 U.S. 216 (1914) (Holmes, J., held statute under which corporation was convicted of selling agricultural machinery over "real value" void for vagueness. *See also* United States v. Cohen Grocery Co., 255 U.S. 81 (1921); Notes, 40 Corn. L. Q. 195; 109 U. Pa. L. Rev. 67 (1960).

293. RESPA, § 7(b); Act of Dec. 22, 1974, P.L. 93-533, § 7(b), 88 Stat. 1727; 1974 House Report at 5.

294. Contract Buyers League v. F. & F. Inv., 48 F.R.D. 7 (N.D. of Ill., 1969), 300 F. Supp. 210 (1969), rev'd *sub nom.* Clark v. Universal Builders, 501 F.2d 324 (C.C.A. 7, 1974), cert. den., 95 Sup. Ct. 657 (1974).

295. *Compare* Fed. Res. Bd. correspondence No. 628, issued under Regulation Z, reprinted in Barron, *supra* n. 68, at 257.

296. RESPA, § 7(c); Act of Dec. 22, 1974, P.L. 93-533, § 7(c), 88 Stat. 1727; 1974 House Report at 5.

297. *See* Appendix 6A *infra*, text @ n. 20.

298. RESPA, § 14(b)(1); 12 U.S.C. § 2612(b)(1) (1977 supp.); 1974 House Report at 8. This idea would not encourage competitiveness or change in our present patterns of conveyancing, and might reduce a borrower's present remedies against servicers of the loan by destroying any argument of borrower privity with the negligent servicer. 1975 House Hearings, at 194-98.

299. Where a statute required further study and reporting to Congress, the agency charged can take no action that might narrow the alternatives open to the decision makers considering the recommendations of such study. Parker v. United States, 309 F.S. 593, aff'd. 448 F.2d 793 (CCA 10, 1971), cert. den., 405 U.S. 989 (1972) (wilderness act study of suitable area held up timber sale).

300. 24 C.F.R. § 3500.8 (1977), and Appendix A. Regulation X, para 82.7(k) (1975).

301. Early regulations provided that attorney's fees need not be disclosed on the form where the "attorney is not retained to perform the title search or other services required by the lender and the borrower or seller, as the case may be, independently elects to be represented by an attorney and independently selects the particular attorney." *Id.,* para. 82.7(i) (1975). This exception did not apply if the borrower selects an attorney from a lender-approved list of less than

three "recommended" attorneys; all three attorneys could have been from the same law firm and all of this still left open the question of whether the borrower must then have paid for both his and the lender's counsel. (*Id.,* para. 82.7(i)(4) (1975)) or whether the borrowers might urge lenders to use their attorneys without a lender's incurring disclosure and a borrower's doubling his legal costs. *Id.* para. 82.7(i)(3) (1975), which stated that where the lender required legal counsel for borrowers, disclosure was necessary. These complicated regulations were eliminated in 1976, and a "P.O.C." (paid outside closing) on the form is now intended to handle this. 24 C.F.R. § 3500.8(b) and Appendix A, where HUD-1 instructions say title search and certification charges need not be differentiated. *Id.*, "Line Item Instructions," lines 1100, 1102-03.

302. HUD has ruled that none of its authority under RESPA is delegated to its field offices. Regulation X, amended January 9, 1976, para. 82.3, 41 Fed. Register 1672 (Jan. 9, 1976) (hereafter Regulation X-1), superseded to same effect by Regulation X, § 3500.3, 41 Fed. Register 22704 (June 4, 1976), as amended through July, 1977 (hereinafter Regulation X-2).

303. Regulation X-2, § 3500.9(3) (1977); Regulation X-1, para. 82.9 (1976). HUD's refusal to delegate interpretive authority to its field offices is understandable in light of past experience of field-office scandals in appraising and loan-underwriting approvals. *See* text *supra* at n. 102. All questions and comments on RESPA regulations must be addressed to Washington. Regulation X-1, para. 82.3 (1976).

304. Regulation X-2, § 3500.8(b) (1977); Regulation X-1, para. 82.8(b) (1976).

305. *See supra* n. 101. Regulation X, para. 82.7(j) (1975), not found in Regulation X-2, § 3500.8 and Appendix A.

306. 1975 House Hearings, at 35.

307. *Id.; see also* Regulation X-2, § 3500.9(3) (1977); Regulation X-1, para. 82.8 (1976).

308. RESPA, § 12; 12 U.S.C. § 2610 (1977 supp.).

309. RESPA, § 8; 12 U.S.C. § 2607 (1977 supp.).

310. RESPA, § 9; 12 U.S.C. § 2608 (1977 supp.).

311. New York Inv. Inc. v. Manhattan Beach Bathing Parks Corp., 229 App. Div. 593, 129 N.Y.S. 921 (2d Dept., 1930), aff'd. 256 N.Y. 162, 176 N.E. 6, 243 N.Y.S. 548 (1931).

312. *See* text *supra* at n. 87; *see* Barron, *supra* n. 268, at 41.

313. 1975 House Hearings, at 167-69.

314. *See* text *supra* at n. 90.

315. RESPA, § 8(a)-(c); 12 U.S.C. § 2607 (1977 supp.); 1974 House Report at 5-6.

316. *See* Regulation X-2, § 3500.14(f)(1)(a)-(b), (g)(1), and Appendix B (1977).

317. 1975 House Hearings, at 62.

318. *Id.,* and similarly proscribed are "loss-leader" services for builders. Regulation X-2, § 3500, Appendix B, ¶3; *cf.* text on § 9 *supra* @ n. 313-14.

319. *Id.,* at 63.

320. Regulation X-2, § 3500.14(f)(4) and Appendix B (1977).

321. 1975 House Hearings, at 63.

322. *Id.; see also* Regulation X-2, § 3500, Appendix B, ¶8 (1977).

323. Daniel v. Paul, 395 U.S. 298 (1969) (enjoining denial of recreation facility membership to blacks proper because snack bar served food moving in interstate commerce). The federal commerce clause is either a tool of economic regulation or a jurisdiction grant of power coextensive with federal power to enact legislation for which there is a strong social need.

324. Goldfarb v. Va. State Bar, 421 U.S. 775 (1975).

325. *Id.,* at 776.

326. *Id.,* at 778.

327. *Id.,* at 783: Price fixing requires only a showing that prices are not negotiable, rather than a showing that prices could be lowered by competition.

328. *Id.,* at 788.

329. *Id.,* at 792-93.

330. The tort foundation of the antitrust laws was established by the Supreme Court in 1906. *See* Chattanooga Foundry & Pipe Works v. City of Atlanta, 203 U.S. 390 (1906). This negates the need of plaintiffs as in *Goldfarb* to show injury. *See* 15 U.S.C. § 1 (1976).

331. United States v. Loews, Inc., 371 U.S. 38 (1962).

332. RESPA, § 8(d)(2); 12 U.S.C. § 2607(a)(2) (1977 supp.).

333. Fed. R. Civ. Proced., Rule 23.

334. Regulation X-2, § 3500.14(c) (1977), and *see* Interstate Circuit, Inc. v. United States, 306 U.S. 208 (1939).

335. The fact of parallel business conduct is not itself a showing of a conspiracy, only circumstantial proof of it. The question is whether independent decisions or an agreement, express or implied, form the basis of the decision to conform to a practice. Theatre Enterprises, Inc. v. Paramount Film Distrib., 346 U.S. 537 (1954).

336. Camp, "Bar Units Told to Repay Reston Fees," Wash. P. (Nov. 16, 1976) at C1, C4.

337. *Id.*

338. RESPA, § 10(1); Act of Dec. 22, 1974, P.L. 93-533, § 10(1), 88 Stat. 1728.

339. RESPA, § 10(2); Act of Dec. 22, 1974, P.L. 93-533, § 10(2), 88 Stat. 1728.

340. 12 U.S.C. § 2609 (1977).

341. *Id.,* § 10(2).

342. *See generally* Barron, *supra* n. 268, at 42.

343. RESPA, § 13; 12 U.S.C. § 2611 (1977 supp); 1974 House Report at 8.

344. RESPA, § 14(b)(3); 12 U.S.C. § 2612(b)(3) (1977 supp.); 1974 House Report 8.

345. *Id.*

346. RESPA, § 14(b)(2); 12 U.S.C. § 2612(b)(2) (1977 supp.); 1974 House Report at 8.

347. 1975 House Hearings, at 20, contains this and subsequent regulatory history.

348. *Id.,* at 326.

349. S.2327 (1975); H.R. 5352 (1975); H.R. 10283 (1975).

350. 1975 House Hearings at 182, 418.

351. This and the following paragraphs are based on Berry, "The Real Estate Settlement Procedures Act: A Small Law for a Small Industry"; *ibid.,* "The Magical Power of Letters from Home" (unpublished monographs dated May 18, 1976). Both are sponsored by the Alicia Patterson Foundation, New York City, N.Y.

352. 1975 House Hearings, at 19-23.

353. S.2327 (1975).

354. Committee on Banking, Housing and Urban Affairs, United States Senate, 94th Cong., 1st Sess., "RESPA Amendments," Rept. No. 94-410 at 1 (Oct. 6, 1975) (hereafter 1975 House Report).

355. Committee on Banking, Housing and Currency, United States House of Representatives, 94th Cong., 1st Sess., "Report on S.2327" at 1 (Nov. 14, 1975).

356. No examples were cited.

357. 1975 House Hearings, at 150, 209, 231.

358. *Id.,* at 189, 367 (testimony of title insurance company representatives).

359. *Id., at 418.*

360. *Id.,* at 182.

361. *Id.,* at 43, 260.

362. Act of Jan. 2, 1976, P.L. 94-205, 89 Stat. 1157.

363. RESPA, § 3(1); 12 U.S.C. § 2602(1), as amended (1977 supp.).

364. 1975 House Hearings, at 32.

365. Regulation X-2, § 3500.5(d)(1) through (8) (1976).

366. *Id.,* §§ (d)(5)-(6) (1976).

367. RESPA, § 3(1)(B)(iii); 12 U.S.C. § 2602(1)(B)(iii), as amended (1977 supp.).

368. *Id.,* § 2602(1)(B)(iv) (1977 supp.).

369. 12 U.S.C. § 2603(a) (1976).

370. Regulation X-2, § 3500.9(a)(1)-(4) (1977).

371. 41 Fed. Register 22703, c. 1 (June 4, 1976).

372. Regulation X-2, § 3500.8(d)(1)-(2) (1976).

373. *Id.,* § 3500.8(b) (1976).

374. Financial privacy is little discussed. *But see* California Bankers Ass'n v. Shultz, 416 U.S. 21 (1974) (upholding the constitutionality of disclosure of certain bank transactions), noted 20 N.Y.L.F. 416 (1975); A. Miller, "The Right of Privacy: Data Banks and Dossiers," in Final Report, *Privacy in a Free Society* 74 (Roscoe Pound—Am. Tr. Law. Fdn., 1974). Harper & James, *Torts* § 9.5, at 678-79, collect early cases in which the right of privacy was premised on a property right. In a litigation context, financial privacy has been upheld in discovery proceedings under Fed. Rules Civ. Proced., Rule 26; *see* McClure v. Boegar, 105 F.S. 612, 613 (D.C. Pa., 1952). *See* Advisory Committee Comments to Rule 26 Amend. (1970). *Cf.* Nader v. General Motors, 25 N.Y.2d 560, 255 N.E.2d 765 (1970) ("the mere gathering of information about a particular individual does not give rise to a cause of action," for one's privacy is invaded only if "confidential information" is sought in an "unreasonably intrusive" way. Warren & Brandeis, "The Right of Privacy," 4 Harv. L. Rev. 193, 214-15 (1892) (suggests a balancing of public and private interests). Tollesafson v. Price, 247 Or. 398, 430 P2d 990 (1967) (selling of plaintiff's note with public advertisement gave rise to cause of action for invasion of privacy where "private facts" advertised). If recorded with a mortgage, would the facts thereby disclosed become "public" for this purpose?

375. Regulation X-2, § 3500.8(c) (1976).

376. Regulation X-2, § 3500.10(a) (1976).

377. Regulation X-2, § 3500.10(c) (1976).

378. *Id.,* § § (d).

379. 1975 House Hearings, at 35.

380. RESPA, § 5(c); 12 U.S.C. § 2604(c) (1977 supp.).

381. Regulation X-2, § 3500.7(b) (1976).

382. *Id.,* § § (d)(2).

383. *Id.*

384. *Id.,* § 3500.6(a).

385. *Id.,* § 3500.6(b)-(c).

386. *Id.,* § § (a).

387. P.L. 94-205 (Jan. 2, 1976); the repeals are summarized at 41 Fed. Register 1672, C.1-2 (Jan. 9, 1976).

388. 1975 House Report, at 4.

389. *Id.,* at 5.

390. *Id.,* at 5-6.

391. *See* text *infra* at n. 76.

392. Act of Jan. 2, 1976, P.L. 94-205, § 7 89 Stat. 1158, amending 12 U.S.C. § 2607(c).

393. "Amendments to the Real Estate Settlement Procedures Act are Explained by HUD General Counsel," 62 Am. Bar Ass'n J. 222 (1976); Hirschler, "RESPA Revised," R. Prop. Prob. & Tr. News (Feb., 1976) at 5.

394. Act of Jan. 2, 1976, P.L. 94-205, § 19 89 Stat 1158 (Jan. 2, 1976).

395. RESPA, § 13; 12 U.S.C. § 2611 (1977 supp.).

396. RESPA, § 14(b)(3); 12 U.S.C. § 2612 (1977 supp.) requires a report to Congress by HUD if the Secretary "concludes there is a necessity for new legislation." This report should be made mandatory.

Appendix 6A:
Great Britain:
A Comparison

The proposition that debate over conveyancing costs is fruitless without concurrent consideration of systemic changes in conveyancing patterns gains support after studying the English debate over conveyancing costs. American conveyancers have long envied the changes that have simplified the system of landed estates and modernized conveyancing in Great Britain. Changes in its real-property law have occurred over the last hundred years, but mostly since the Law of Property Act of 1925.[1] Interests in land have been abolished or simplified; the "dead-hand" control of testators has been stayed,[2] and of particular interest here, conveyancing procedures have been streamlined.[3] From the American perspective, the important point is not the direction of change but the fact of the change itself, for our system has evolved far more slowly.

Why did Britain's system progress so rapidly? Some have argued that the holders of real property there constitute a small upper class, that conveyancing is therefore an upper-class service performed efficiently just because of the clientele.[4] It might be said, however, that they can equally well afford the expense of a cumbersome service. Conversely, some have argued that the small number of landholders makes reform easier (Britain has a lower percentage of owner-occupied dwellings than does the United States); or that change has come because of a lack of skilled conveyancers to man the older system;[5] or that the number of attorneys situated in Parliament to resist change is comparatively small.[6]

Adoption of Past Reforms (the Torrens System) to English Practice

The evolution from a title-deeds system of unregistered conveyancing to what was initially a Torrens system and is now a title-registration and guarantee system has taken over a century.[7] Long-range governmental attention to improve conveyancing patterns is a prerequisite to conveyancing improvement.

As originally conceived, the Torrens system of title registration and transfer establish a system whereby a judicial decree confirmed title in a named person(s). The process was expensive; it required bringing a judicial action. The title confirmed, with the state as a guarantor, the boundaries established by exact survey, which added still further to the expense. But since the process was voluntary, it could not generate the volume that might allow for reduced fees.

These three aspects of a Torrens system—its judicial nature, the measurement of exact boundaries, and the dependence on voluntary, costly participation—doomed it to failure, both in England and the United States.[8] At the turn of the century Professor Percy Bordwell wrote:

Voluntary registration of title has, in general, been a failure in both the United States and England. Its heavy initial cost alone would insure this. . . .[9]

Wherever title registration did survive in the United States, it either attained very high standards of boundary surveying so that land developers could utilize it as a substitute for an *in rem* quiet-title action (Massachusetts);[10] or was supported by a few large landowners (Hawaii);[11] or did not require the registration of boundaries and used administrators instead of judges (Minnesota); or was promoted heavily.[12]

Monopolies and Cost Controls in English Conveyancing

One must look to English practice and the attitudes of the English legal profession for explanations of the century-long modernization of English conveyancing, long dominated by solicitors. As a result of a series of lawsuits and a political settlement involving revenues needed by the younger Pitt, the solicitor's branch of the legal profession gained a statutory monopoly of conveyancing[13] in 1804.[14] In 1903 the barristers agreed to recognize this monopoly.[15]

The correlative duty of the solicitor's statutory monopoly was that his fees became subject to taxation or audit by court-appointed Masters of the Lord Chancellor's office. The first occurred in 1729 not as a response to conveyancing problems but as a general regulation of the legal profession.[16] In time clients were also permitted to challenge fee levels before boards of the Law Society, the professional association for solicitors.

From 1883 on, however, basic conveyancing fees were determined according to a statutory scale, fixed as a percentage of the amounts involved in the transaction;[17] the scale used either the purchase price or the loan amount as its basis for computation, depending on whether the solicitor represented the purchaser or the lender. Originally, this scale was regarded as a step beneficial to the client in that it permitted him to ascertain the charges before the transaction was closed. At its inception, it may have been a method of reducing these charges, even though it contained an escalation factor as real property values rose. So far as the client was concerned, "scale fees" became a double-edged sword.[18]

Since 1941 each solicitor must be recertified annually by the Law Society.[19] As part of this process, he must have his conveyancing and other financial records audited and submit the results to his superiors in the Law Society.

In the twentieth century fees set by scale, combined with procedures to discipline lawyers and prevent undercutting these fee levels, fixed the maximum rate. The rule against undercutting scale fees was established in the 1930s. In 1934, "it was made clear that the offense of touting was an offense under Section 5 of the Solicitors' Act, 1932," and *touting* was defined to include undercutting and "the acceptance by solicitor of remuneration at less than the statutory or customary rate with the object or result of attracting . . . business." As Zander has written:

Scale fees in conveyancing matters are fixed by the Lord Chancellor's Committee under the Solicitors' Remuneration Orders, but the rules permit the substitution of special local scales which must not, however, be greater than the national maximum. The local scales are fixed by the Local Law Societies. In 1950, the Law Society tried to enforce 80-85 percent of the national scale as the minimum.

English Conveyancing Procedures

From the American viewpoint English conveyancing patterns have some distinctive features, although, as in the United States, they are largely a matter of custom and usage and have been developed mostly to handle out-of-the-ordinary transactions in which a complication develops. "Most conveyancing transactions are completed without a hitch."[20] More documents are involved in an English conveyance than in the United States. Some are executed before the agreement of sale is signed, before the equitable conversion takes place and the executory period commences.

The first document is the vendor-estate agent (real estate broker) listing contract.[21] It is normally in writing. Some estate agents insist on signing a preliminary contract once a prospective purchaser is found.[22] This contract is signed "subject to contract," and binds neither party, although it may protect the estate agent's right to a commission. If no agent is involved, the parties themselves agree to buy and sell "subject to contract," a well enough known phrase. The signing of a contract is also subject to the carrying out of a detailed inspection on the condition of the house, conducted by a "surveyor" who reports his findings to the purchaser. Many estate agents conduct inspection services as a part of their business.

Only when this preliminary agreement is signed does a solicitor enter the transaction. As in the United States, "it is rare that he [the solicitor] has been instructed by either party before a sale has been agreed between them."[23] The vendor's solicitor, by letter, customarily notifies the purchaser or his solicitor that a formal contract will be forthcoming after certain preliminary matters are arranged. Once the vendor's solicitor receives the title deeds or registration certificate, he drafts a contract, forwarding it to the purchaser's solicitor.[24] If a mortgage is outstanding, the title documents will have to be obtained from the building society or lender. Such requests are made by letter in which the solicitor undertakes to hold the documents on behalf of and on the instructions of the mortgagee. By the same letter, the solicitor notifies the lender of the intent to redeem the mortgage by the vendor.

When the purchaser's solicitors have received the draft contract, they undertake the search of local government records back about four years to discover any outstanding encumbrances imposed by private parties, local governments, taxing, or planning authorities.[25] "Preliminary inquiries" in standard form will also be made of the vendor's solicitor. They involve ownership of boundary objects, existing disputes about boundaries, easements in use, pending notices received or served, warranties of fitness from builders, insurance, covenants, bonds, defects, services, shared facilities, adverse rights, planning status, fixtures, tax assessments, and existing leaseholds.[26] Taken together, these constitute a more complete examination of the title to a property than is normally undertaken in the United States. When these are returned and if the draft contract proves satisfactory and the purchasers obtain a new mortgage, copies will be signed and exchanged between the parties and their solicitors.[27]

After contracting, the vendor submits the past title deeds to the purchaser's solicitor who examines title and raises any objections he deems necessary. At this time he also submits a draft conveyance to his opposite number.

With this procedure, the executory period is usually shorter in England than in the United States. Since many inquiries are handled before formal contracting, the parties can know more about the property before they are formally bound to go through with the transaction. The English contract, once signed, contains fewer "subject to" clauses than its American counterpart.

In both countries, however, the title search occurs during the executory period and involves a search of a national "land charges register," recently computerized at Plymouth but formerly maintained for unregistered conveyances in eleven locations in England.[28] It contains a list of less-than-fee encumbrances registered against the title. With so many matters covered by the preliminary inquiries and the abstract already received, the search is really an up-date or "bring-down" and is conducted twice, the second time just before "completion," as the closing is called in England.

While the search of the land charges registry is going forward, the vendor's solicitor prepares the draft conveyance, arranges the time and place for completion (usually in his chambers), and prepares a completion statement prorating transfer service and utility charges. The purchaser's solicitor reviews this statement and compares the abstract against the original title documents if this has not already been done.

At completion, payment by banker's draft is exchanged for the keys. Once completed, the purchaser's solicitor sees to the stamping of the conveyance and if necessary, applies for a first registration. In cases where the property is already registered, the procedures just described are the same except that the investigation of title is confined to the public register. Registration does not reduce the role of the solicitor, though it may simplify it.

Since some days may elapse before the vendor's mortgage is formally discharged, the vendor's solicitor gives his opposite number a written understanding to discharge it soon after the completion.[29]

Some Comments on the Process

The solicitor in any conveyancing matter may undertake many more diverse inquiries than would his American counterpart, particularly at the precontract stage. No available statistics suggest just how often such inquiries are more than a matter of form and result in "so far as is known" answers or how frequently diligent searches are necessary concerning these matters. Also unclear is the liability of the solicitor for his failure to discover information pertinent to these inquiries. There is no English counterpart of a mechanic's lien or a security interest attaching to the land for nonpayment of real property taxes so the potential of liability for incompetently undertaken searches would seem to be less in England than in the United States.

The cost of the solicitor's services in 1974 was £80-150 on a £8,000-20,000 house if the solicitor acts for the purchaser and about a third less if he acts for the vendor who does not have the expense of procuring a mortgage.

Public Debate over Conveyancing Fees

The appropriateness of conveyancing fees has long been debated in Parliament. There are several possible origins of this controversy, including the 1958 Cost of Leases Act. It stated simply:

Notwithstanding any custom to the contrary, a party to a lease shall, unless the parties thereto agree otherwise in writing, be under no obligation to pay the whole or any part of any other party's solicitor's costs of the lease.[30]

The effect of this legislation was to change the customary procedure whereby the leasee paid the lessor's costs.[31] The statute was enacted a year after the Solicitor's Act of 1957.[32] One of the periodic statutes governing the decision-making process to determine solicitor's remuneration, the latter statute gave exclusive power to a parliamentary committee whose drafts must be referred to the Council of the Law Society for comment before enactment.[33]

With such procedures in effect, the periodic petitions of the Law Society to raise their conveyancing and other rates were bound to receive public attention.

Indeed, the law profession agitated for increases in the scale from 1956 on, the last increase having been in 1944.[34] There is a good deal of antilawyer feeling in Parliament, which is not as dominated by attorneys as the United States Congress and state legislatures are.[35] In 1950-56 solicitors were more concerned with establishing minimum conveyancing charges than with getting new types of work;[36] one economist saw this as an attempt to consolidate the solicitors' conveyancing[37] monopoly. Also, since the English profession is not as large as the American and since other professions, e.g., accountants, have taken up much of the tax work, solicitors' livelihoods have become heavily dependent on conveyancing,[38] which comprises 55 percent of their workload.

Moreover, as the Cost of Leases Act indicates, the first glimmer of a debate over conveyancing costs came in the area of nonfreehold transfer. English citizens grew accustomed to the idea of widespread homeownership later than Americans; in the United States, homeownership became a common goal after World War I and received the sanction of government policy in the 1930s. In Britain only 45 percent of all households achieve homeownership[39] as compared to 63 percent in the United States.[40] For a large proportion of British house purchasers in the 1950s and early 1960s, this was their first purchase. Furthermore, with housing prices rising 43 percent between 1956 and 1963, purchasers attempted to offset these increases by reducing solicitor's fees.[41]

In addition, there were two more specific reasons for keeping the cost controversy fueled. In the Cost of Leases Act, a business practice of having one party pay for the costs of another was reversed, with each party now paying his own costs. What happened in many conveyancing transactions when the same solicitor acted for both sides to the transaction?[42] Who paid for what services, and who was protected? The law was silent. Client frustration with dual representation produced demands for inquiries in the early 1960s.[43] No reduction in fees for either party resulted from this dual representation, although some simplistic solutions were proposed. For example, M.P. Robert Edwards introduced a bill reducing all conveyancing fees by half.[44]

A second reason is that solicitors are the branch of the legal profession that regularly meets the public, and they remain the one large profession where bills are not paid by national insurance programs. One of the times when the public meets a solicitor is a house purchase, and understandably, his bill produces shock and surprise. The uniqueness of the solicitor's place among professionals surely accounts for some of the public outcry. Taken together, this remarkable combination of factors has kept the issue before the public.[45]

Solicitor Responses

One response to these persistent inquiries on costs was the Law Society's proposal for a "title certificate." This proposal emerged full blown out of a

Society committee. Briefly, the idea was that at completion, the purchaser's solicitor would present his cleint with a certificate, which stated that he had examined the title and would guarantee its marketability as of the date of completion.[46] The certificate's practical effect would be that, upon any subsequent transfer, the period of time covered by the certificate need not be researched; only an update search of title and a new certificate would be necessary. The issuance of a certificate would replace the vendor's duty to present title deeds.[47] Critics said that the idea was only as good as the solicitor's liability insurance (and in the process another possible alternative, American title insurance, was ridiculed as worthless); anyway, they said, nation-wide title registration was the real solution. On the grounds that under this scheme the solicitor was to insure his client regardless of the former's negligence, at least one local law society openly criticized it. It thought that the extension of registration and a shorter title-search period for unregistered conveyances were better solutions.[48] In the end, few were prepared for the idea of a title certificate, and it met a chilly reception.[49] The Law Commission, established in 1965 by Parliament, eventually rejected the certificate idea in favor of a crash program to extend registration.

This proposal did not abate the criticism of solicitors through 1966.[50] Debates in the Oxford Union and economic studies on restrictive practices in the profession were presented in the legal journals.[51] One journal editor concluded:

The question whether remuneration should be by scale or not is one on which there can be two views.[52]

He thought, however, that the public preferred the certainty of scales. Many solicitors wrote to the editors[53] of various law journals, justifying higher charges in light of other price increases.[54] Parliamentary concern was with raising fees on the lower end of the scale.[55]

Two documents dominated the debate during the last years of the 1960s: the commencement in 1968 and subsequent completion of the Prices and Incomes Board's (PIB) "Report on the Remuneration of Solicitors"[56] and a survey by the largest consumer magazine, Which?, on conveyancing.[57]

The latter report concluded that good conveyancing is to be had from a good solicitor,[58] but it did not indicate how to tell good conveyancing from bad. The consumers surveyed—all members of the Consumers' Association publishing Which?—expressed the greatest satisfaction when their solicitors communicated frequently with them.[59] This lesson was not lost in the law journals.[60]

However, it was the PIB report that had the greater impact. The pay-as-you-go rule of the Cost of Leases Act had, throughout the various negotiations over scales, been consistently ignored. The PIB report enunciated the rule that one legal service should pay its own way and not be subsidized by another legal activity, no matter how meritorious or socially beneficial these activities might be. One law journal interpreted this prohibition of cross-subsidies to mean that "fees should attract the necessary human capital" to render legal services.[61]

Yet the report's conclusion flew in the face of the record of the ongoing negotiations over scale increases that year when, as before, trade-offs were urged as a compromise. One journal reported that the government had decided on a "package deal" wherein increases in trial court and some conveyancing charges were to be offset by reductions in other conveyancing charges.[62] More important to the M.P.s were the increases in the lower end of the conveyancing scale made in the early 1960s and increases in the rates levied by building societies on estate builders—all of which hurt the poorer mortgagors and new houseowners, respectively.

1970-1972

Negotiations for higher scale rates had in 1970 pushed charges upward, particularly steeply at the lower end of the scale. In this year a compromise was reached. A PIB proposal to limit solicitors' acting for both parties to one and one-half times the scale fee was dropped. Scales on estates' houses in developments of 100 or more dwellings were reduced 10-25 percent for purchasers. Where one solicitor served both mortgagor and mortgagee, a right to appeal his fee to the Law Society was established. Finally, scales were increased on the lower end of the price scale but abolished for homes costing over £30,000.[63] Homes costing over £30,000 were subject to customary or negotiated fees. One letter to an editor said that the period of intensive controversy of 1966-70 seemed "like a bad dream."[64]

Parliamentary debates soon reflected private member sentiments to annul this 1970 order.[65] Although this sentiment was unsupported by any party leadership, a second PIB report on solicitors' costs opposed any scale increases in March 1971 rates.[66]

By the end of 1971, the press and journals frequently reported that scale fees might be abolished altogether. The lord chancellor wanted all scales regarded as maximums, negotiable on transactions over £10,000, and reduced still further where the solicitor acted for both parties.[67] On May 1, 1972, the attorney-general stated in question time in the House of Commons that the lord chancellor "hopes that an order may be made in the near future which will have the effect of abolishing scale charges and minimum charges."[68] The lord chancellor, Lord Hailsham, said a short time later than an order was already drafted and would be submitted to the statutory committee in June 1972 operative in the early fall.[69] Responses to this proposal came quickly: It was "welcomed" in one journal;[70] the Law Society said that "it would not have chosen to alter the system of scale," but "abolition is the best alternative now available."[71]

Officially, the action was justified as a method for promoting competition.[72] To this, PIB responded that no resulting cut in the prices of conveyancing services was likely, and no cost accounting existed to set fees at other than customary levels.[73] Probably the lord chancellor was "being loyal," going along with the policy of his Conservative government when presented with a reasonable, if not compelling, basis for doing so.[74]

The leadership of the Law Society was criticized as this debate over abolition progressed. Their position was criticized as unaggressive and "less than straight-forward."[75] There were requests for a polling of member preferences in the matter,[76] and several letters from members of the more aggressively conservative British Legal Association took the Law Society to task for passivity.[77] Gradually, however, this criticism subsided as members realized that the Law Society would enforce a "fair and reasonable"[78] standard for fees.[79] Under the new order a client was given the right to file for a review by a committee of the Law Society Council of the fee sought by the solicitor.[80]

The energies of this debate appear spent. By 1975 discussion was flagging, revived occasionally by prosecution under the Solicitor's Act of 1957 of an unauthorized conveyancer. More such were promised, according to the new secretary-general of the Law Society. The government got rid of a persistent problem on a reasonable premise, and the Law Society achieved self-regulation and an opportunity to indefinitely continue the status quo. The burden of challenging a fee shifted to the client who must now file for a Law Society review, while the criteria for reviewing a fee remains custom and usage. Nothing in the course of this debate impelled solicitors to rationalize their services, and nothing except the good-will of the solicitor makes them more comprehensible to the client.

Notes

1. 1925, c. 20; 15 Geo. 5, c. 20.
2. *Id.,* § 1.
3. Land Registration Act of 1925, c. 21, 15, and 16 Geo. 5, c. 21; *see generally* D. Barnsley, *Conveyancing Law and Practice* 9 (1973).
4. Fiflis, "Security and Economy in Land Transactions: Some Suggestions from Scotland and England," 20 Hast. L. J. 171, 206 (1968).
5. *Id.,* at 201; *see also* Fiflis, "English Registered Conveyancing: A Study of Effective Land Transfer," 59 N.W.U. L. Rev. 468 (1964).
6. Interview by author with Prof. S. Cretney, Oxford Univ., June 25, 1976.
7. A brief summary is contained in O. Browder, R. Cunningham, J. Julin, *Property* 1001-1010 (2d ed., 1973).
8. *Id.*
9. Bordwell, "Registration of Title to Land," 12 Iowa L. Rev. 114 (1927).

10. Mass. Stat. Ann., ch. 185 (1974).

11. Haw. Stat. Ann., ch. 342 (1974).

12. Minnesota Stat. Ann., ch. 508 (1974).

13. Solicitors' fees could be "taxed" or, in other words, reviewed by court officials as early as 1729. The renewal of the taxing legislation in 1739 gave rise to the establishment of the "Society of Gentlemen Practicers." This was the first trade association for solicitors in Great Britain. As two chroniclers of the history of the English Bar have written,

The most important achievement of the Society of Gentlemen Practicers . . . was to win for the legal profession a statutory monopoly of conveyancing. The Society first sought to secure this monopoly in 1748. It was ultimately obtained in 1804 as the result of what appears to have been a deal between the Society and the Younger Pitt. During the latter part of the 18th century, taxes had been imposed on attorneys' and solicitors' annual practice certificates and on articles of apprenticeship. The main purpose of the Act which gave solicitors a monopoly of conveyancing was to increase these taxes; and the monopoly appears to have been given as a *quid pro quo* for the higher duties. Although the taxes themselves were reduced in the middle of the 19th century and abolished in the middle of the 20th, the monopoly remained and became the foundation upon which the prosperity of the junior branch of the profession was later to be built. [B. Abel-Smith & R. Stevens, *In Search of Justice* 42 (1968).]

Conveyancing in the Solicitor's Act of 1957 means just that, the preparation and execution of a transfer document. So services ancillary to the conveyance are not subject to the monopoly. One for profit service today, the National House Owners Society provides ancillary services (contracts, property inspections) at reduced rates and "assists" its members in their preparation of a deed. ["Conveyancing," *Which?* (March 1970) reprinted in "Buying and Selling A House" 23, 33 (1970).]

14. *See* B. Abel-Smith & R. Stevens, *Lawyers and the Courts* 23 (1967); *id., in Search of Justice* 124 (1968); M. Zander, *Lawyers and the Public Interest* 171-180 (1968).

15. B. Abel-Smith & R. Stevens, *Lawyers and the Courts* 196-206 (1967).

16. *Id.,* at 19-20. In 1883 the first scale fees were a percentage of the purchase price or loan amount of the property sold. These fees were first controlled by General Orders (Solicitors' Remuneration Orders, 1883-1970). When first introduced, they had as their principal objective the reduction of conveyancing costs and as their further objective the advanced disclosure and determination of these fees.

17. C. Chavasse, *Conveyancing and Other Non-contentious Costs* 7 (5th ed., 1972).

18. B. Abel-Smith & R. Stevens, *Lawyers and the Courts* 377 (1967).

19. *Id.,* at 41 (1968).

20. E. Bowman & E. Tyler, *Elements of Conveyancing* 1 (1972).

21. *Id.,* at 2.

22. In Scotland solicitors display unsold housing inventories in their offices and so act as an estate agent for a 1 percent commission if the transaction is completed under their auspices. English solicitors increasingly act as stakeholders for the deposit. "Current topics: Second Report on Conveyancing," 110 Sol. J. 197 (1966). "Conveyancing in Scotland," *Which?* (June 1971), noted in "Conveyancing North of the Border," 115 Sol. J. 475 (1971).

23. Bowman & Tyler, *supra*, n. 20, at 2.

24. *Id.*, at 43.

25. *Id.*, at 4.

26. "Enquiries before Contract," Con 29 (Long form), January 1974.

27. H.W. Wilkinson, *Standard Conditions of Sale of Land* 1 (1972), contains a brief history of this standard printed form, tracing some of its clauses back to 1804. The first version was published around 1902, and eighteen editions have been published since that time. The Law Society undertook publication of its form in 1926. Local law societies sometimes publish their own versions. *See also* "Estate Developers' Standard Forms of Contract," 110 Sol. J. 259 (1966).

28. In unregistered conveyancing, a root of title thirty years old is normally acceptable, and twenty-five years is customarily accepted in many cases. The Land Registry is normally satisfied with a fifteen-year-old root of title. V. Hackell & E. Nugee, "Root of Title-I," 110 Sol. J. 179, 201 (1966). Law Commission, Com. Paper No. 9, "Transfer of Land: Interim Report on Root of Title to Freehold Land" 2, 5, 6, 7, 8-12 (1967) emphasizes the extent of the search period has always been a matter of convention; at common law, the period was sixty years, changed in

a. 1874 to forty years, and
b. 1925 to thirty years, after passage of the Reform of Property Act.

This report (at 11-12) proposed a further reduction to twelve to twenty years, twelve being the number of years needed for adverse possession. The advantages of this proposal are best known to solicitors, and it is "easier for experts to know an answer than to prove it." *Id.*, at 14. No statutory root of title definition exists, and this report would not recommend one. *Id.*, at 16. That was left up to agreement between the parties.

29. Occasionally the courts remind solicitors that these undertakings are serious obligations. *Re* Mallows (1960) 176 E.G. 1117, where the High Court enforced a solicitor's undertaking; he had undertaken to remove two second mortgages; the mortgages would not later cooperate, and the solicitor was liable for resulting damages.

30. Cost of Leases Act, § 1 (1958), 6 and 7 Eliz. 2, c. 52, noted at 108 L. J. 761 (1958), 22 Mod. L. Rev. 302 (1959), 100 Sol. J. 354, 476 (1959).

31. Conveyancer's Notebook, Costs of Leases Act, 1958, 22 Conv. and Prop. Law 321 (1958).

32. "Conveyancer's Notebook, Solicitor's Remuneration," 32 Conv. and Prop. Law 310-11 (1968).

33. There is in the House of Commons a solicitor's caucus, but it is only informally involved in this rate setting.

34. "Conveyancing Costs," 106 L. H. 375 (1956).

35. L. Friedman, *History of American Law* 560 (1973).

36. Q. Johnstone & D. Hopson, *Lawyers and Their Work* (1967).

37. D.S. Lee, *Economic Consequences of the Professions* (1966), quoted at 30 Conv. and Prop. Law 81-83 (1966).

38. Prices and Incomes Board, "Standing Reference on the Remuneration of Solicitors: First Report," Com. Paper No. 4217 (1969).

39. D. Mandelker, *Housing Subsidies in the United States and England* 17 (1973) puts the homeownership rate in England at 50 percent of all households; D. Donnison, *The Government of Housing* 205 (Table 16) (1967) makes an estimate of 43 percent based on a 1961-62 survey; *see generally* C. Abrams, *Man's Struggle for Shelter in an Urbanizing World* 30-36 (1964) for comparative statistics. "Conveyancers Notebook, Price of Land," 24 Conv. and Prop. Law 24 (1960): "In the last four years the number of home owners has risen in a most spectacular fashion. . . ."

40. 1972 Stat. Abst. of the United States 688 (Table No. 1156).

41. (1974) Whittaker's Almanac 597, gives the 1956 average cost of a three-bedroom house as £1,448 (or £1.58/sq. ft.) and in 1968, as £3,864 (or £4.02/sq. ft.); "Conveyancer's Notebook, Conveyancing Costs," 28 Conv. and Prop. Law 187 (1964).

42. Interview with A. Mellows, Temple Chambers, June 24, 1974, in London.

43. Note, 79 L. Q. Rev. 25 (1963), debate continued in "Current Topics," 114 Sol. J. 381 (1970); *re Evill* (1951) All E.R. 108 for a justification of full scales when acting for both parties. The new 1960 scale satisfied few and was reported to be "still on the low side." Conveyancer's Notebook, "The New Scale of Costs," 24 Conv. and Prop. Law 5-7 (1960); Sol. Remun. Order, 1959, S.I., No. 2027; Sol. Remun. Order, Registered Land, 1959, S.I. 1959, No. 2028.

44. "The Sale of Houses and Land" (Legal Costs) Bill, § 1 (1963), reported in "The Conveyancer's Notebook," 28 Conv. and Prop. Law 242 (1964).

45. "Conveyancer's Notebook, Title Certificate Scheme," Conv. and Prop. Law 419 (1965).

46. A similar idea has been proposed by attorneys in suburban counties outside Washington, D.C.

47. E. Bowman & E. Tyler, *Elements of Conveyancing* 6 (1972).

48. *Id.,* at 420.

49. Interview with Cyril Glasser, Bernard Sheridan and Company, June 19, 1974, in London.

50. "Conveyancer's Notebook, Gresham's Law," 30 Conv. and Prop. Law 81 (1966).

51. *Id., see* D.S. Lee, *Economic Consequences of the Professions* (1966).

52. *Id.,* at 83.

53. "Current Topics," 172 Sol. J. 401, 426, 446 (1968).

54. *Id.,* 114 Sol. J. 158 (1970).

55. *Id.,* 113 Sol. J. 190 (1969).

56. Com. Paper 3529 (1968), noted at 32 Conv. and Prop. Law 81 (1968).

57. "Conveyancing," *Which?,* March 1970, reprinted in "Buying and Selling a House," 23 (1970); noted in "Current Topics," 114 Sol. J. 197 (1970).

58. *Id.,* at 34.

59. *Id.,* at 28.

60. The *Which?* report also surveyed alternative conveyancing services offered by the National House Owners' Association for registered land. *Id.,* at 33.

61. "Conveyancer's Notebook, Remuneration of Solicitors," 32 Conv. and Prop. Law 81 (1968).

62. *Id.,* "Solicitor's Remuneration," 32 Conv. and Prop. Law 310 (1968).

63. "New Conveyancing Remuneration Rates," 115 Sol. J. 21 (1971); "Conveyancing Charges," 121 N.L.J. 25 (1971); "Conveyancer's Notebook, Conveyancer's Remuneration," 35 Conv. and Prop. Law 69 (1971); Sol. Remun. Order, 1970, S.I. No. 2021.

64. 115 Sol. J. 48 (1971).

65. "Conveyancing Charges," 121 N.L.J. 124; *see* Hansard's Reports, H.C., Feb. 11, 1971, col. 803-04; "Westminster and Whitehall," 115 Sol. J. 115 (1971).

66. "Conveyancing Charges: Prices and Incomes Board Report," 121 N.L.J. 304 (1971); Letters to the editor, 115 Sol. J. 794, 815 (1971); "Conveyancer's Notebook, Report of the Prices and Incomes Board," 35 Conv. and Prop. Law 143 (1971).

67. *E.g.,* "Scale Fees in the Balance," 115 Sol. J. 917 (1971).

68. "Farewell to Scales," 122 N.L.J. 398 (1971).

69. *Id.*

70. *Id.*

71. *Id.*; full statement reprinted at 122 N.L.J. 409 (1972). *See also,* "Current Topics: No More Fee Scales," 116 Sol. J. 341 (1972); "Notes and News," 116 Sol. J. 44 (1972).

72. "Schedule II Competition and the Public Interest," 122 N.L.J. 390 (1972).

73. *Id.*

74. Interview with Cyril Glasser, *supra* n. 49.

75. "Conveyancer's Notebook, Conveyancing Scales," 36 Conv. and Prop. Law 73 (1972).

76. Letter to the editor, 116 Sol. J. 419 (1972); the idea failed for want of two signatures on a petition, 116 Sol. J. 682 (1972).

77. *Id.,* 116 Sol. J. 377 (1972).

78. "Conveyancer's Notebook, Solicitor's Remuneration," 36 Conv. and Prop. Law 226 (1972).

79. Letters to the editor, 116 Sol. J. 105, 429, 448, 487 (1972).

80. Sol. Remun. Order, 1972, S.I. No. 1139.

Afterword

The underlying theme of this book is that title records are the key to our conveyancing system. The evolution of the title-related aspects of our conveyancing patterns has largely been a response to the way these records are indexed, maintained, and finally provide (or fail to provide) title evidence. Improvement in these records will improve the patterns themselves, but improvements, to be feasible, should proceed in discrete stages; that is, each improvement must be self-contained, improving the records in its own right, and laying the groundwork for further improvements. Legislation can prepare the way for improving the records, particularly if existing records must be rearranged in the process; but the marketable-title acts and the variety of curative statutes so far enacted are of little practical value to title searchers and raise their own problems as well.[1] This being so, improvements in the records themselves are a next step, to establish tract indexes and then more comprehensive title-related records. As more types of records are included in the indexes and records, however, administrative control over their contents will be necessary to provide constitutional safeguards in the case of nonconveyancing, ex parte records.[2]

The need for administrative controls could be lessened if accessibility to the records were controlled: if, for example, the "public" records were made accessible only with the written permission of the fee owner. But downplaying the public aspect of the records is perhaps as difficult as any attempt to control the validity of the interests that appear on them. Changing the legal effect of the record system is at this point no greater an administrative problem than the alternative of controlled access. As Professor Barnett has written of the marketable-title acts, if all the effort expended on this legislation were redirected toward implementing a registration system, greater benefits would have been achieved without making the task appreciably more difficult.

Better records may of course induce people to rely on them to a greater extent than many do today, when the recording system provides only chronological evidence of title without confirming its validity. However, successive recordings establish only a chain of evidence down to the date on which the last purchaser becomes a vendor, so each owner knows "if I don't record, I won't have good title." Changing this knowledge of the effect of the recording system to a positive, "if I record, I will have good title," is the effect of a registry.[3] Changing the inconclusive legal effect of recordation may also provide a basis for increasing the federal role in modernizing our conveyancing patterns. Over the last six years, federal regulation of settlement costs and patterns has proved a difficult task.[4] Initially concerned with high costs of settlements, the government proved unable to define what *high* meant. In light of the inconclusive nature of title proof and recordation, this is not surprising. After all, a purchaser may not know what he is buying no matter what he pays at settlement.

215

At a time when the federal government is seeking a role in modernizing these patterns, I have argued that it—and any person interested in changing our conveyancing—must first select particular jurisdictions in which to work. In spite of the fact that the recording system is administered in every county in the country, the benefits of better title records will not be as readily apparent in every county—not as apparent in Washington, D.C., as in Sioux Falls, for example. The reason is that Washington, D.C., has learned to cope with its poor records through the maintenance of private title plants. In fast-growing counties, the public benefits of improved records could be more dramatic. Each year in this country a geographic area the size of Rhode Island is undergoing urbaniza-tion—or rather, suburbanization, the changing of raw, previously agricultural or forrested land into suburban lots. This is an astoundingly large acreage to convert annually, and it also means that there are more than a million new separate parcels of land created every year.[5] Attending their monumentation are the numerous boundary, contractual, and title problems that are grist for the conveyancer's mill. We do not know by what magnitude title problems multiply with the suburbanization of land, but the increase is probably dramatic.

Urbanizing jurisdictions need, and are least likely to possess, title records able to cope with this multiplication of parcels and title problems.[6] Initial attention should therefore be paid to such counties. It is here that federal aid—grants in aid, bonds, or loans—can be most helpful. However, since there are 252 metropolitan areas recognized as such by the Bureau of the Census and many of these are multicounty areas, further selection should provide aid to those suburban counties:

1. In states having enacted marketable-title acts (there are now sixteen) and curative legislation; such states will have in place laws to allow land titles to undergo the change to urban status with the least uncertainty. The lesson of our experience with marketable-title acts is that it is precisely in such long and complicated title searches such as must be undertaken as a precondition to land development, that such laws will be most useful.

2. Which have converted their title records to parcel indexes. Such indexes are accessible for a variety of purposes, not just to conveyancers, but to land planners, tax assessors, surveyors, and public officials. It would permit the monitoring of the urbanization process; there is much in title records maintained today of use to these monitors—land prices, parcel sizes, ownership names, and terms of financing—which will allow public officials to understand that process better. It is unnecessary to add to the informa-tion on the title records to improve them. Much improvement in the way we handle the information we now collect—much of it useful in anticipating, monitoring, and servicing urban growth as well as conveyancing—is possible.

In the process of aiding urbanizing jurisdictions, we would be enabling conveyancing to proceed on the basis of the traditional attorney-client relationship, including the conveyancing bar as an ally of change, rather than its opponent.

From the federal perspective, HUD has been in existence a decade and largely has failed to find a clientele for its programs, much as the Agriculture and Commerce Departments earlier were able to. HUD was established to bring under one roof a collection of urban programs in which mortgage bankers, city planners, land developers, and the low-income sectors of the country participate.[7] These clienteles have very different programmatic interests. Planning and housing production are its twin goals, often in conflict. From HUD's point of view then, undertaking an overhaul of the conveyancing records might be a step toward building a united constituency for the agency. A further interest might be in simplified conveyancing: Converting recording offices into registries once land records are improved would help builders market their houses and lenders finance them. The fact that many builders around the country are advertising new homes available "with no settlement costs" indicates that our conveyancing system is getting in the way of housing production and needs help.

Notes

1. *See* ch. 3, *infra.*
2. *See* ch. 4, *infra.*
3. *See* ch. 5, *infra.*
4. *See* ch. 6, *infra.*
5. K. Zeimetz, *et al.,* "Dynamics of Land Use in Fast Growth Areas," United States Department of Agriculture, Agric. Econ. Rept. No. 325 (1976) at i; Burke, "Federal Intervention in the Conveyancing Process," 22 Am. U. L. Rev. 239 (1973).
6. C. Haar, *Between the Idea and the Reality* 15-34 (1976).
7. C. Edson & B. Lane, *Low and Moderate Income Housing* 1-2 through 1-12 (1972).

Index

Index

Abstract of title, 18, 21
Abstractor, 14, 17-18, 22, 165; certificate issued by, 23; efficiency, 40; liability, 22
Adverse possession, 106, 115. *See* registration of title
Alberta, Province of, 106
American Bankers' Association, 170
American Bar Association, 140
American Bar Foundation, 143
American Land Title Association, 139, 142, 149
Antitrust laws, x, 36, 143, 166
Appraisers, 14
Attorneys, 14-15, 17, 23, 36; agents of title insurers, 164; fees, 3; opinion on title, 32
Assembling title information, 13
Australia, 105

Barnett, Walter E., 215
Barrett, William, 148
Basye, Paul, 65
Bordwell, Percy, 110, 202
British Columbia, Province of, 106-107
British Legal Association, 209
Brock, William E., 151
Brokerage, 15-17; District of Columbia, 35; fees, 3, 6, 16; South Dakota, 21

Canada. *See name of Province*
Caveat Emptor, doctrine of, 14
Caveats, 107
Closing, 14, 39; closing statements, 152
Commission on Mortgage Interest Rates, 136
Commissioners on Uniform State Laws, xi, 65
Computers, x
Contracts, ix; binder contract, 15; contract of sale, 13, 21; economic function, 16; exclusive right to sell contract, 36; listing contract, 15
Conveyance, ix
Conveyancing, patterns of, 17-19, 31-33
Costs of Leases Act, 1958, 205-207
Cost of Living Council, 143
Council of Housing Producers, 139
Cranston, Alan, 153
Credit Reporting Agencies, 14; fees, 4
Curative acts, xi, xii, 59-60, 65-67, 103, 176, 215-216

Deed of release, 39
Disclosure, 154-163, 173-175. *See also* Real Estate Settlement Procedures Act
Discount points, 3, 6, 138, 142
District of Columbia, 35-40
Due process of law, 70, 85-94; state action, 87

Emergency Home Finance Act of 1970, 136-137, 150
English conveyancing, 203-205; completion, 204, debate over fees, 205-209; estate agent, 203; preliminary agreement, 203; preliminary inquiries, 204; solicitors, 202
Equity and conveyancing, 67-69, 70; equitable interests, 68
Escrow agents, 14, 33-34, 39; fees, 4, 39; instructions to agents, 34; legal theory, 34; regulation of accounts, 168-169, 174-175
Executory period, xi, 13, 118

Falde v. Chadwick, 26
Federal aid to land records, 169-170, 176-177, 216-217
Federal Housing Administration, Department of Housing and Urban

Federal Housing Administration (cont.)
  Development, 137-139; Housing
  and Home Finance Agency, 135;
  mortgage underwriting fee, 4, 5,
  137; role, 137; sample of under-
  written loans, 141. *See also* United
  States
Federally related mortgage, 147, 153
Formation of new households, 134
Fuentes v. Shevin, 91

General Accounting Office, 135
General welfare clause, 60, 66, 70
Goldfarb v. Virginia State Bar, 166-
  167, 168
Government patent, 20
Gude, Gilbert, 148

Hailsham, Lord, 208
Hawaii, 106, 108, 202
Hazard and fire insurance, 5
Holstein, Thomas, 139
Homeownership, xii, 138, 206; access
  to, 134; new households, 134
Homesteading, 20-21
House inspection fees, 4; house inspec-
  tor, 14; practice in England, 203
Housing and Urban Development Act
  of 1972, 147
Hunt v. Luck, 106

Illinois, State of, 108
Indemnification, 32, 38. *See also* title
  insurance
Indexing of conveyancing documents,
  79-80. *See also* tract indexes
Information needed for settlement,
  6-7
Installment land sale contracts, 25-27;
  contract for a deed, 25
Institute for Urban Life, 135
Interest, 5
Interest groups, 142

Kickbacks, 151-152, 154; regulation,
  163-166, 175

Land Charges Registry, British, 204
Land locators, 21
Law Commission, British, 207
Law of Property Act, 1925, 201
Law Society, England, 202, 205, 206,
  208-209
Lawyers Title guaranty fund, 29
Legal description of land parcel, 82,
  106
Legislation, x
Life insurance fees, 5
Lis pendens, doctrine of, 83, 87, 90,
  93-94
Lobbying, 170

Manitoba, Province of, 106
Marketable title, xi, xii, 15, 68-69
Marketable-title act, 23, 59-62, 103,
  215; root-of-title, 63
Massachusetts, 105, 106, 108, 202
Mechanic's liens, 83, 91, 106
Minimum fee schedule, 29, 166
Minnesota, 108, 110
Mitchell v. W.T. Grant Co., 92
Mortgage, 15, 27; discount points, 3;
  loan commitment, 14; mortgage
  lending, 14
Mortgage application fee, 5
Mortgage Bankers Association, 140,
  149
Mortgage Credit Act of 1970, 136

Name index, 80
National Association of Home Build-
  ers, 139-140
National Association of Real Estate
  Boards, 140, 143
National Housing Conference, 140
Nebraska Code, 66
New South Wales, 105
*North Georgia Finishing, Inc. v. Di-
  Chem, Inc.*, 93
Notice, 90, 116

Office of Management and Budget,
  142

Off-record risks, 31

Packwood, Robert, 153
Parcel identifier, 82
Parcel index. *See* tract indexes
Parliament, 201; House of Commons, 208
Patman, Wright, 145, 147
Payne, John, 139-140
Powell, Richard, 110, 112
Preliminary certification of title, 23
Preparation-of-document fees, 5
Prices and Incomes Board, 207
Privacy of assets, 176
Privity of contract, 7, 22
Processing fees, 3
Professional custom, 19
Proxmire, William, 144, 149, 151, 153
Public land records, 19, 27, 59, 88, 116, 144
Public Works Administration, 134
Puerto Rico, 108

Real Estate agent, 13, 15-17. *See also* Brokerage
Real Estate Cost Reform Act of 1972, 145
Real Estate Settlement Procedures Act of 1974, 153-170; amendments, 172-175; disclosure of selling prices, 151, 153, 158-162, 174; disclosure of settlement costs, 152, 153, 156-158, 173-174; escrows, 108; exemptions, 172; good faith estimates, 173; hostility to, 170; information booklets, 150, 152-153, 154-156, 173; kickbacks, 163-168; legislative history, 144-145, 147-153; settlement sheet, 162-163; title information improvement, 169-170, 176-177
Real estate taxes, 5
Real estate transfer industry, 14; fragmentation, 175
Recording, x, 14, 69, 79, 89, 103, 107-108, 215; fees, 6; recordable documents, 86; recorders of deeds, 119; relation to equity, 89
Registration of title, 103-120; administrative process, 117; adverse possession, 106, 115; assurance fund, 104, 107, 109-110; certificate of title, 103, 106, 118, 120; constitutionality, 117; constructive notice, 105; defeasible certificate, 105, 115; experimentation, 113; general boundaries, 106; guarantee, 117; initial cost, 111; initial registration, 105, 108; interests registered, 106; mirror principle, 104; misdescriptions, 110; modifications, 105-107; registrar, 105; registry, 103; universality, 107
Replevin, 91
Romney, George, 146, 148, 150

Saskatchewan, Province of, 106
Secondary national mortgage market, 137
Settlement costs, x, 3, 133; amortization, 7; federal regulation, xii, 153-175; settlement process, x; settlement services, ix, 3. *See also* Real Estate Settlement Procedures Act
Settlement statement, 150, 162-163
Shelly v. Kraemer, 87
Simes, Lewis, 65, 120
Sioux Falls, South Dakota, 13, 19. *See also* South Dakota
Slander of title, 84
Sniadach v. Household Finance Corporation, 92
Solicitors, 202, 204. *See also* English conveyancing
Solicitor's Act of 1957, 205, 209
South Dakota, 19-34, 109; Beadle County, 110; Roberts County, 110
Special warranty deeds, 39
Statutes of limitations, 60, 116
Stephens, Robert G., 148, 150
Stevenson, Adlai, 153
Suburban housing, 134

Sullivan, Lenore, 135, 153
Survey fee, 4; surveyor, 14

Termite inspectors, 14; fees, 5
Title binder, 38
Title Charge Reduction Act of 1971, 145
Title-examination fees, 4
Title guaranty fund, 28, 29-30
Title information system improvement, 169, 176
Title insurance, 31-32; indemnity, 32, 38; lender's coverage, 32; owner's coverage, 32; title insurance premium, 5, 24, 38; title insurer, 14, 17, 36, 117
Title opinion, 38
Title plants, 19, 22, 33, 37, 64, 216; capital investment, 64; labor specialization, 65; take off, 63; take off expenses, 64
Title records, 59. See also Public land records
Title searches, x, 31, 36-37, 108
Title standards, 23, 69
Torrens, Robert Richard, 104
Torrens titles, 28, 60, 103-104, 107, 111, 201; experimentation with, 107-112; judicial nature, 110; modifications, 107
Tract indexes, xii, 79-80; cost, 82; encumbrance on, 84-85; ex parte documents, 86, 90-91; expunging interests from, 84; hearing, 91; legal description, 82; organization, 80-82; self-indexing device, 83; size of recording district, 80. See also Recording
Transfer taxes, 5, 27

Unauthorized practice of law, 21, 34
Uniform disclosure-settlement sheet, 162-163
Uniform Land Transactions Act, xi
Uniform settlement statements, 172
United States, Department of Housing and Urban Development, 137-139, 140-141, 143-144; preliminary report on mortgage settlement costs, 141-142; Report on Mortgage Settlement Costs, 145-147. See also Antitrust laws; Federal Housing Administration; Real Estate Settlement Procedures Act
United States, Department of Justice, 143
Urbanization, x, 114, 216
Use-deprivation, 92

Veterans' Administration, 135, 137, 141

Washington Post, 145, 153
Weitzel v. Leyson, 26
Which?, 207

Zander, Michael, 203

About the Author

D. Barlow Burke, Jr. graduated from Harvard College, the law schools of the University of Pennsylvania and Yale, and from the University of Pennsylvania's Graduate School of Fine Arts (in city planning). He has taught city planning and is currently a professor of law specializing in real property, at American University's law school in Washington, D.C.

DATE DUE

GAYLORD   PRINTED IN U.S.A